I0803112

IMAGES of America

DUBOIS AND THE WIND RIVER VALLEY

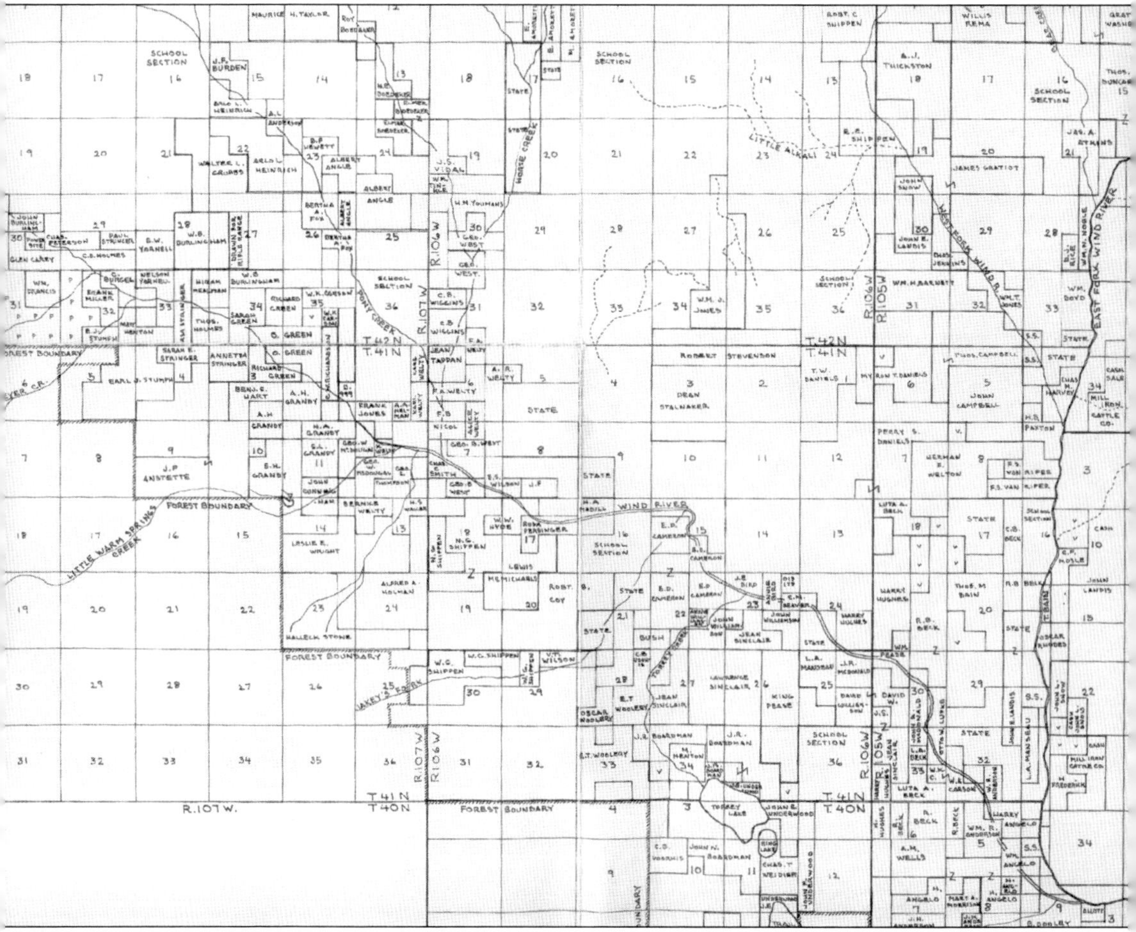

An early homestead map of the upper Wind River Valley shows land ownership in the area around the settlement that became the town of Dubois. The map also shows land ownership along some of the Wind River's tributaries. (Courtesy Mary Allison.)

On the Cover: Joan Trego, at lower left, and twins Jean and Ann White look down from their high perch on Warm Springs Mountain. Wyoming Tie and Timber Company's headquarters camp on Warm Springs Creek in the Wind River Mountains is spread out below. Trego's father was the company's accountant and bookkeeper, and she grew up in their headquarters camp. (Courtesy Dubois Museum.)

IMAGES
of America

DUBOIS AND THE WIND RIVER VALLEY

Norma Williamson

ARCADIA
PUBLISHING

ISBN 978-0-7385-9308-1

Published by Arcadia Publishing
Charleston, South Carolina

Printed in the United States of America

Library of Congress Control Number: 2011937271

For all general information, please contact Arcadia Publishing:
Telephone 843-853-2070
Fax 843-853-0044
E-mail sales@arcadiapublishing.com
For customer service and orders:
Toll-Free 1-888-313-2665

Visit us on the Internet at www.arcadiapublishing.com

To Mary Allison, who preserved the early days in the upper Wind River Valley, and to Joan Trego (Pinkerton) Tucker, who brought to vivid life the story of the Scandinavian tie hacks

Contents

ACKNOWLEDGMENTS

Dubois and the Wind River Valley is my gift to the people of the upper Wind River Valley who have given me friendship and support for over 20 years. It has been a great privilege to learn more about the unique individuals who created a lasting community in a beautiful but unforgiving environment.

The assistance of Katrina Krupicka, director of the Dubois Museum, made it possible for me to work with the museum's wonderful historical photograph collection. Melinda Bobo, museum curator, had the tedious and tiring task of scanning photographs from the collection I identified for use in the book into digital format. Melinda has earned my deep gratitude. I would also like to express my gratitude to Wayland Duerschmidt, June Bonasera, and Anna Moscicki, who took the time to read the book's text files in the final days of editing.

The majority of the images I have included in *Dubois and the Wind River Valley* are from the Dubois Museum collection unless otherwise noted. The Shoshone National Forest also provided me with access to its extensive historical photograph database, and I deeply appreciate the cooperation and assistance of forest archaeologist Kyle D. Wright. The contributions of longtime residents of the Dubois area were invaluable. Alice Hart, Jean Werts, John Finley, Dolores Haslam, and St. Thomas Episcopal Church graciously allowed me to digitize irreplaceable photographs and documents from their collections. I am grateful for their trust.

Finally, this book would not have been possible without the information Dubois historian Mary Allison collected with such dedication for *Dubois Area History*. The same can also be said of Joan (Pinkerton) Tucker, who used photographs taken by her father, A.B. Trego, and others to tell the story of a vanished way of life in *Knights of the Broadax*. Both books are now out of print but still available in some museums and libraries.

INTRODUCTION

In the years between 1840 and 1870, a quarter of a million people traveled through the area that is now Wyoming on the Oregon-California Trail, but few lingered. Wyoming was not organized as a territory until 1869 and did not achieve statehood until 1890. The upper valley of the Wind River, however, remained a frontier into the early years of the 20th century. In many ways, it is still a frontier today. The national forest lands surrounding the upper Wind River Valley contain some of the most remote wilderness in the lower 48 states, the closest towns are almost 80 miles away, and the nearest metropolitan areas are several hundred miles away in any direction.

The first permanent settlers in the Wind River Valley chose to live in the lower end of the valley, where it is at its widest point and 2,000 feet lower in elevation. Other factors also played a role in the settlement of the lower valley first. When gold was discovered at South Pass in 1865, a handful of the hundreds of gold-seekers stayed on in the lower Wind River Valley after the short-lived gold rush ended. In 1868, the US government set aside 2.7 million acres in the Wind River Valley as a reservation for the Eastern Shoshone. A military fort (Fort Augur) was established in 1869 on the site of present-day Lander, and this encouraged development of a small, permanent community that remained after the military fort was moved to Fort Washakie on the reservation. The rugged terrain of the upper Wind River Valley further discouraged settlers from venturing north, and the Wind River Reservation formed a barrier of sorts between the upper and lower portions of the valley.

Although scattered bands of Indians hunted in the upper valley for hundreds of years and a party of fur traders led by Wilson Price Hunt traveled through in 1811, the upper valley of the Wind River remained largely unknown territory. Hunt's party crossed the Wind River Mountains west of present-day Dubois on a broad, level pass that is known today as Union Pass. This pass is a triple divide where the Wind River, Absaroka, and Gros Ventre mountain ranges rise, and streams flowing from these ranges are the headwaters of the Colorado, Columbia, and Missouri river systems. Jim Bridger, the famed mountain man and guide, also spent time in the upper Wind River Valley and is credited with naming Union Pass.

By the late 1880s, lured by free land promised by the 1862 grazing act, a handful of families began to venture into the upper Wind River Valley. They found a beautiful valley that narrows like the prow of a ship at its head where the Wind River and Absaroka mountain ranges join at Togwotee Pass and the Wind River begins in Wind River Lake. Those first homesteaders found little land suitable for cultivation in the upper valley, and early settlements developed along Wind River's tributaries. Scottish immigrants settled along the East Fork of the Wind River, and a thriving community developed based on sheep and cattle ranching. Small settlements were also established along other tributaries and creeks. Most of the early communities had post offices and one-teacher schools that testified to the importance placed on education.

Most early settlements in the upper Wind River Basin were based on agriculture, but little more than hay could be grown successfully in an area where the average growing season is 38 days. Understandably, people who were homesteading land and planned on growing crops to earn their living became discouraged. Today, there are only traces of most early settlements, but the tiny community established along the Wind River remained and thrived as a center of commerce for outlying areas.

Outlaw Butch Cassidy and his partner Al Heiner spent the fall and winter of 1889–1890 in a cabin on Horse Creek, a tributary of the Wind River, a few miles north of Dubois. Some accounts of Cassidy's life suggest that he and his partner were stealing horses in the vicinity of present-day Cody, Wyoming, and bringing the horses across the Absaroka Mountains for resale in Idaho. Why Cassidy left Dubois is not known, but it is known that he became involved in a highly publicized crime spree after he left Dubois.

By the time homesteaders arrived in the upper Wind River Valley, the establishment of Yellowstone National Park in 1872 was already charting a different future for the upper Wind River Valley. In 1891, the federal government set aside the first in a series of timberland reserves designed to protect the nation's first national park. The Wind River Range and other lands south of the park were added to the timberland reserves in 1902. The portion of timberland reserve that is now the Shoshone National Forest became the country's first national forests in 1908.

Construction of the Chicago & North Western Railway line across Wyoming was responsible for bringing forest-based industry to Dubois. In the early 1900s, the Wyoming Tie and Timber Company began a railroad tie–cutting operation in the national forest near Dubois. The tradition of harvesting the forest's abundant natural resources continued after the cross-tie operation shut down in the mid-1940s. Louisiana Pacific Lumber Company operated a sawmill on a 75-acre parcel of land southeast of Dubois from the late 1940s until 1987.

With Yellowstone National Park as a next-door neighbor and the first national forest surrounding the town, it was only natural for enterprising citizens to see the potential for income from visitors passing through Dubois on their way to visit Yellowstone National Park. Two of the oldest continuously operating guest ranches in Wyoming are located in the Dubois area.

Long before the first white settlers came to the upper Wind River Valley, ancestors of the present-day Eastern Shoshone tribe established village sites in the Wind River Mountains at elevations above 11,000 feet, and artifacts found at one such high-elevation site are estimated to be 1,500 years old. Some of the extensive rock art in the Dubois area has been dated as 3,000 years old, and archaeological exploration of a site in the East Fork of the Wind River drainage found evidence of use by native people as far back as 10,000 years ago. However, our story concerns the white settlers who began to move into the upper Wind River Valley in the late 1880s.

One

Early Years in the Upper Wind River Valley

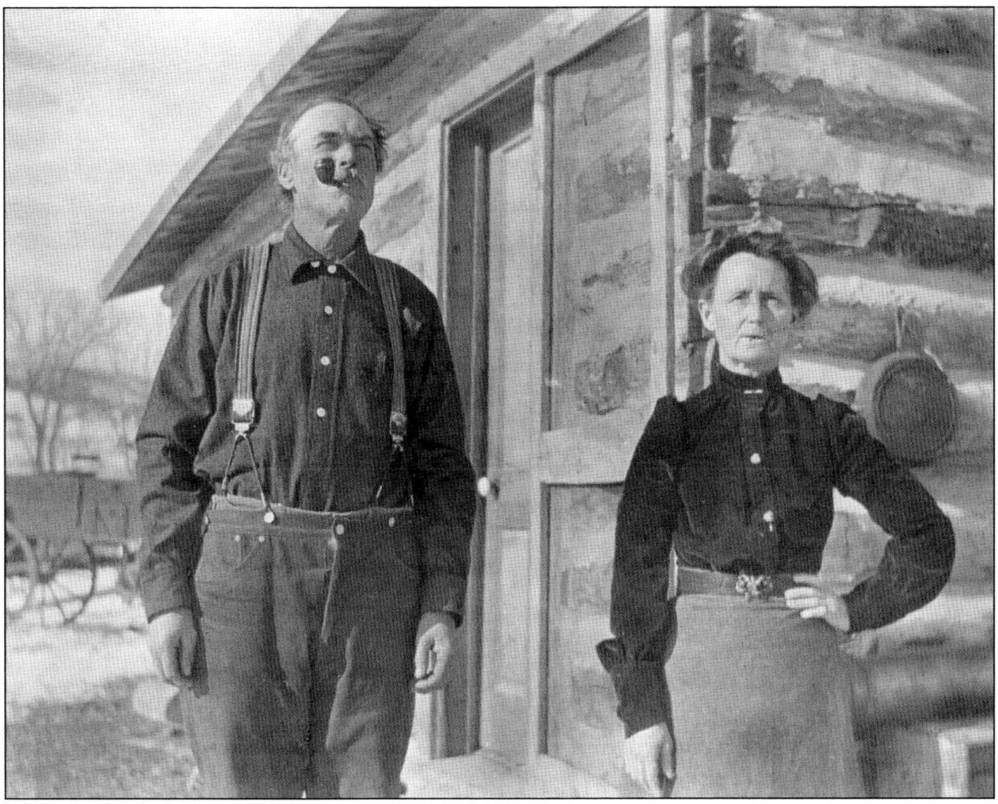

John and Mahala Burlingham are pictured in the early 1900s in front of their cabin west of present-day Dubois. The Burlinghams came to the area in 1889 with their seven children and built a cabin along the Wind River where the rural Stoney Point subdivision is located today. They were the earliest homesteaders in the Dubois area who sought free land through the provisions of the 1862 Homestead Act.

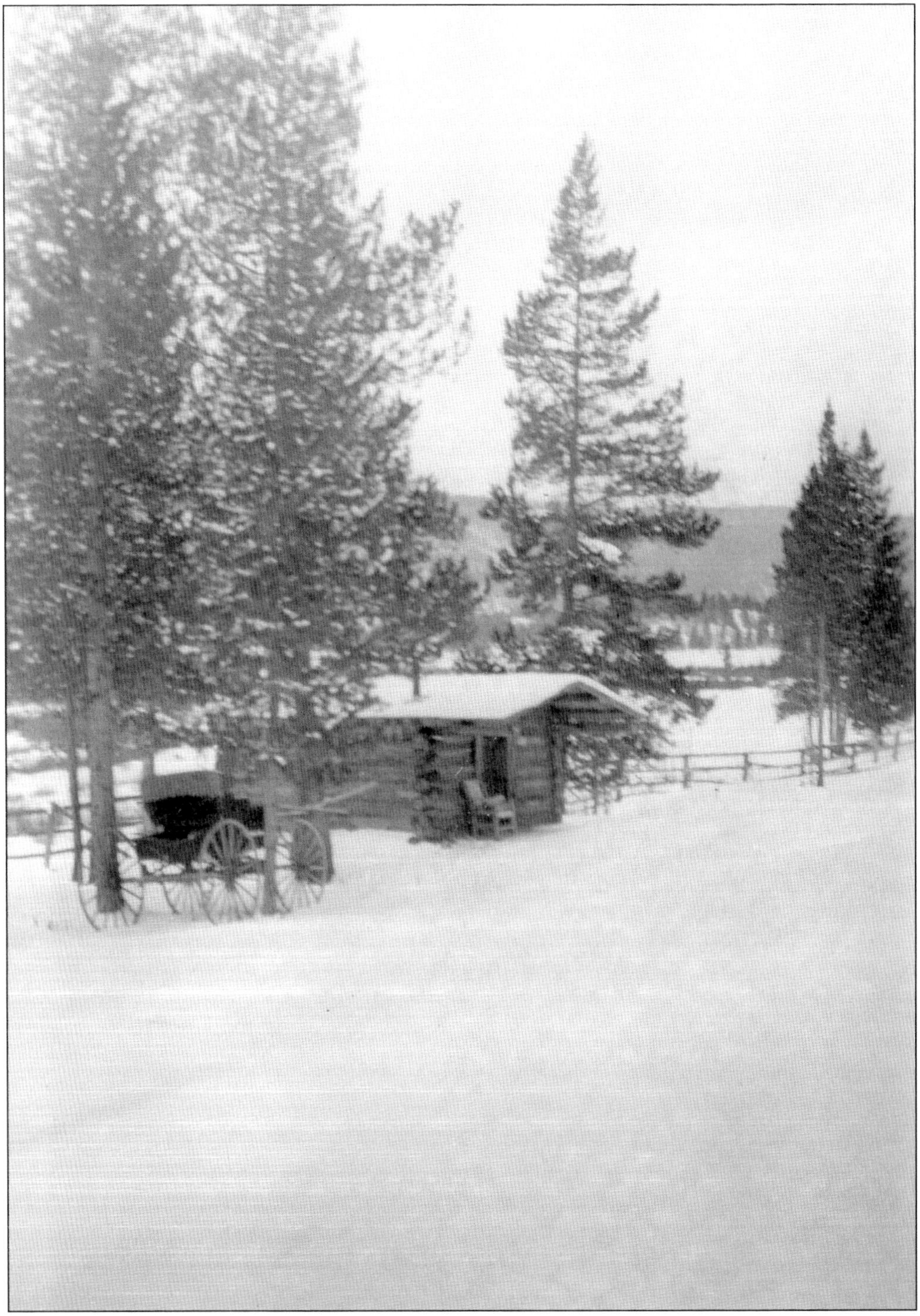

John and Mahala Burlingham's cabin is pictured in the early 1900s surrounded by snow. At first, the cabin had no windows and only a dirt floor. A camp stove with the stovepipe sticking through the roof was the only source of heat. The couple slept on a feather bed and made beds for the children from rows of poles covered with woven and overlapped pine boughs.

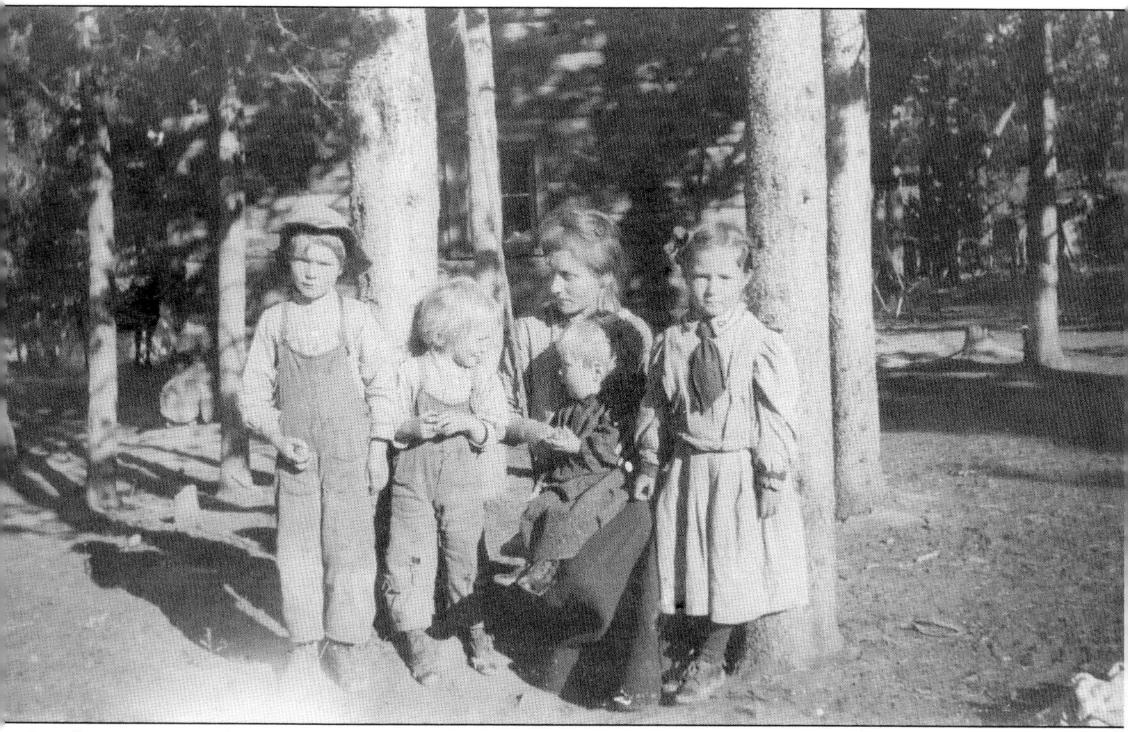

Frankie Moriarty, daughter of John and Mahala Burlingham, poses with her young children in front of the Moriarty cabin at Wagon Box Gulch in 1906. Pictured from left to right are Dan, Bill, Jack, and Mary. Frankie's husband, Tom, was the brother of Fr. Dan Moriarty, a Catholic priest for the Arapaho tribe on the Wind River Reservation.

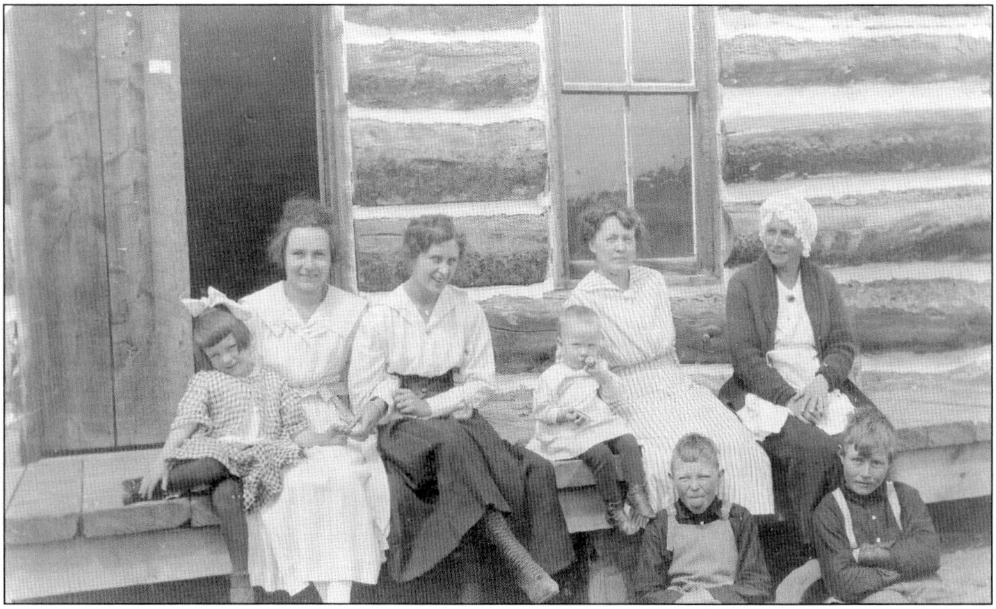

Female settlers in the upper Wind River Valley made their difficult lives more bearable by occasional visits with friends and neighbors. A group of neighborhood women is pictured with Frankie Moriarty, the third person from the left, in 1918 on the Moriarty front porch. Seated to the left of Moriarty are her daughter Mary and Elsie Cross. Two unidentified women and three unidentified children are pictured to the right of Moriarty.

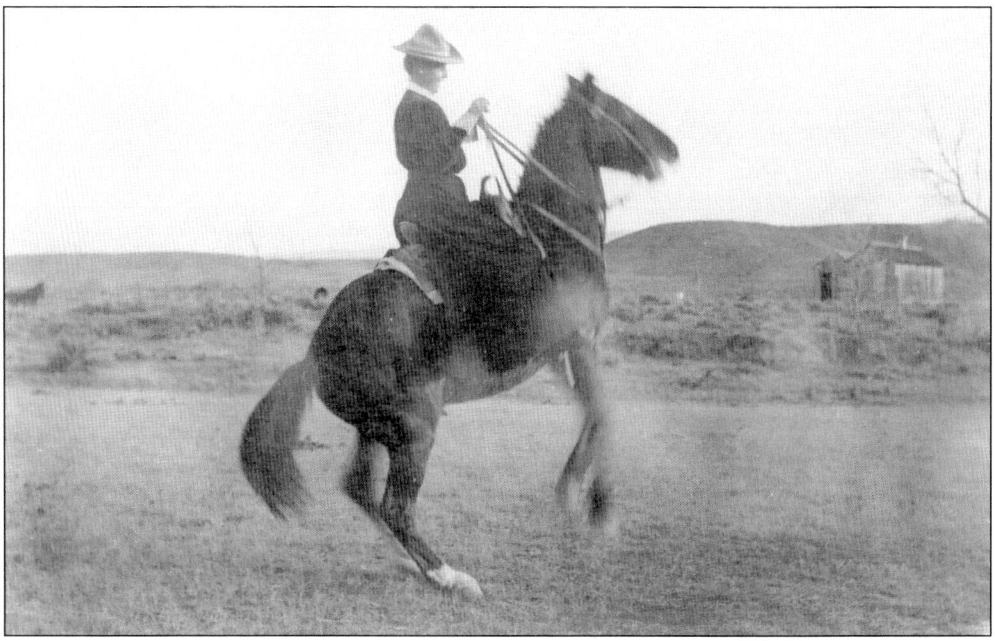

Hattie Burlingham Butler is shown working with her horse Freddie around 1906. She married Ben Butler in 1894 and was the first of John and Mahala Burlingham's seven children to marry, but her marriage eventually ended in divorce.

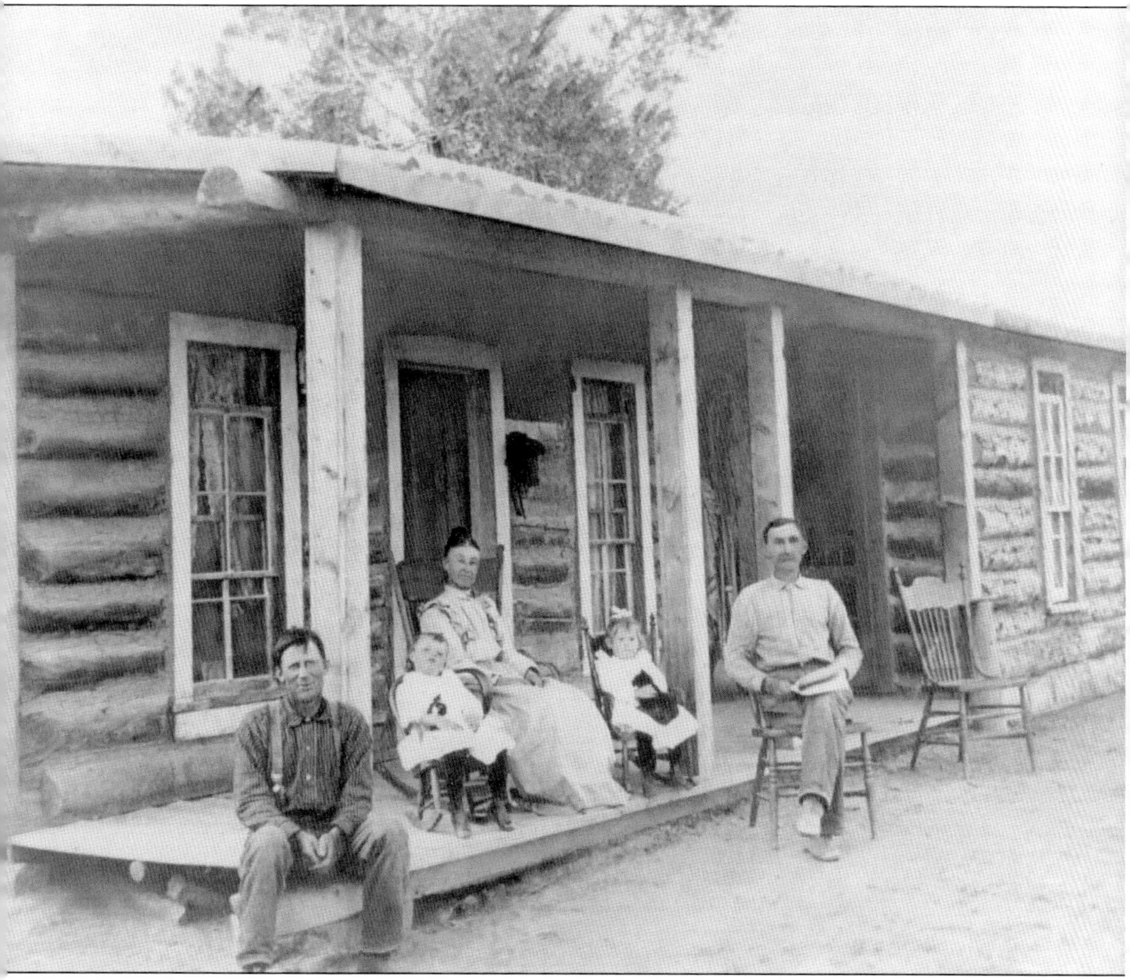

Elwood S. Wilson, a former Texas ranger, his wife, Victoria Spencer Wilson, and daughter Nova moved into a cabin on the Wind River in 1896 near the site where the Dubois Medical Center is located today and operated a sawmill there as well. The Wilsons are shown seated on their front porch in the early 1900s with a man who worked for them at the time and the two granddaughters they took into their home when daughter Nova Locke died giving birth to her second daughter. Wilson is seated in a chair on the right. (Courtesy Alice Hart.)

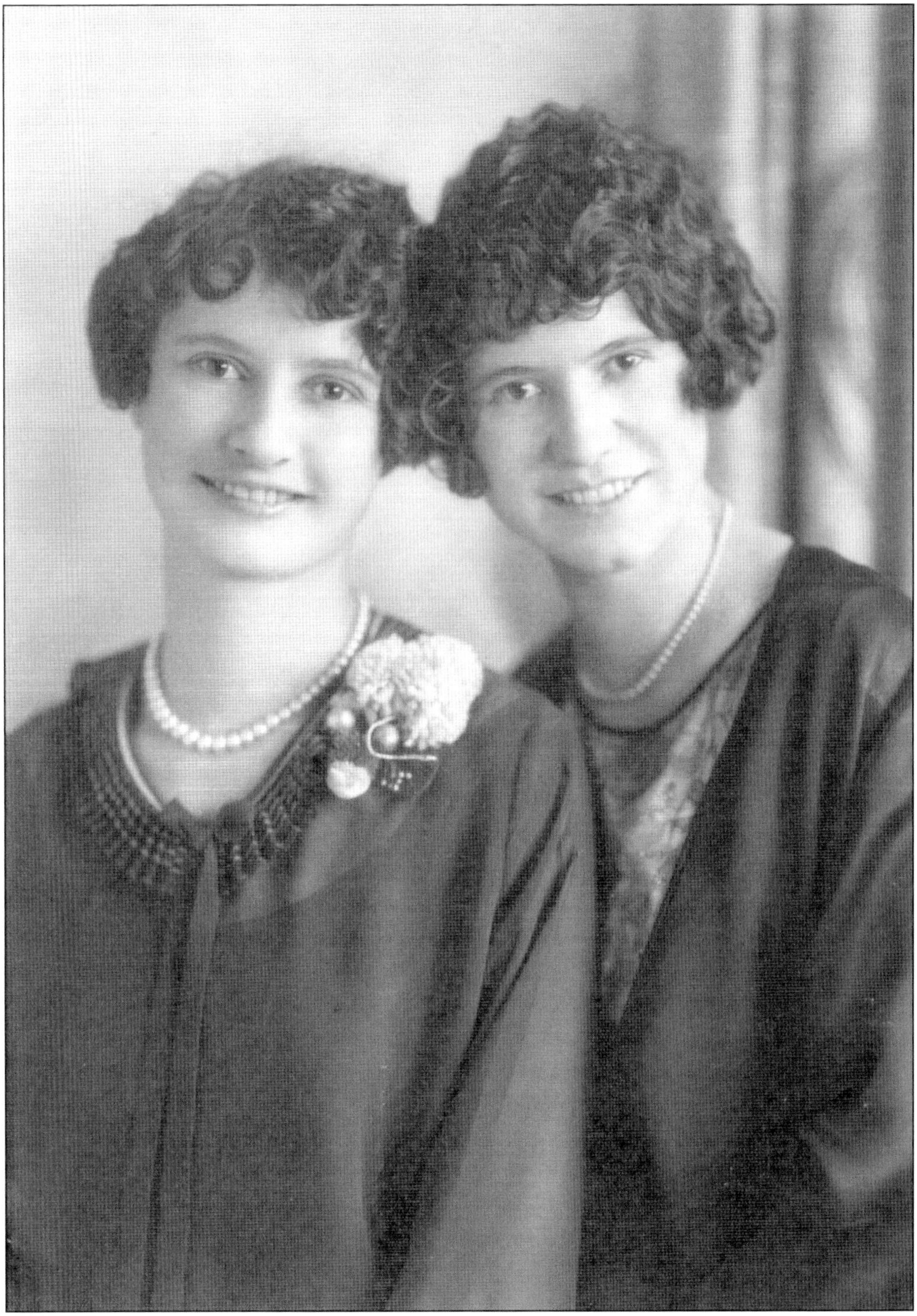

Edwin and Victoria Wilson's granddaughters Verna Locke Leseberg and Nova Locke Gilliland posed together at their double wedding in 1927. The young women's father, James Locke, homesteaded east of present-day Dubois in the early 1900s on land that is now the Painted Hills subdivision. (Courtesy Alice Hart.)

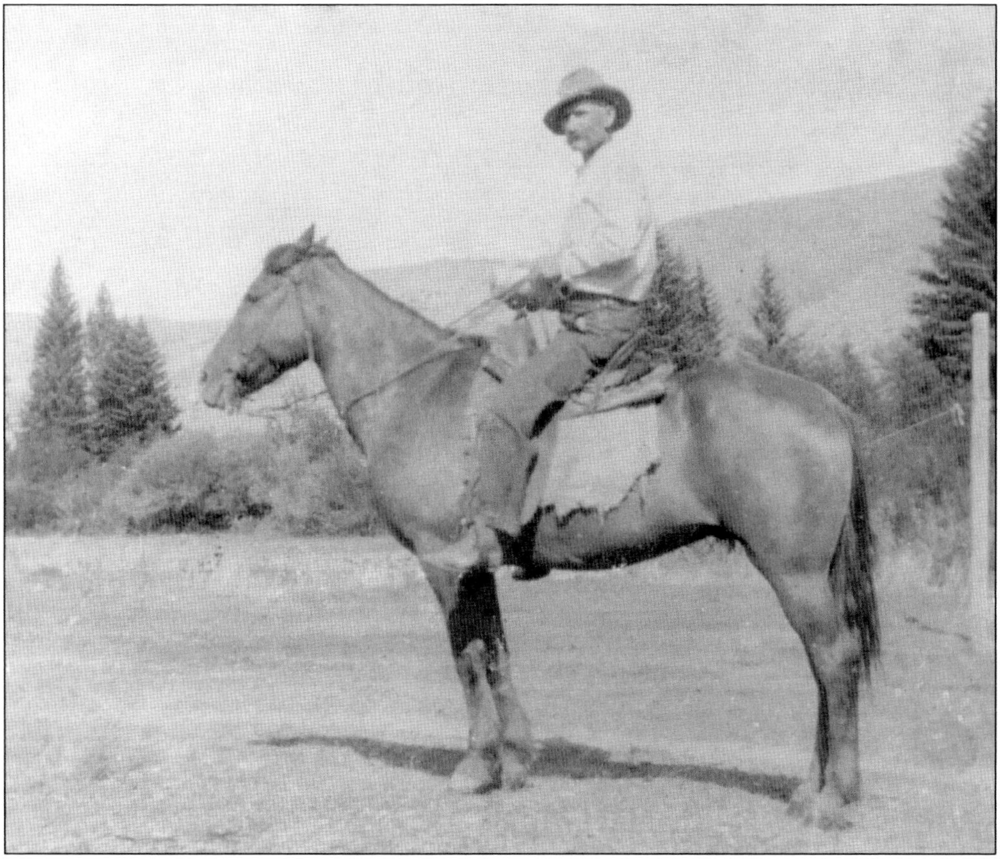

Elwood Wilson is pictured on horseback, likely at the family homestead on Jakey's Fork of the Wind River. Victoria Wilson filed a homestead claim on the property in 1909, and the family lived on it until Elwood Wilson died in 1919 as a result of having his teeth pulled by a traveling dentist. His wife then sold the homestead to Charles C. Moore, who turned the property into a guest ranch. (Courtesy Alice Hart.)

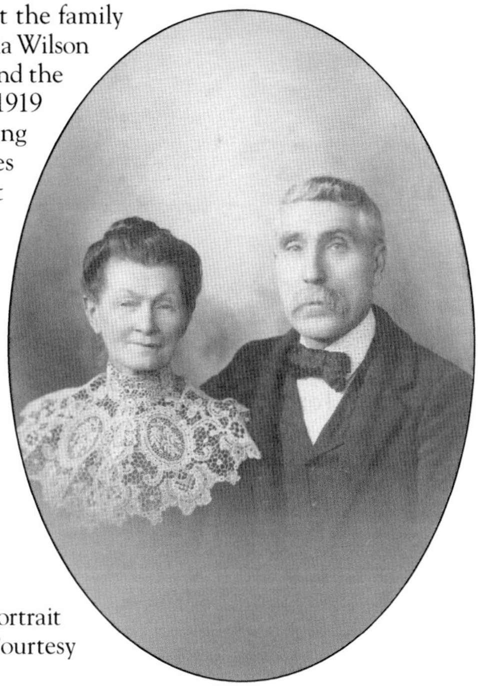

Elwood and Victoria Wilson are shown in a formal portrait taken a few years before Elwood's death in 1919. (Courtesy Alice Hart.)

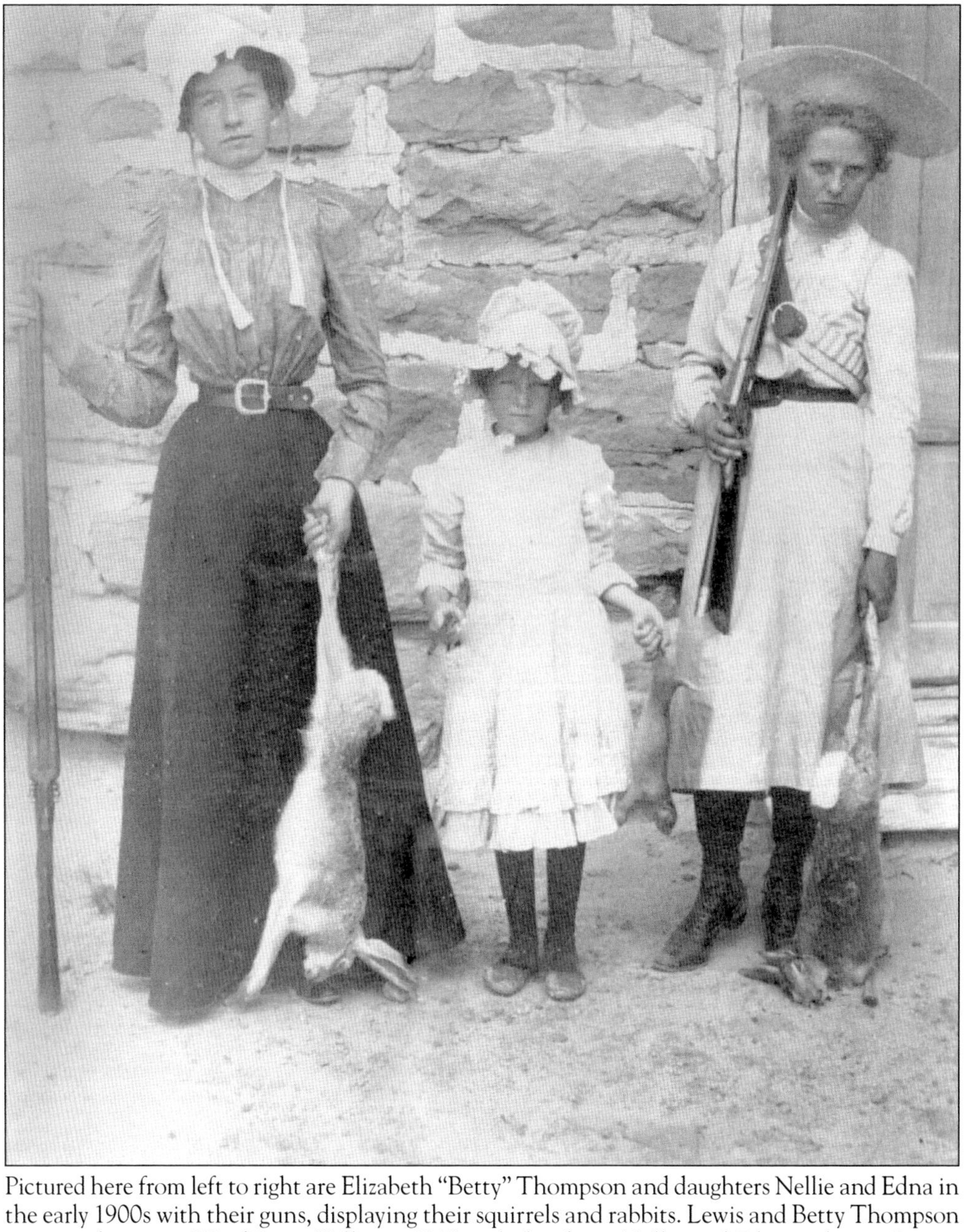

Pictured here from left to right are Elizabeth "Betty" Thompson and daughters Nellie and Edna in the early 1900s with their guns, displaying their squirrels and rabbits. Lewis and Betty Thompson came to the upper Wind River Valley in 1905 with daughters Nellie and Edna and sons George and Richard. They purchased an existing homestead west of present-day Dubois where Warm Springs Creek empties into the Wind River. Notice Betty and her daughters are wearing dresses, and Betty's tiny waist indicates she is tightly corseted.

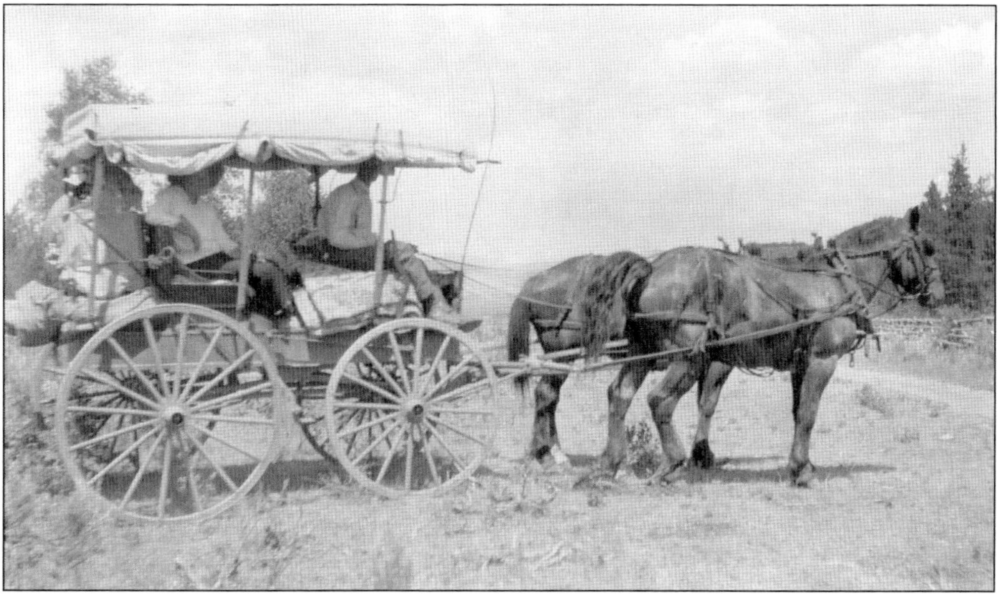

Edna and Roy Nipper and baby Nellie are pictured in their wagon, returning to their homestead at Blacktail Butte in the Snake River Valley near present-day Moose, Wyoming, after a visit with family in Dubois. Edna was the daughter of Lewis and Betty Thompson, and Roy was the son of Grant and Minnie Nipper.

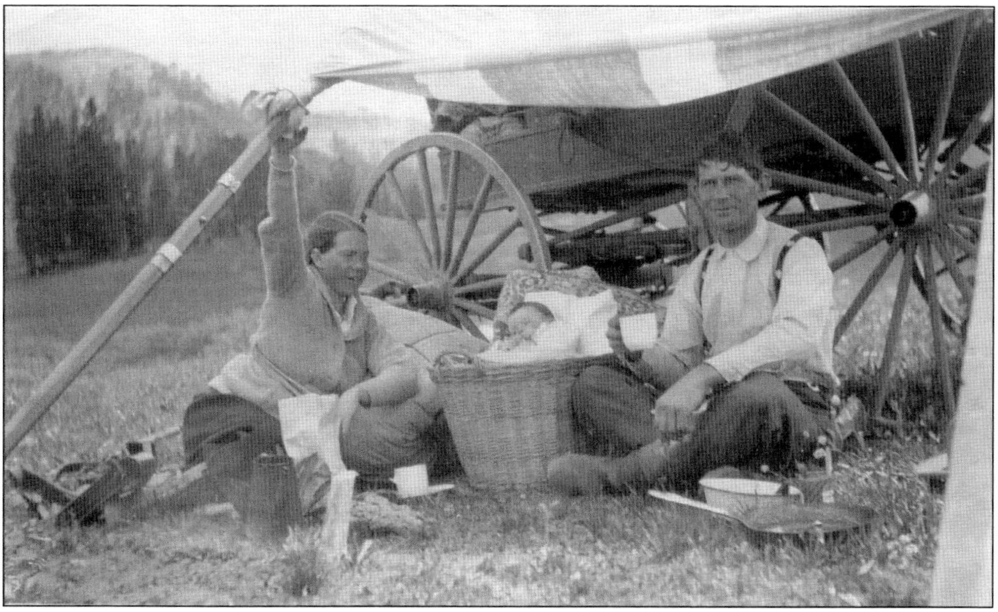

Edna and Roy Nipper enjoy a meal along the way to their Blacktail Butte homestead, while baby Nellie sleeps peacefully under the wagon. The Nippers would have spent several nights on the trail before they reached home.

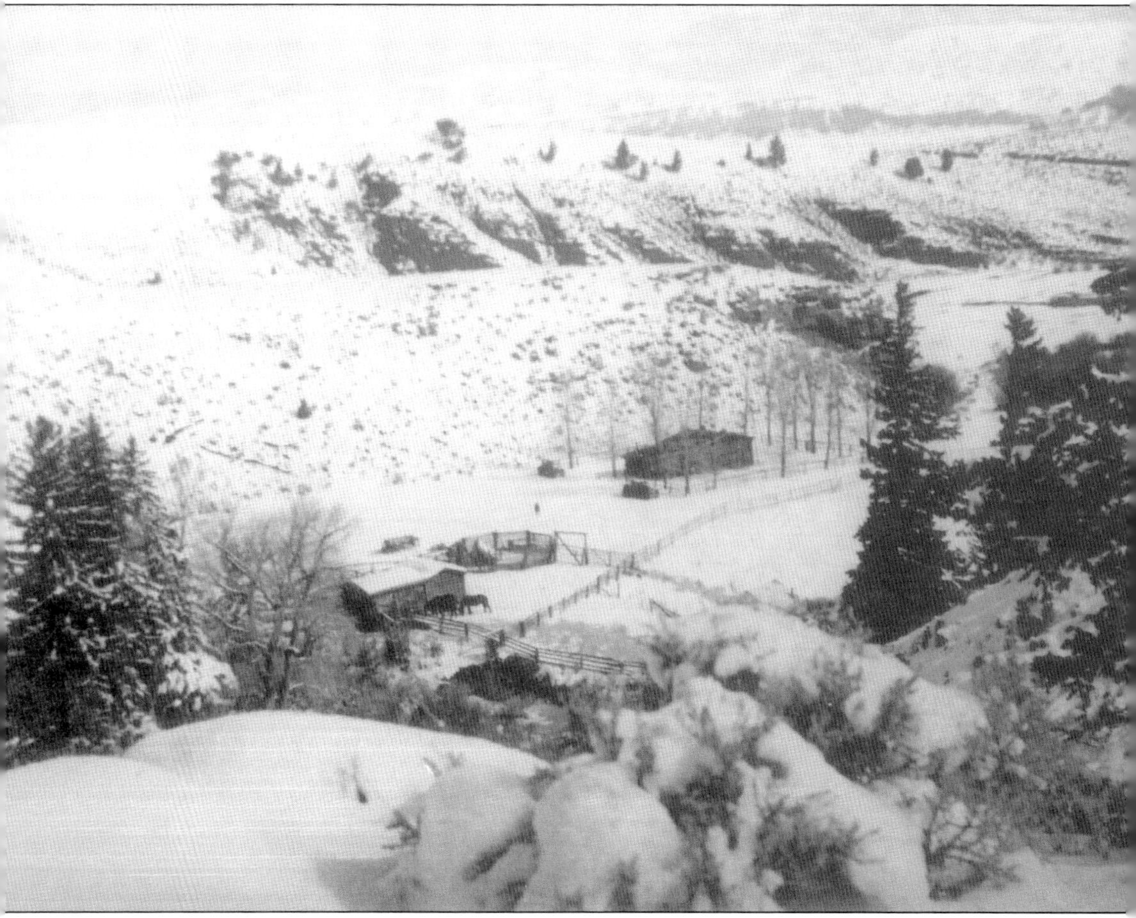

The upper Grandy homestead is pictured in 1931. Stephen Grandy, his wife, Harriet, and son Gus came to the upper Wind River Valley in the early 1900s from a mining community west of Thermopolis, Wyoming, but the family was originally from New York state. The family homesteaded at two sites in the vicinity of upper Little Warm Springs Creek where Grandy raised racehorses. He and his son Gus used horses and farm equipment to dig a reservoir and ditch in the national forest to irrigate their hay fields.

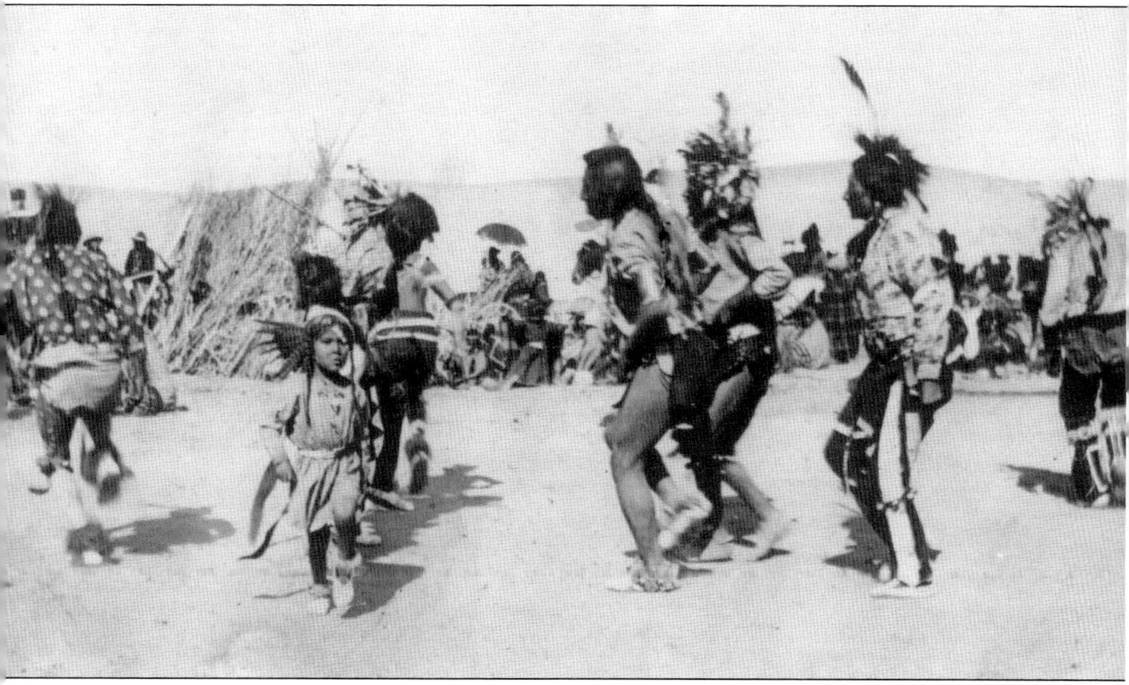

Indian dancers are pictured on the Wind River Reservation in the early 1900s. Some of the early homesteaders, such as the Duncan family on the East Fork of the Wind River, settled on land along tributaries of the Wind River that bordered the reservation.

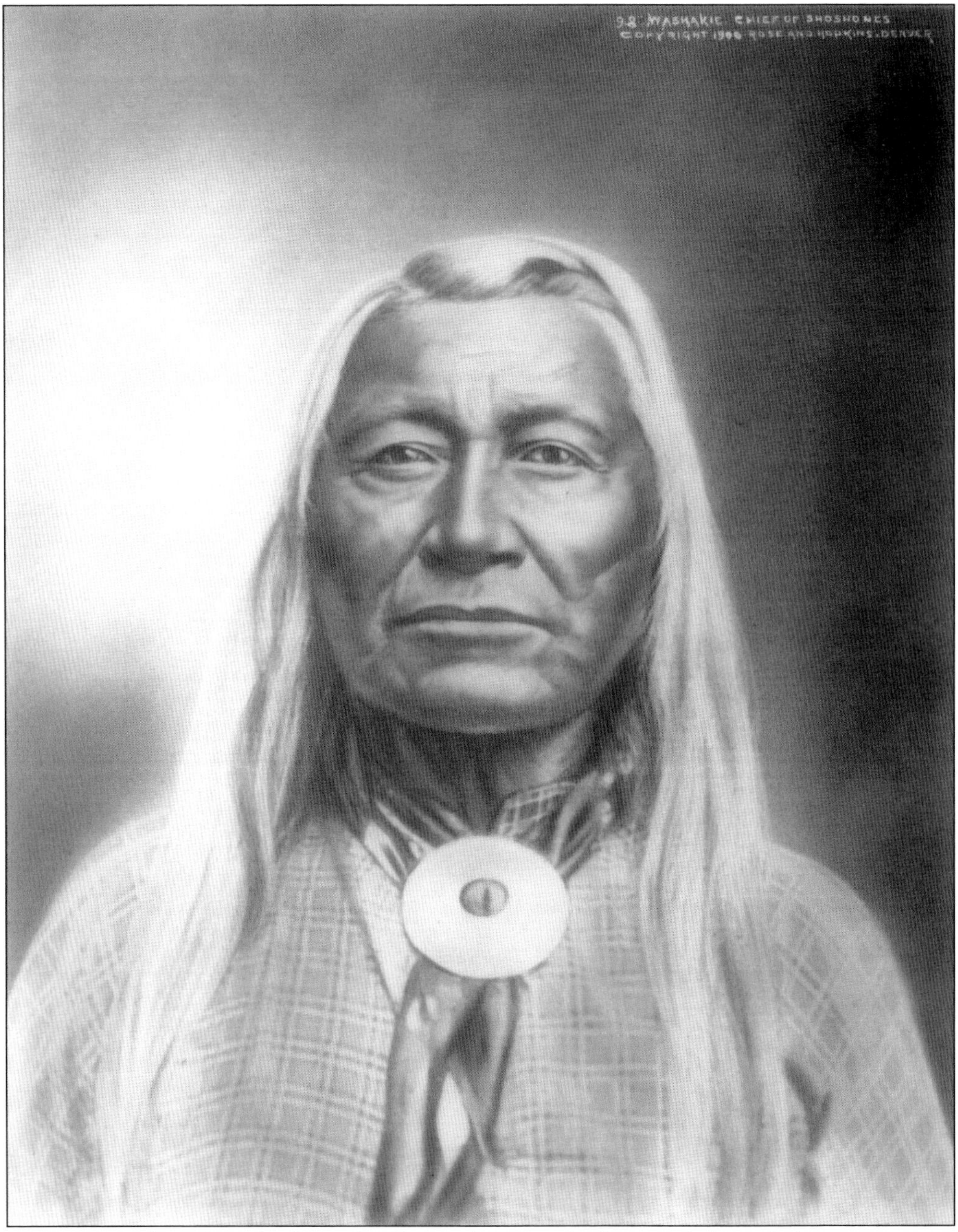

Washakie, the legendary Shoshone chief, knew the survival of his people depended on maintaining peaceful relations with the white settlers moving to the Wind River Valley. The tradition of peaceful relations continued after his death in 1900. This is a photograph of an 1880s painting of Washakie from the C.C. Moore collection at the Dubois Museum.

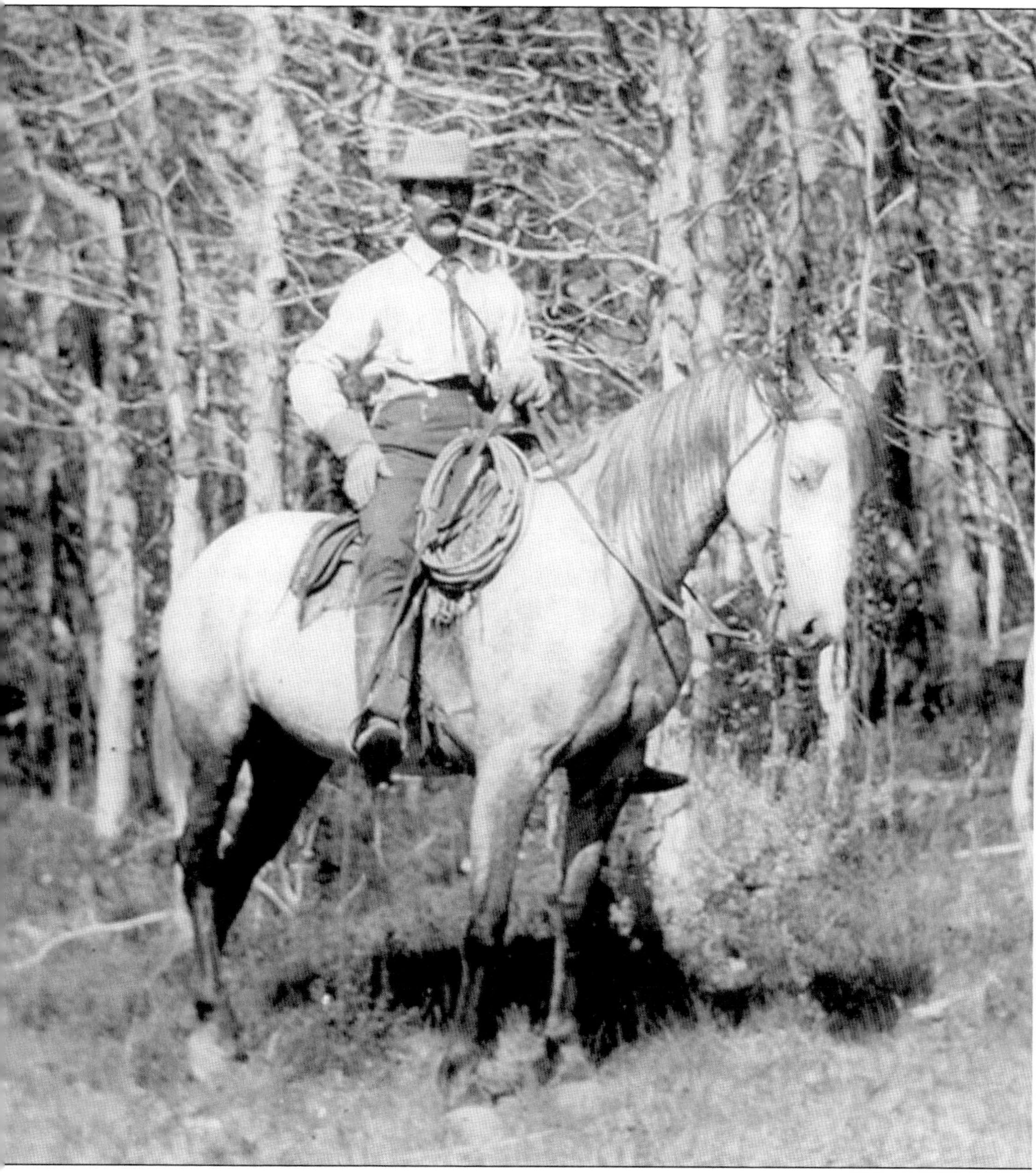

William "Bill" Duncan is shown on horseback in a photograph taken by Margaret "Peggy" McKissock prior to their marriage in 1912. The story of the Duncan community, "Little Scotland," in the valley of the East Fork of the Wind River, began in Ayshire, Scotland, where Bill and his brother Thomas S. "Tom" Duncan grew up in a family of 10 children. Bill sailed for America in 1890, and Tom joined him in 1893. The young men worked several years to learn skills necessary for operating a ranch. By 1900, Bill and Tom had saved enough money to buy sheep and began homesteading in the East Fork Valley.

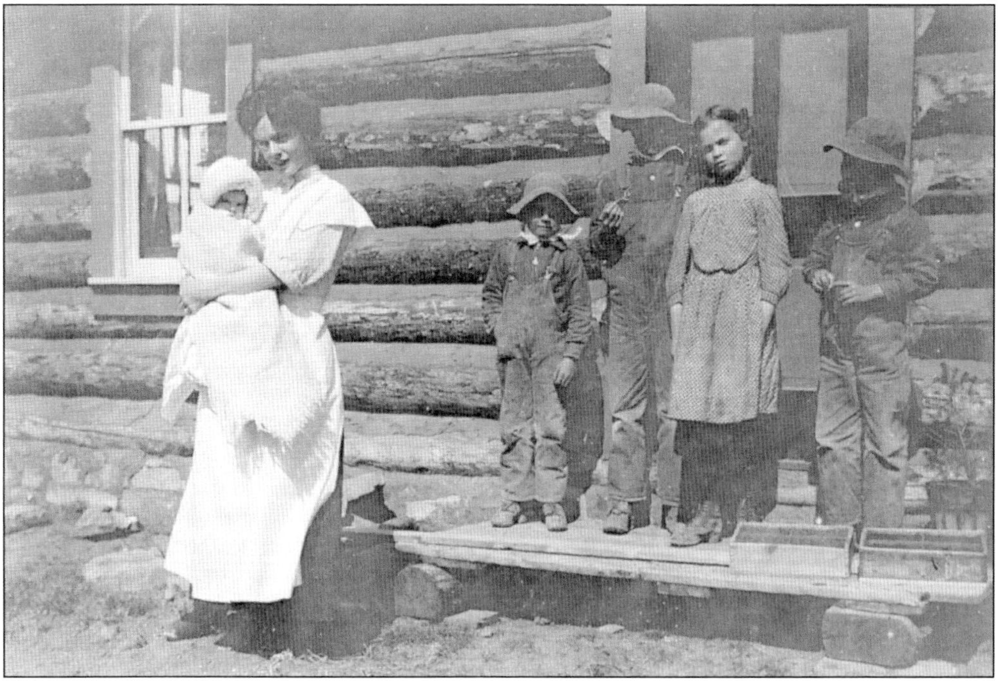

Peggy Duncan is pictured at the Bill Duncan ranch in 1913, holding daughter Marion. Tom and Kate Duncan's children pictured with her are, from left to right, Bill, Bob, Katharine, and Jim. Marion Duncan grew up to marry O. Fred Finley, and their son John still lives on the family ranch. (Courtesy John Finley.)

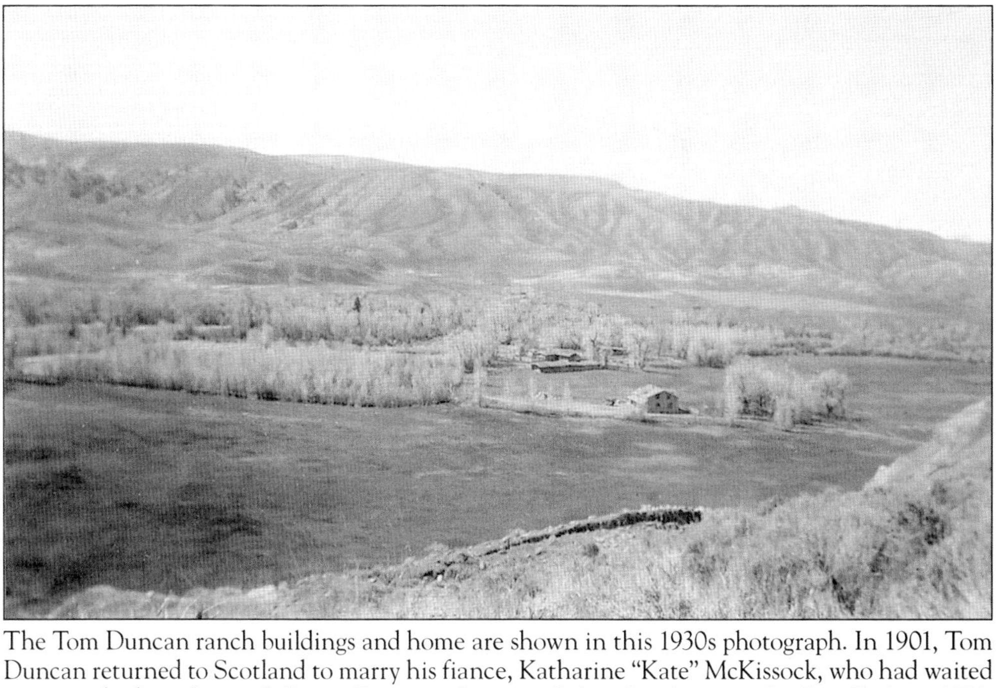

The Tom Duncan ranch buildings and home are shown in this 1930s photograph. In 1901, Tom Duncan returned to Scotland to marry his fiance, Katharine "Kate" McKissock, who had waited six years for him. Jim and Gavin Duncan also joined their brothers on the East Fork in 1901. (Courtesy John Finley.)

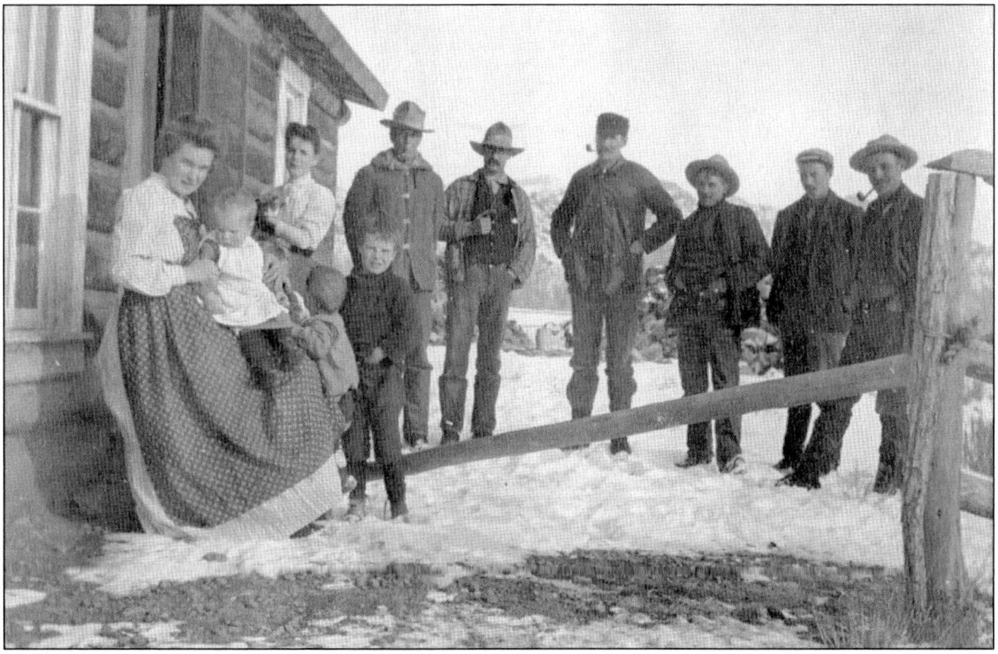

Kate Duncan is shown here in 1907 with her children at the Tom Duncan ranch. Bill is in her arms, and the other children, pictured from left to right, are Jim, Katharine (hiding behind her mother), and Bob. Pictured in the back row from left to right are Jeanie Muir Duncan, Gavin Duncan's wife; Kate's brother John McKissock; Tom Duncan; Gavin Duncan; Bob Campbell; Johnny Campbell; and Jeanie Duncan's brother Gilbert Muir. The Campbell men emigrated from Scotland along with Muir. (Courtesy John Finley.) (Courtesy John Finley.)

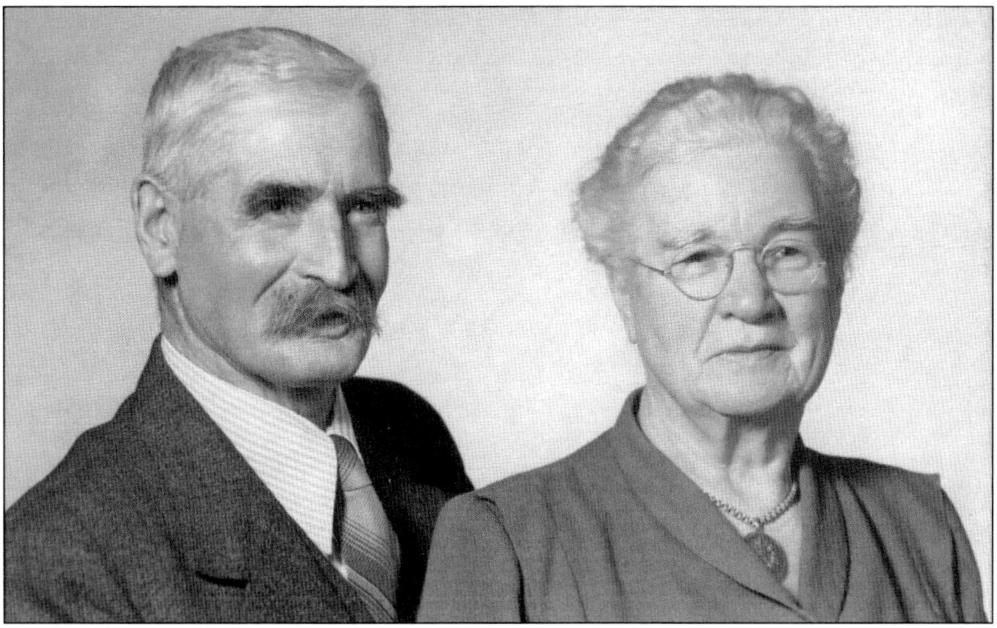

Tom and Kate Duncan are pictured in the early 1950s at their family ranch. Kate continued to speak with a heavy Scottish accent all her life, and local people often found her speech difficult to understand.

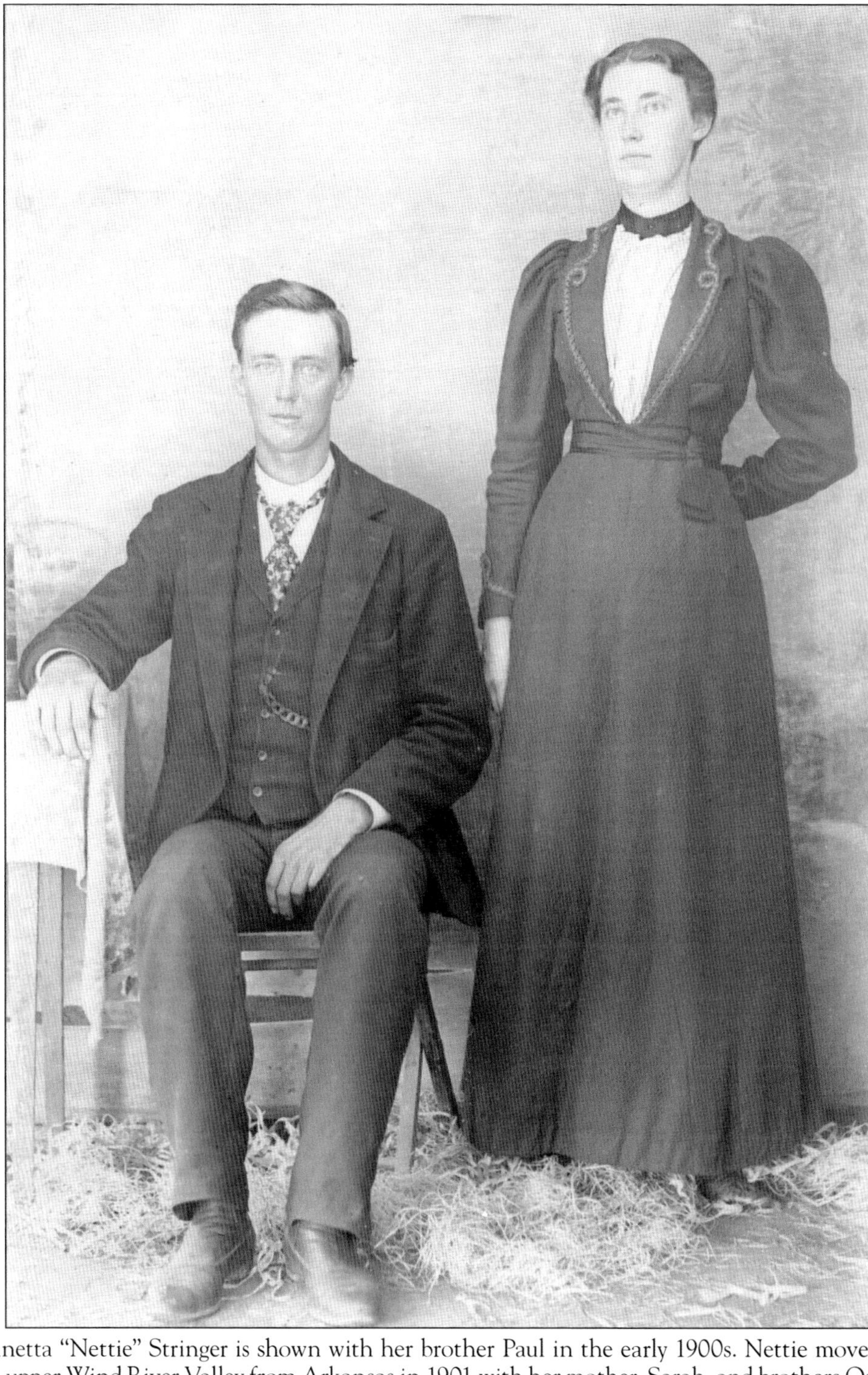

Annetta "Nettie" Stringer is shown with her brother Paul in the early 1900s. Nettie moved to the upper Wind River Valley from Arkansas in 1901 with her mother, Sarah, and brothers Oscar, Albert, Carl, and Ernest. The three older brothers, Asa, Ross, and Paul, had been in the upper Wind River Valley since 1899. The Stringer family settled on the Wind River west of Dubois and filed homestead claims.

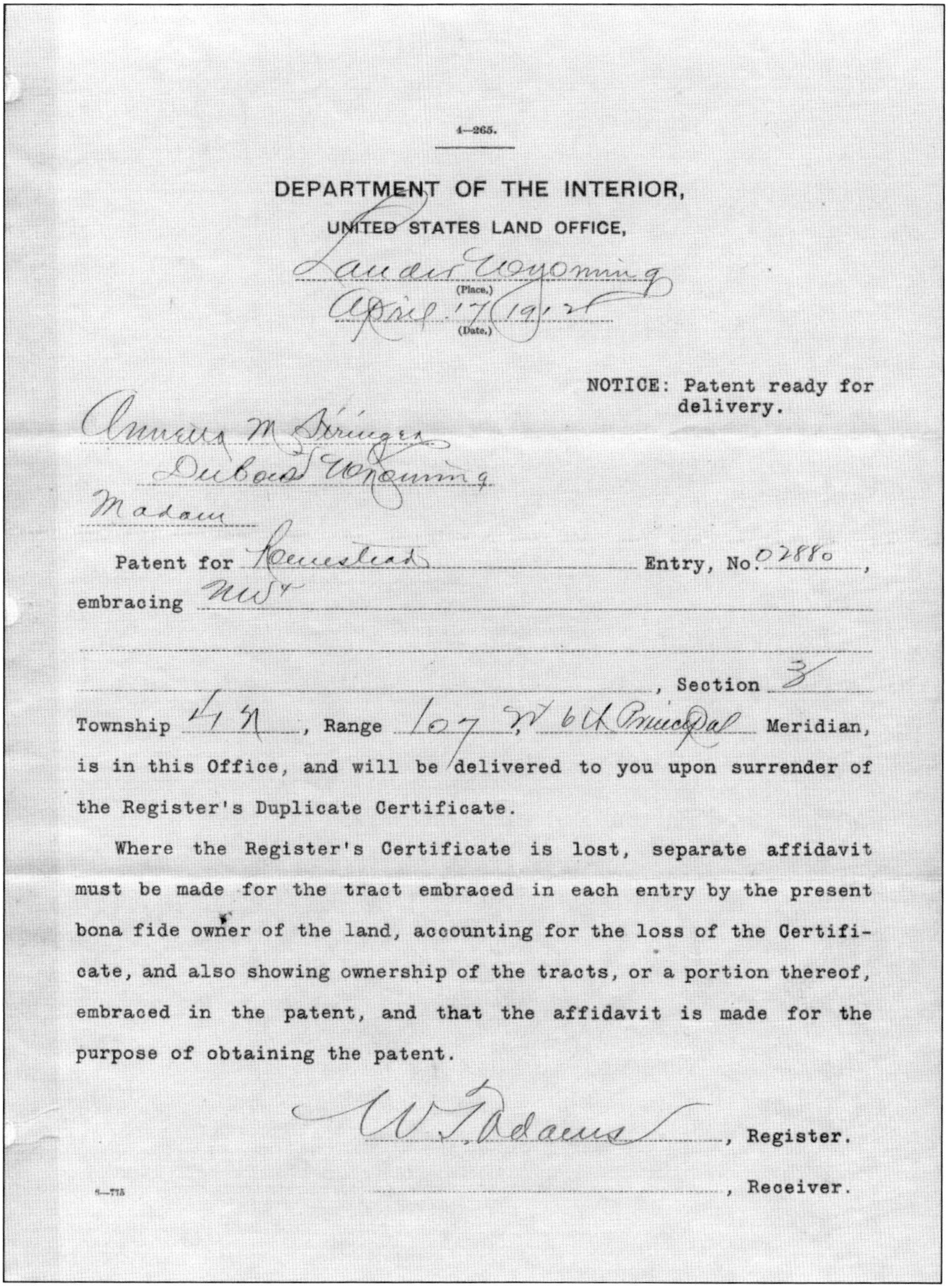

4—265.

DEPARTMENT OF THE INTERIOR,

UNITED STATES LAND OFFICE,

Lander Wyoming
(Place.)

April 17 1912
(Date.)

NOTICE: Patent ready for delivery.

Annette M Stringer

Dubois Wyoming

Madam

Patent for Homestead Entry, No. 02880,

embracing NW4

, Section 3

Township 41 N, Range 107 W 6th Principal Meridian, is in this Office, and will be delivered to you upon surrender of the Register's Duplicate Certificate.

Where the Register's Certificate is lost, separate affidavit must be made for the tract embraced in each entry by the present bona fide owner of the land, accounting for the loss of the Certificate, and also showing ownership of the tracts, or a portion thereof, embraced in the patent, and that the affidavit is made for the purpose of obtaining the patent.

W T Adams, Register.

, Receiver.

8—775

Nettie Stringer filed a homestead claim in 1905 and fulfilled the Homestead Act requirements by the fall of 1912 as indicated in a letter from the US Department of Interior.

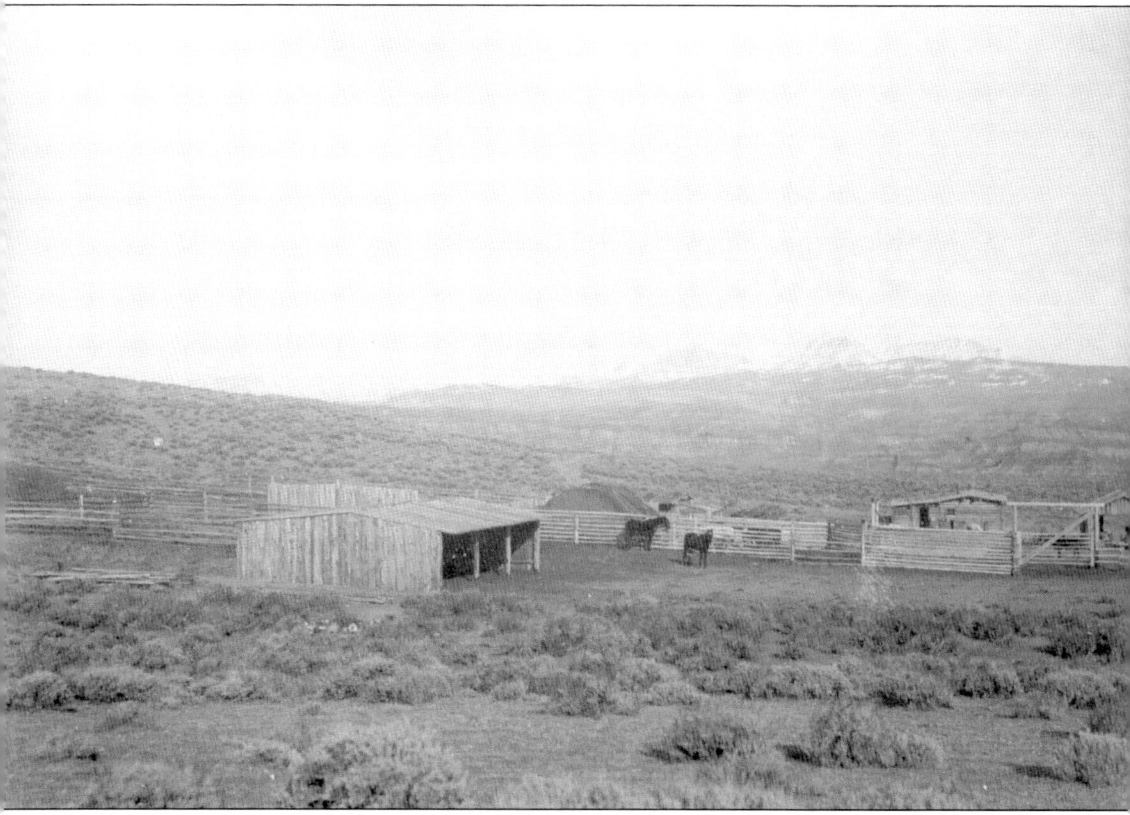

The homestead of Nettie Stringer's brother Asa is pictured here. Nettie ranched on her homestead until 1913 but continued to live with her brother Asa until she moved into town to cook for her brothers at the Stringer Hotel. The hotel was built by Oscar and Albert in 1913 in the village that would incorporate as the town of Dubois the following year.

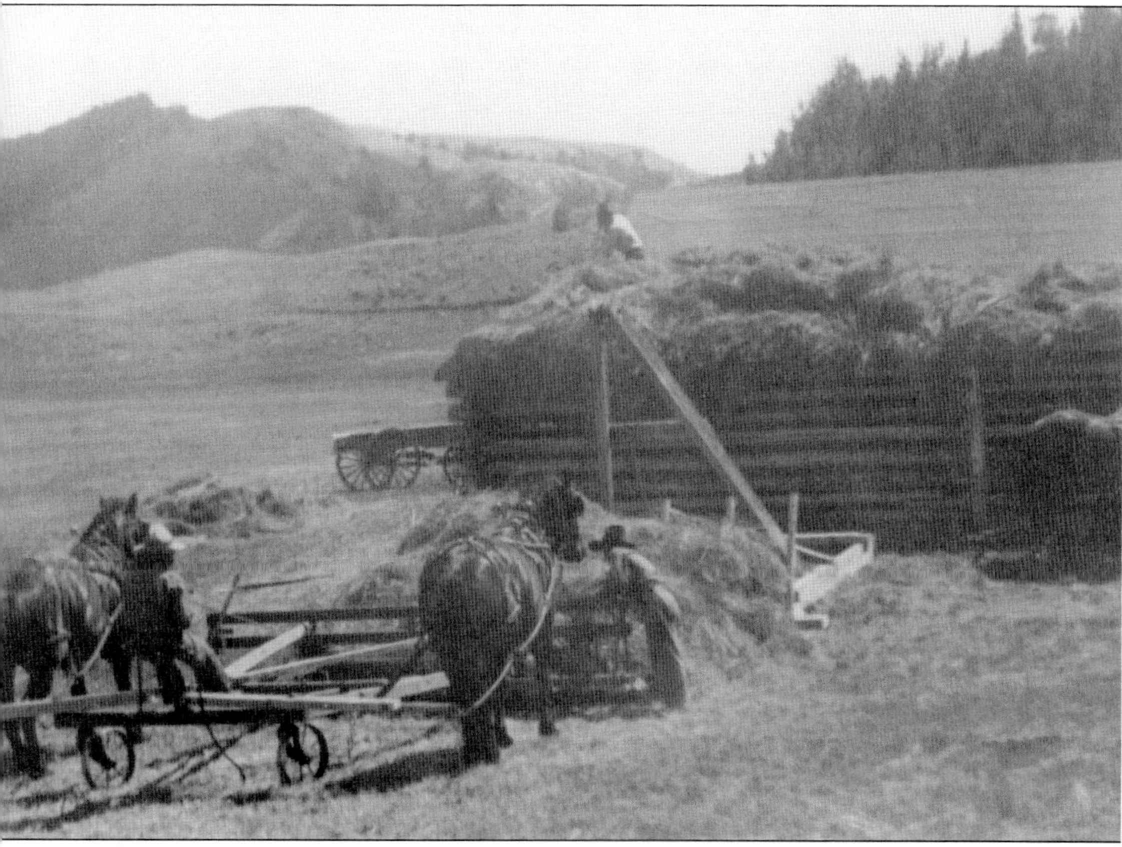

Einar and Augusta "Gussie" Anderson are shown in the late 1930s raking hay at their 120-acre homestead on Plow Creek in the upper Horse Creek drainage. In addition to their homestead acreage, the Andersons held a US Forest Service permit to graze 80 cows in the Washakie National Forest.

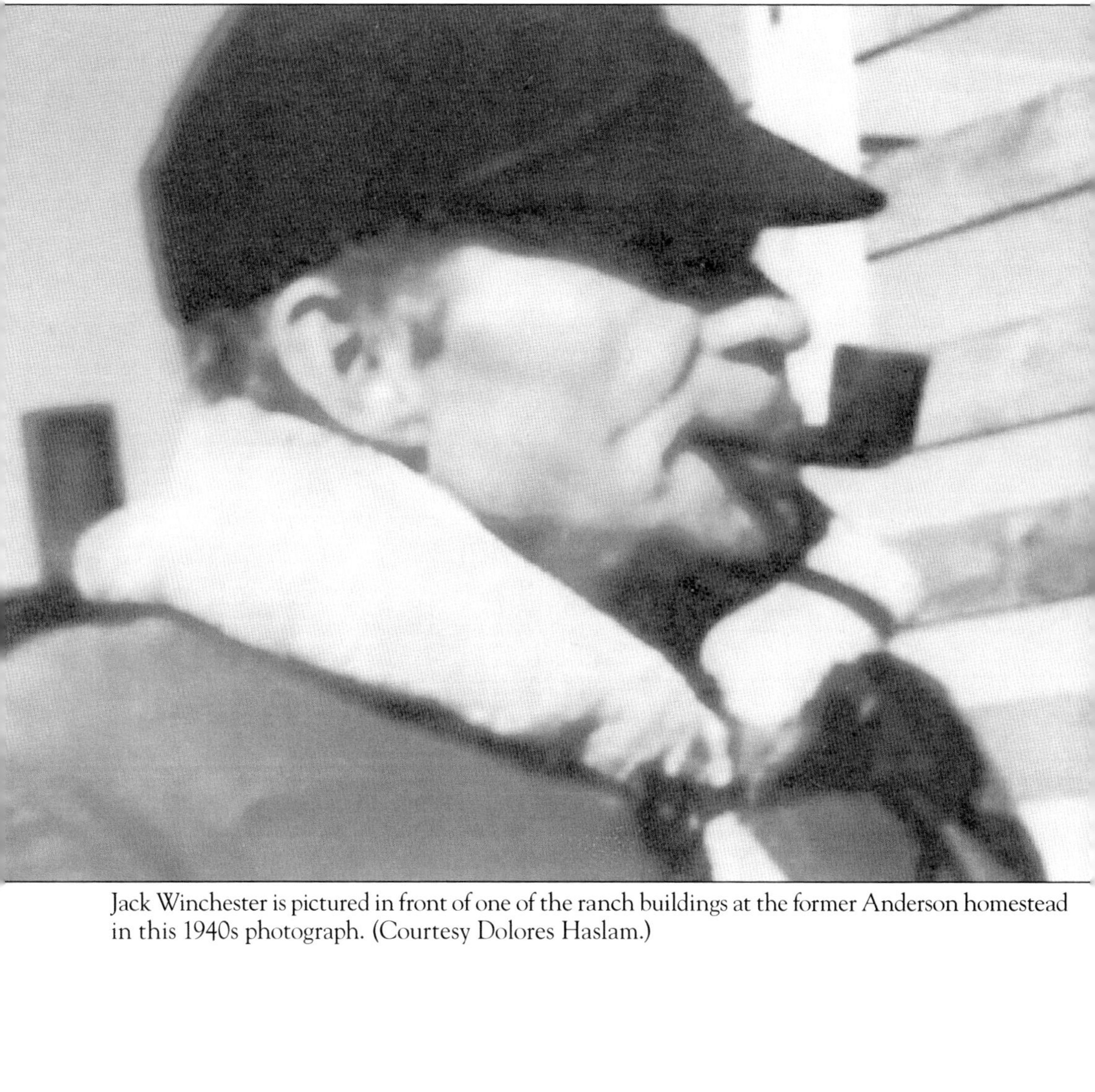

Jack Winchester is pictured in front of one of the ranch buildings at the former Anderson homestead in this 1940s photograph. (Courtesy Dolores Haslam.)

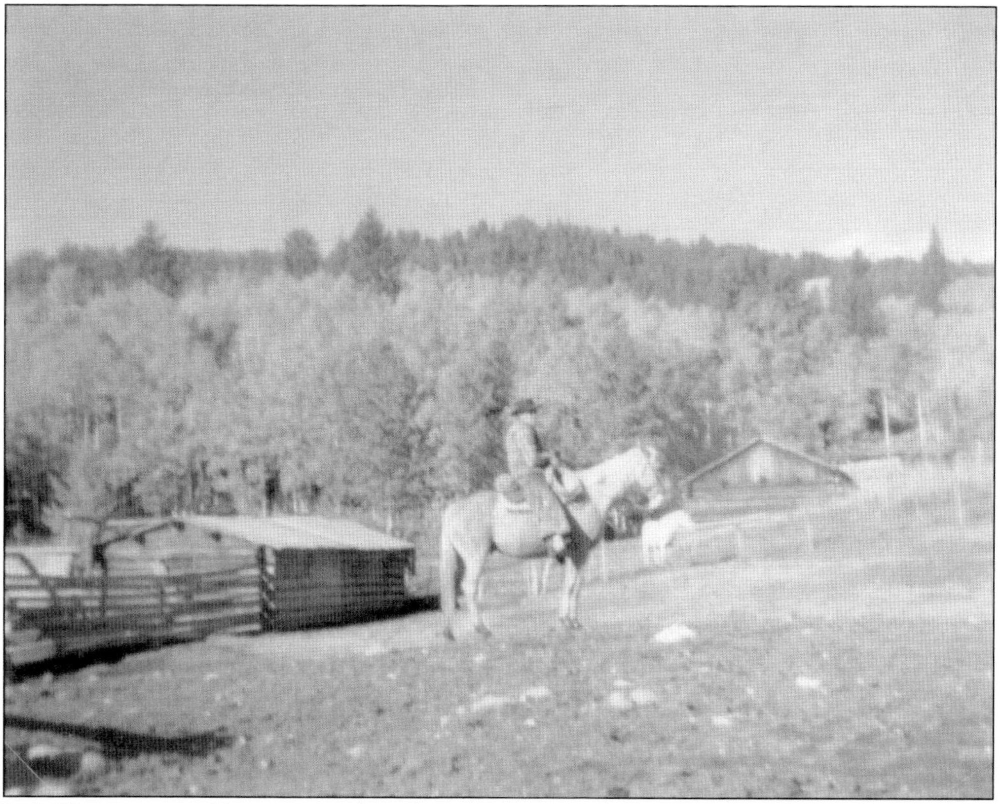

Jack Winchester and his sons purchased the Anderson homestead as summer range for their cattle in 1946. The Winchester family operated their home ranch on the Wind River Reservation near Crowheart, seasonally moving cattle from one ranch to the other. Here, Jack's son Albert is pictured on his horse looking over the former Anderson homestead that his family called the upper ranch. (Courtesy Dolores Haslam.)

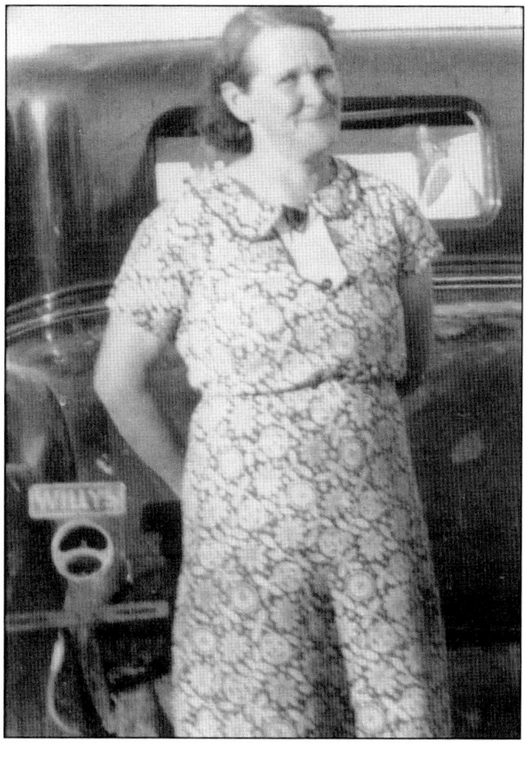

Jack Winchester's wife, Goldie, looking every inch the industrious ranch wife, is shown standing in front of the back of her car in the 1930s. (Courtesy Dolores Haslam.)

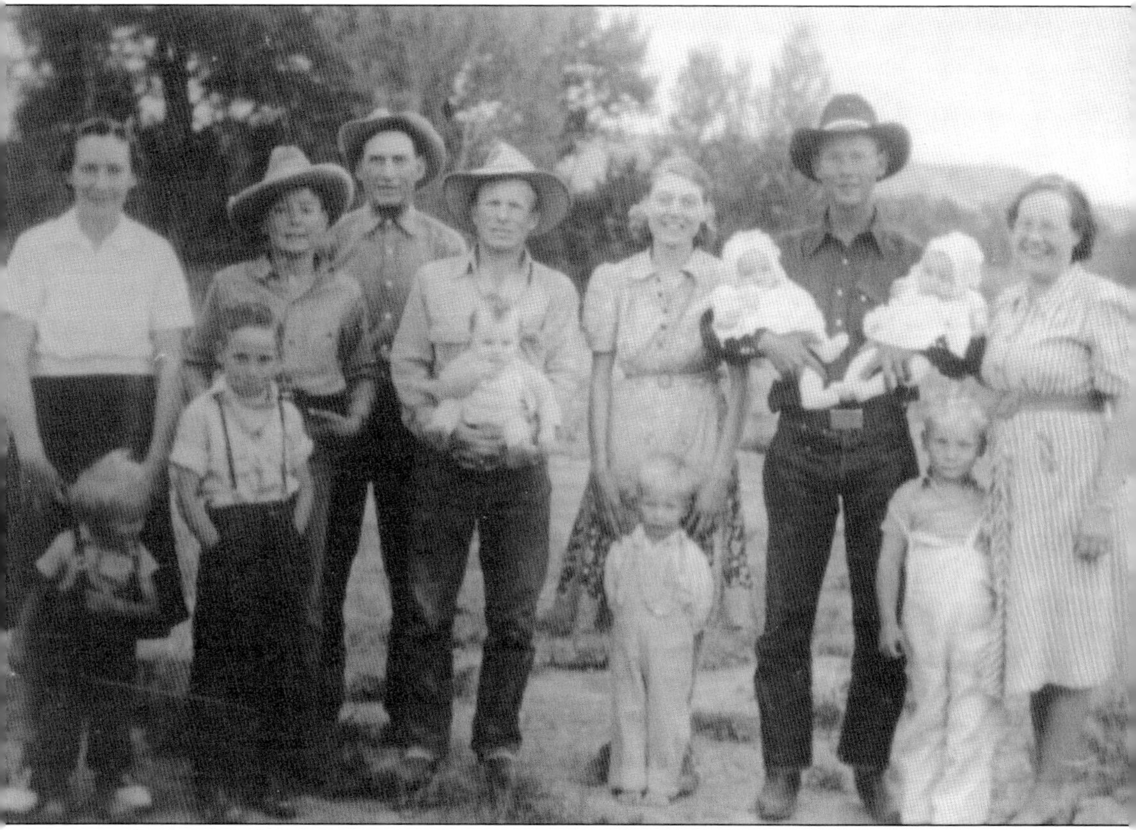

The extended Winchester family is pictured in the 1940s. In the back row from left to right are Winifred Crow, two unidentified hired hands, Harold Winchester holding baby Dolores, Eleanora Winchester, Lee Wickstrom with Hazel's twins Beverly and Barbara, and Hazel Winchester. The children in front, from left to right, are Jackie Winchester, Marvin Thomson, "Booge" Frank, and John L. Frank. (Courtesy Dolores Haslam.)

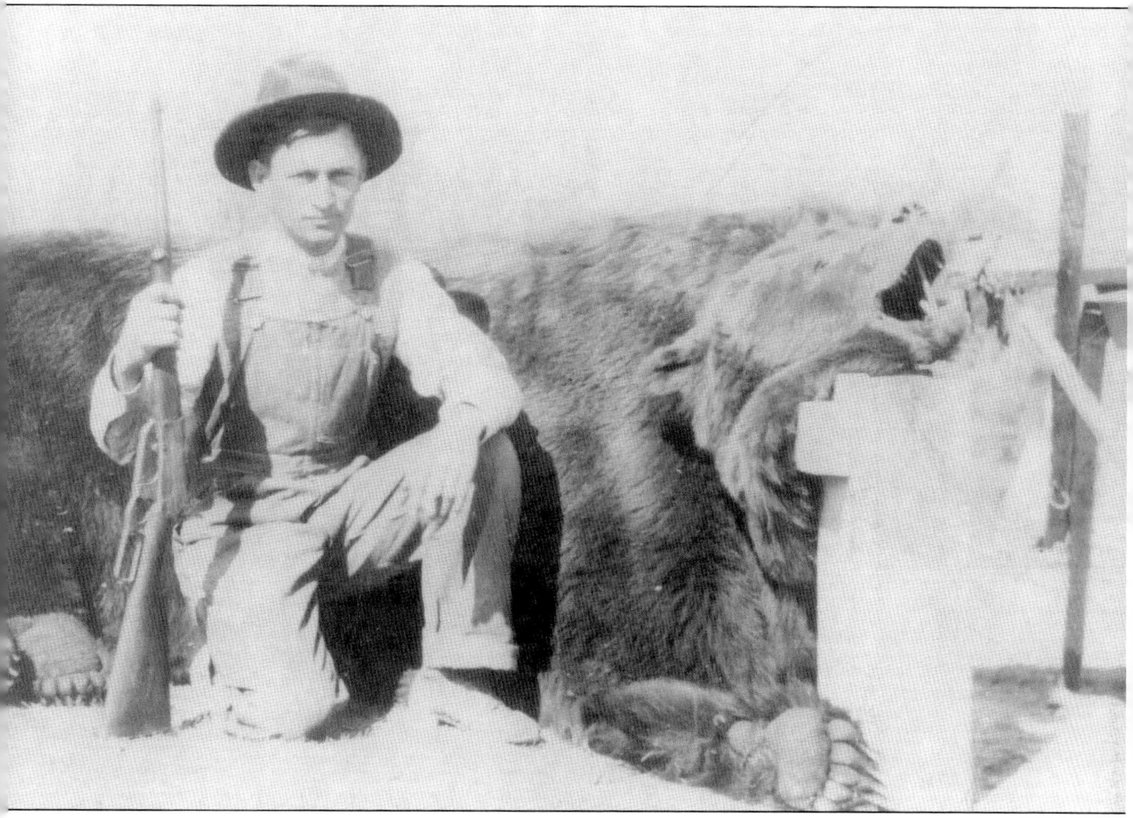

Oliver Wickstrom, grandson of Jack and Goldie Winchester, poses with a bear he shot. Ranching in areas bordering a national forest presented unique problems, such as bears killing ranch livestock.

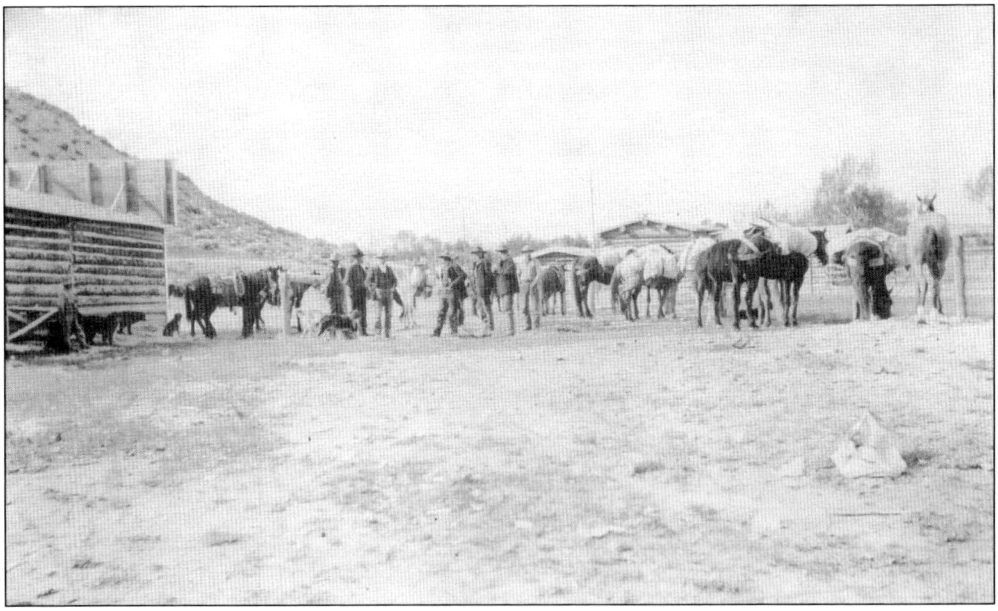

Richard Bartholomay Jr., and his friends have drawn the attention of curious local residents as they pack supplies from F.A. Welty General Merchandise. Charles C. "Charlie" Moore outfitted the hunting party; Moore met these men while working at Marshall Fields in Chicago and attending the University of Michigan.

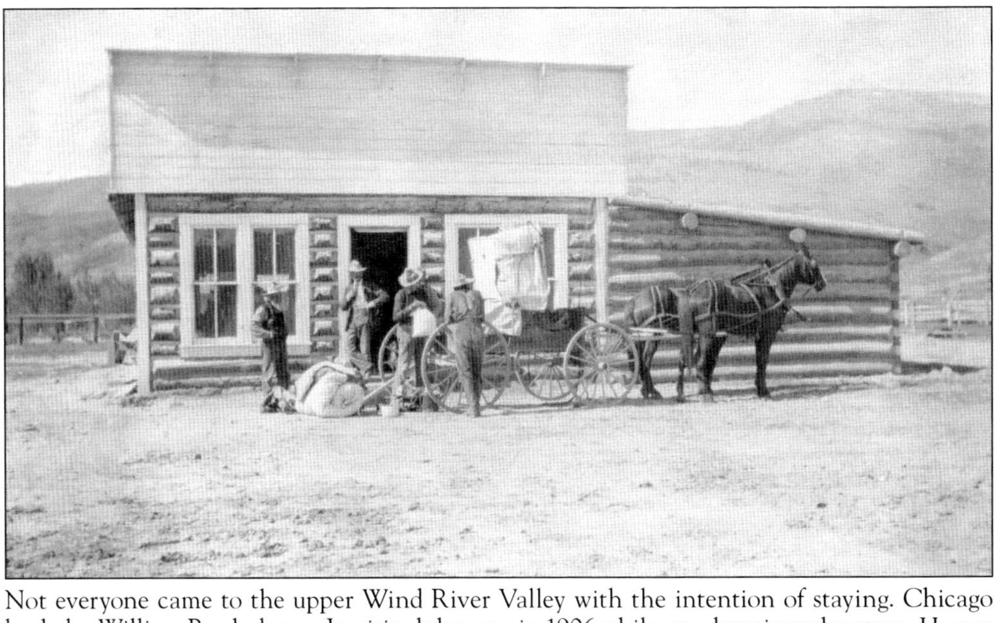

Not everyone came to the upper Wind River Valley with the intention of staying. Chicago bachelor William Bartholomay Jr. visited the area in 1906 while on a hunting adventure. He was accompanied by Conrad Seipp, Edward Uihlein, and Russell Thorpe. The young men are pictured packing supplies they have purchased at F.A. Welty General Merchandise.

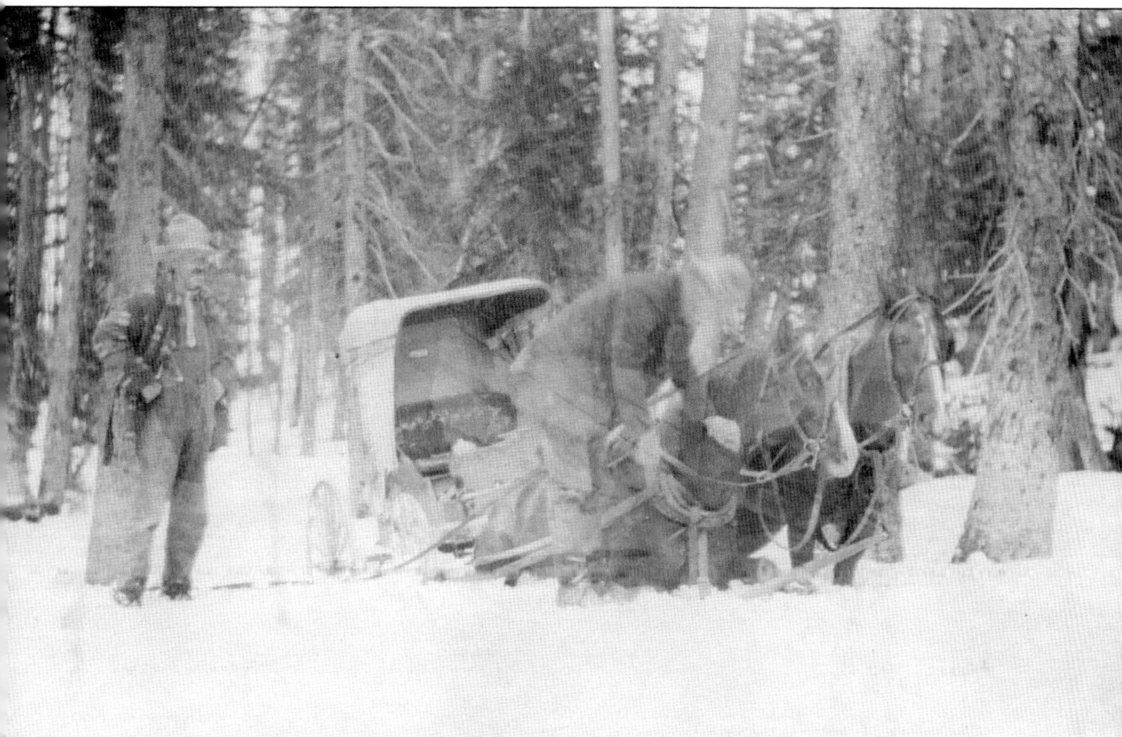

William Bartholomay Jr. and his friends were soon bogged down in deep snow, and their hunting adventure became even more adventurous. At some point during their stay in the upper Wind River Valley, they were joined by writer Owen Wister, who was connected to Bartholomay through a friend, Wyoming native Russell Thorpe.

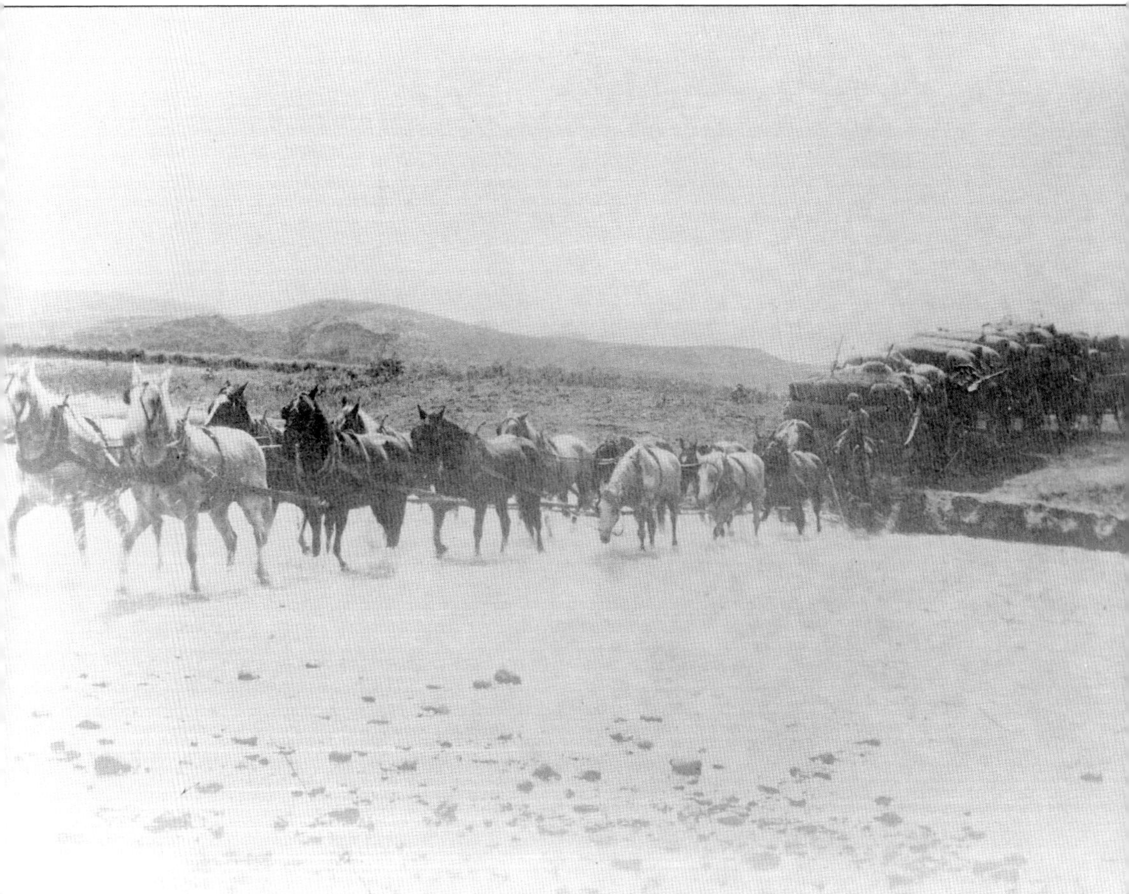

Before automobiles, supplies for homesteaders in the upper Wind River were brought in by freight teams. Willard West's freight team is seen here in the early 1900s at Double Crossing on the Powder River.

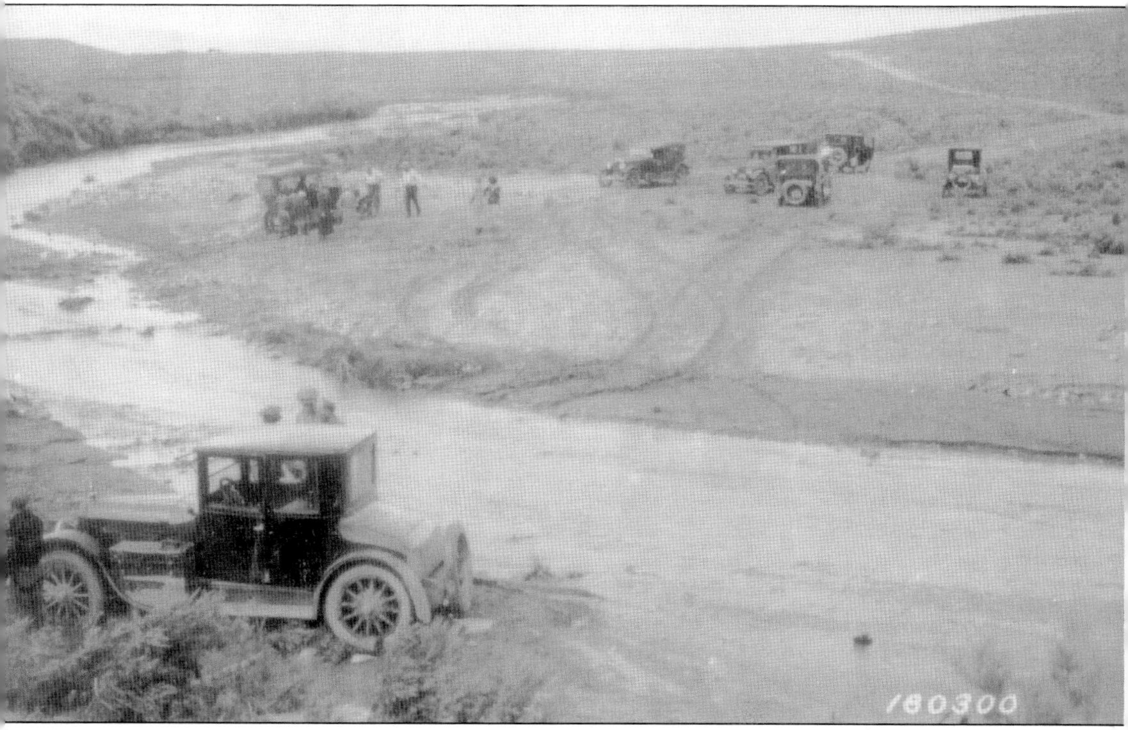

When automobiles became popular in the 1920s, travel to and from the upper Wind River Valley became easier, but it was still difficult. A line of automobiles is pictured waiting to cross the Wind River in the late 1920s.

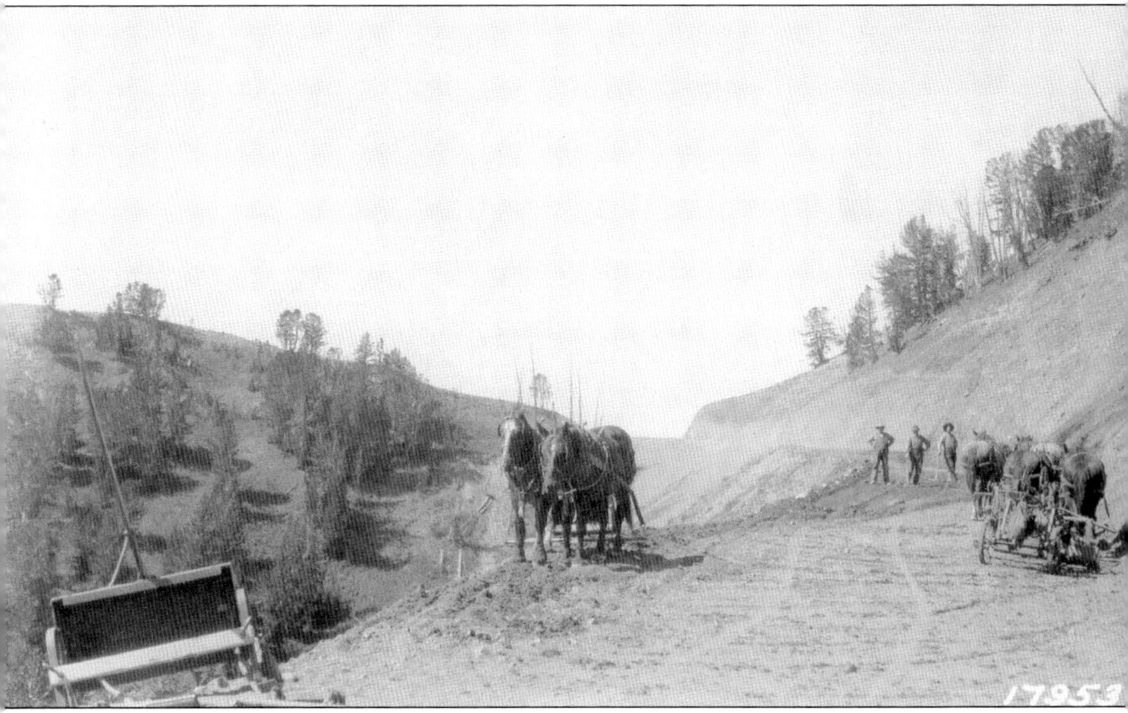

Horse teams are shown in the early 1920s building a section of the original US Highway 287 near Barber's Point on Togwotee Pass. The completed highway connected the upper Wind River Valley to Yellowstone National Park and the Snake River Valley. Capt. William A. Jones of the US Army Corps of Engineers visited Yellowstone in 1873 and recommended building a road across Togwotee Pass, but it was not completed until 1921. The pass is named for Togwotee, a Shoshone chief who guided Jones's expedition. Opening of the highway was celebrated with a ground-breaking ceremony at Togwotee Pass and a rodeo in Dubois.

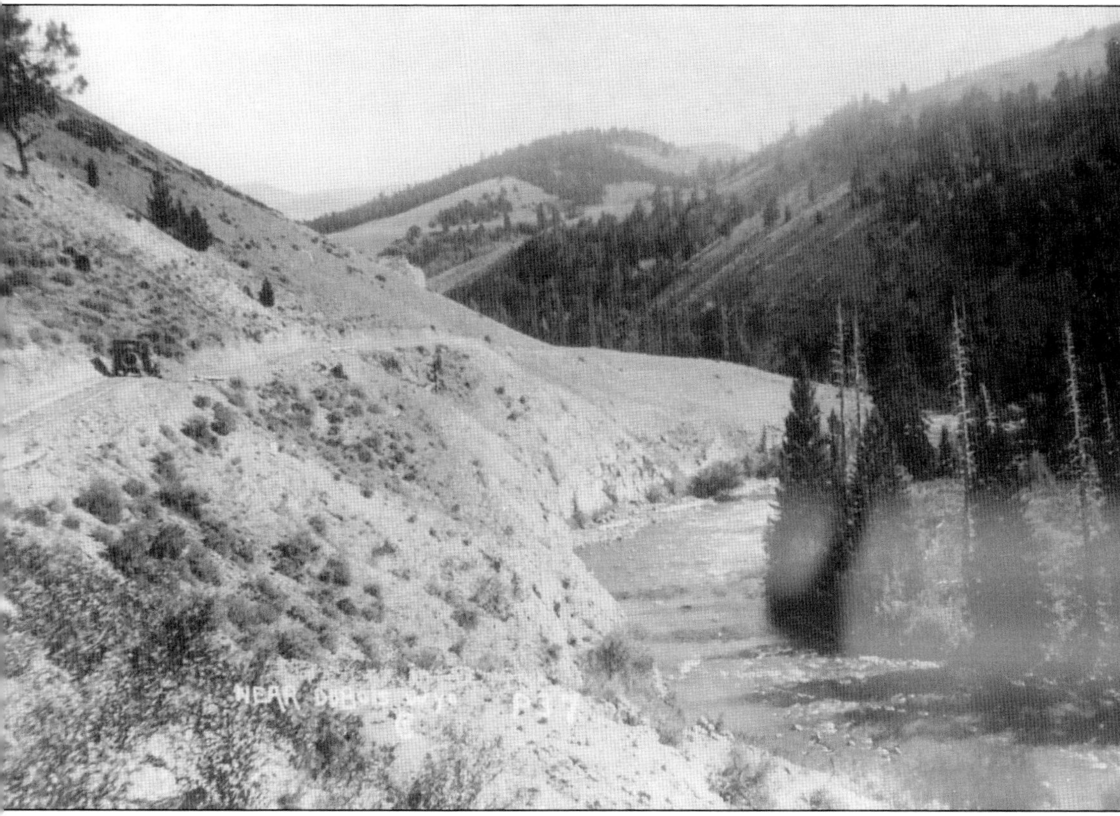

This 1936 photograph of US Highway 287 west of Dubois near Stoney Point illustrates that travel in the upper Wind River Valley was still far from ideal.

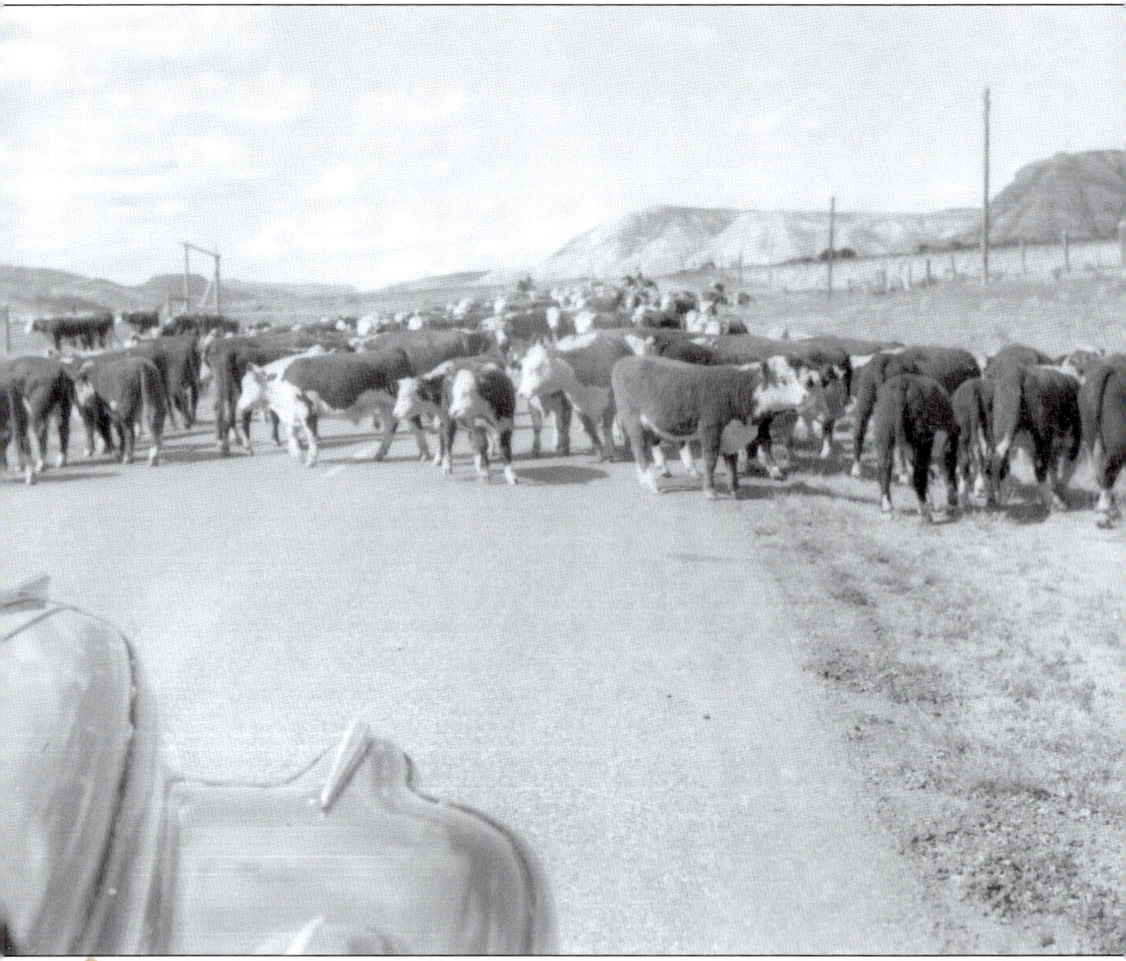

A cattle drive is pictured west of Dubois in the 1940s. Early families of the Dubois area soon discovered that ranching was the only practical use of land in the upper Wind River Valley, where the growing season for plants was so short.

Two

Little Town on the Wind River

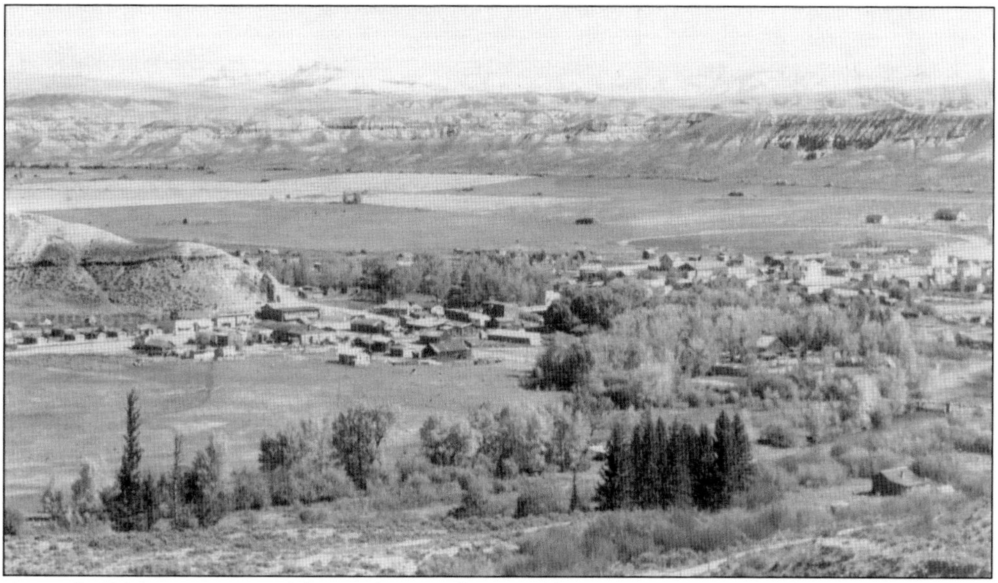

An early 1900s panorama of the settlement that would soon become Dubois shows a small cluster of houses and businesses strung out along the Wind River. The settlement was incorporated as the town of Dubois in 1914. The new town was called Dubois because that name had been given to its first post office in 1889. Names such as Tibo and Never Sweat were proposed at first but rejected. Dubois was deemed an acceptable compromise, because people liked the way Idaho senator Fred Dubois had voted on several important issues. He was also a member of the US Postal Committee at the time.

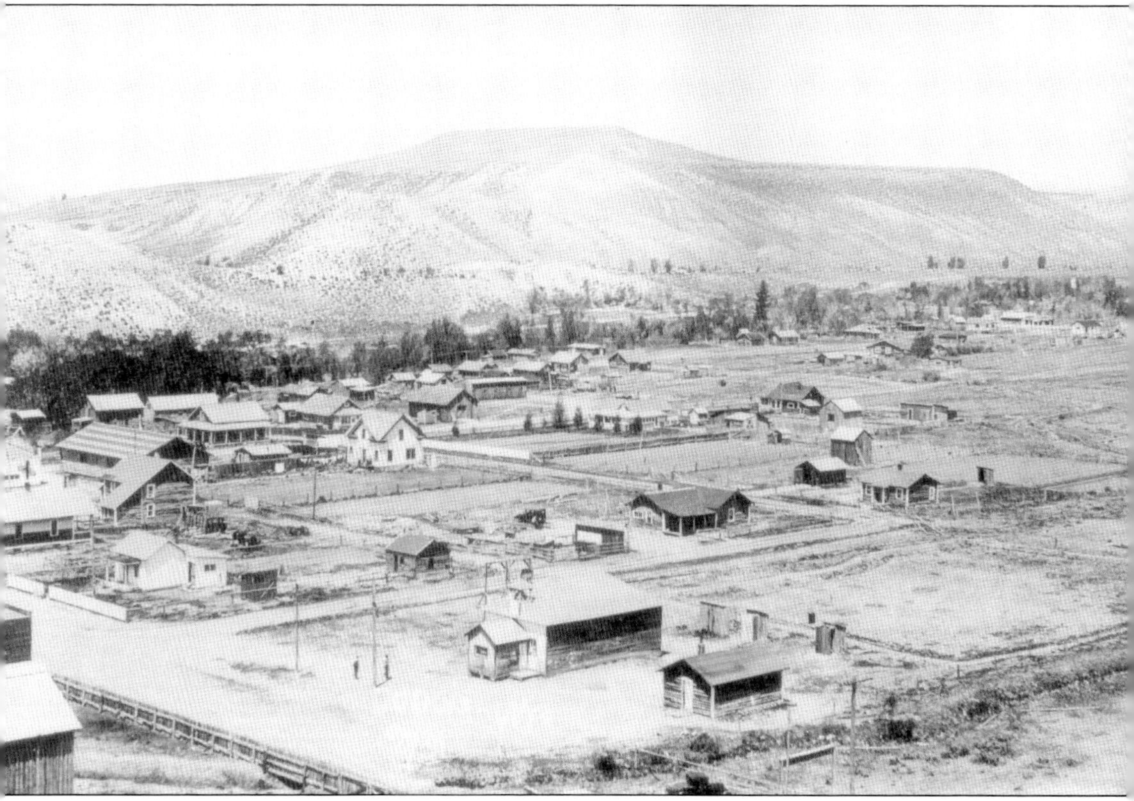

A panorama photograph of Dubois shows the town in 1934. The commercial area has obviously grown, but there are few other changes.

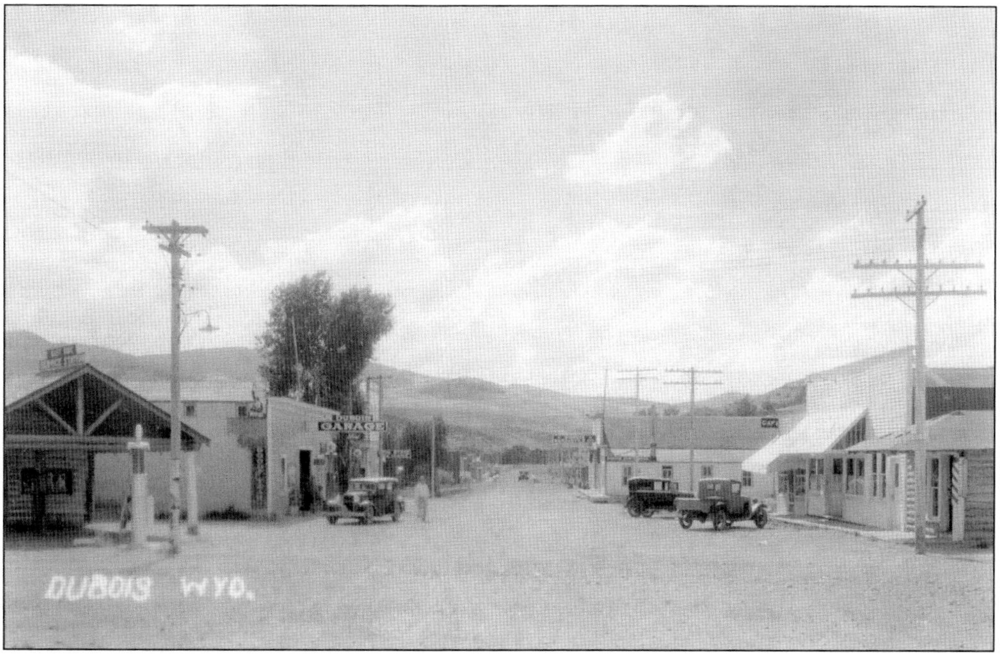

Downtown Dubois is pictured in 1924 looking west down Ramshorn Street from the East Side Service Station and Dubois Garage to Dubois Mercantile.

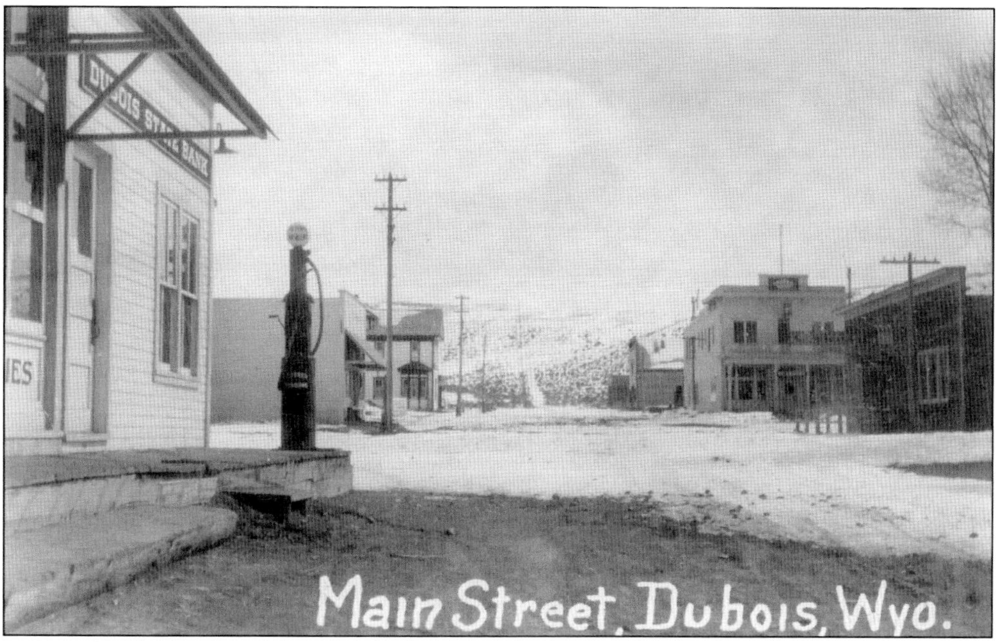

A second view of Ramshorn Street in 1924 faces east toward the wing of Dubois Mercantile that housed the Dubois State Bank. The bank operated between 1918 and 1933, but it was not the first bank in Dubois. The Amoretti, Welty, Helmer and Co. Bank was established in 1913 but failed in 1927.

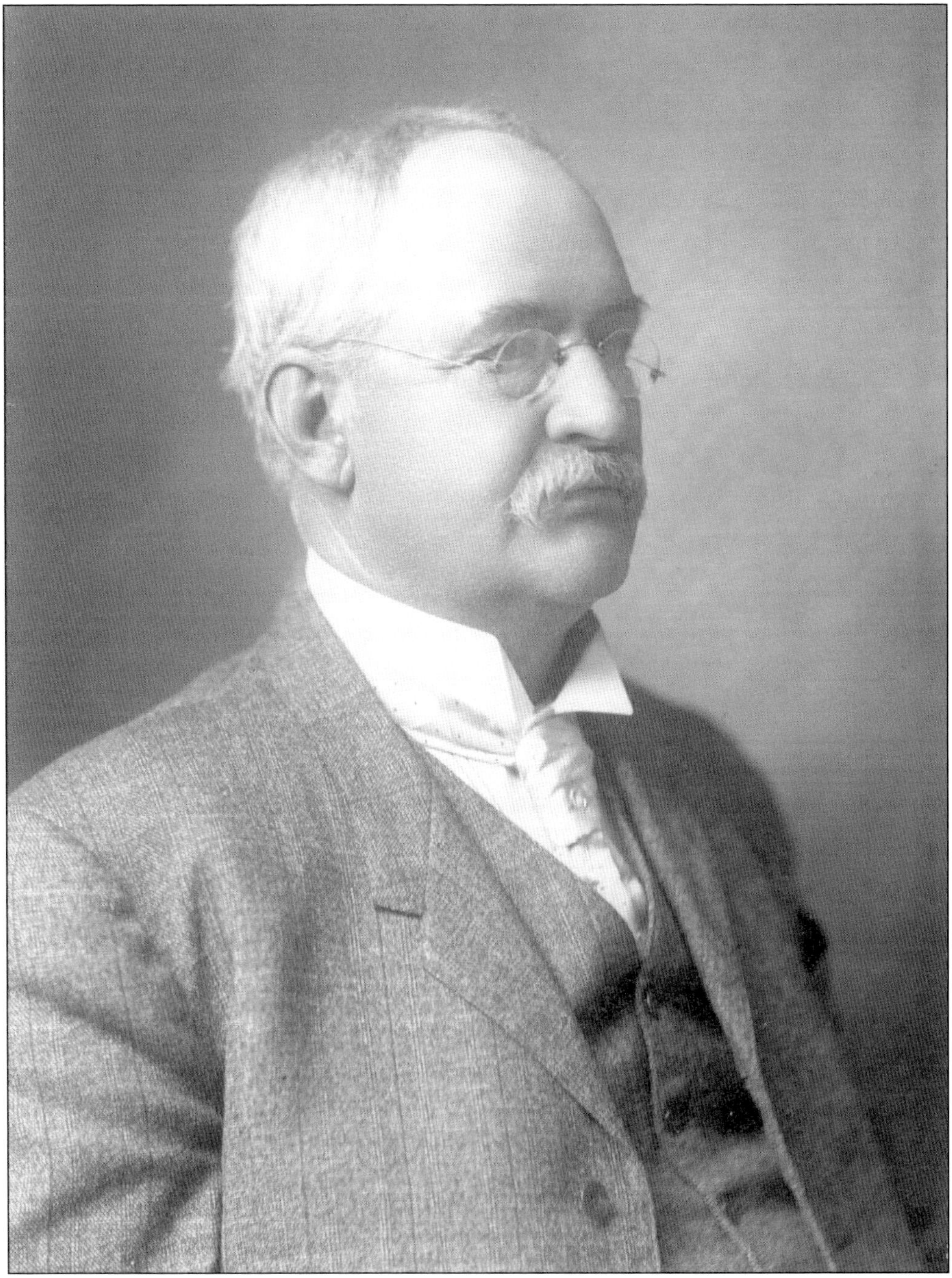

Dr. Frances Welty, pictured in the early 1900s, became the only doctor in the upper Wind River Valley in 1906 after he left his post as doctor for the Indian Agency on the Wind River Reservation and moved to his homestead on Horse Creek. Dr. Welty was elected the first mayor of the newly incorporated town of Dubois in 1915 and was serving a second term in 1919 when he was swept away by floodwaters from an unusually heavy rain that caused Horse Creek to flow over its banks. Dr. Welty was sleeping in his office next to the creek at the time. His body was found several miles downstream a few days later.

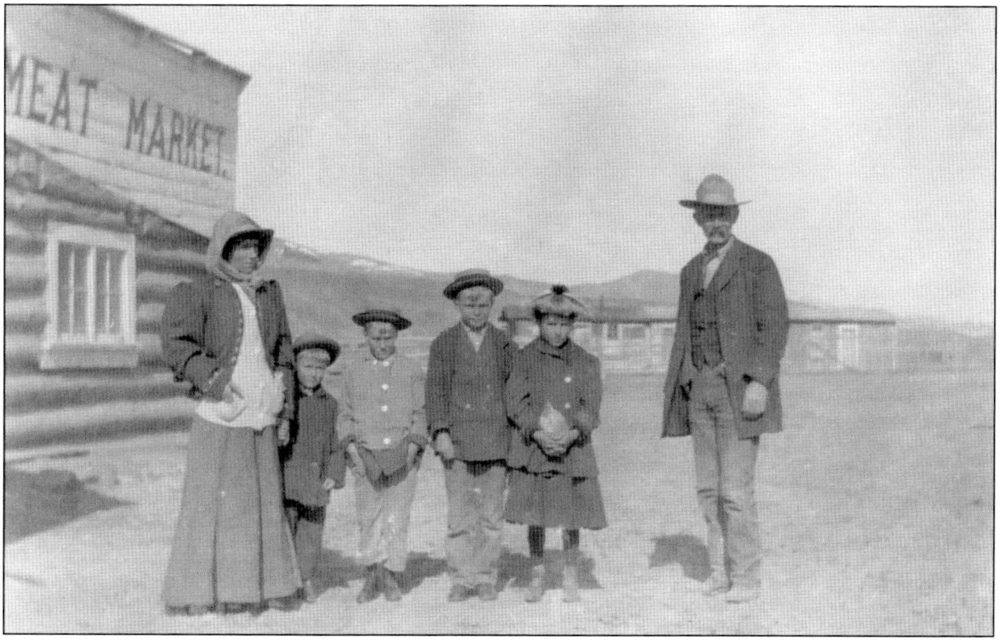

An unidentified family of six poses in front of F.A. Welty General Merchandise and Meat Market around 1900. In 1898, Frank Amoss Welty, son of Dr. Frances Welty, purchased an existing store in the growing village along the Wind River and moved his business. Welty learned merchandising while working summers at J.K. Moore's Trading Post on the Wind River Reservation when his father was a doctor for the Indian Agency. By 1897, young Welty was selling merchandise from a store on his father's Horse Creek homestead.

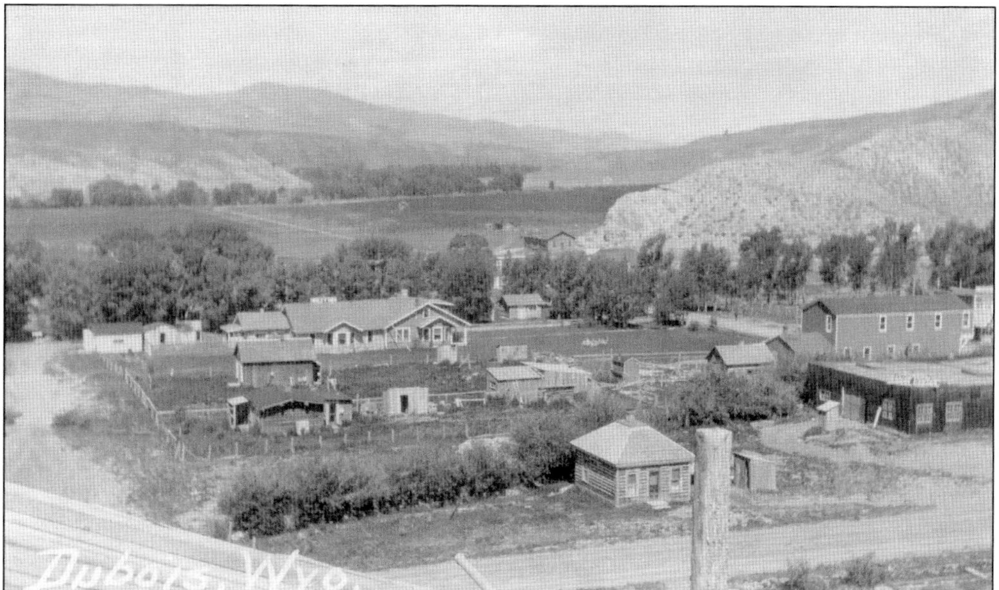

The Welty Inn is shown in the late 1920s. The inn was operated by Gladys Welty, the wife of Frank A. Welty, with cabins constructed near their home. A registered nurse, she was often called when someone was sick during the years after Doctor Welty died and there was no doctor in the community.

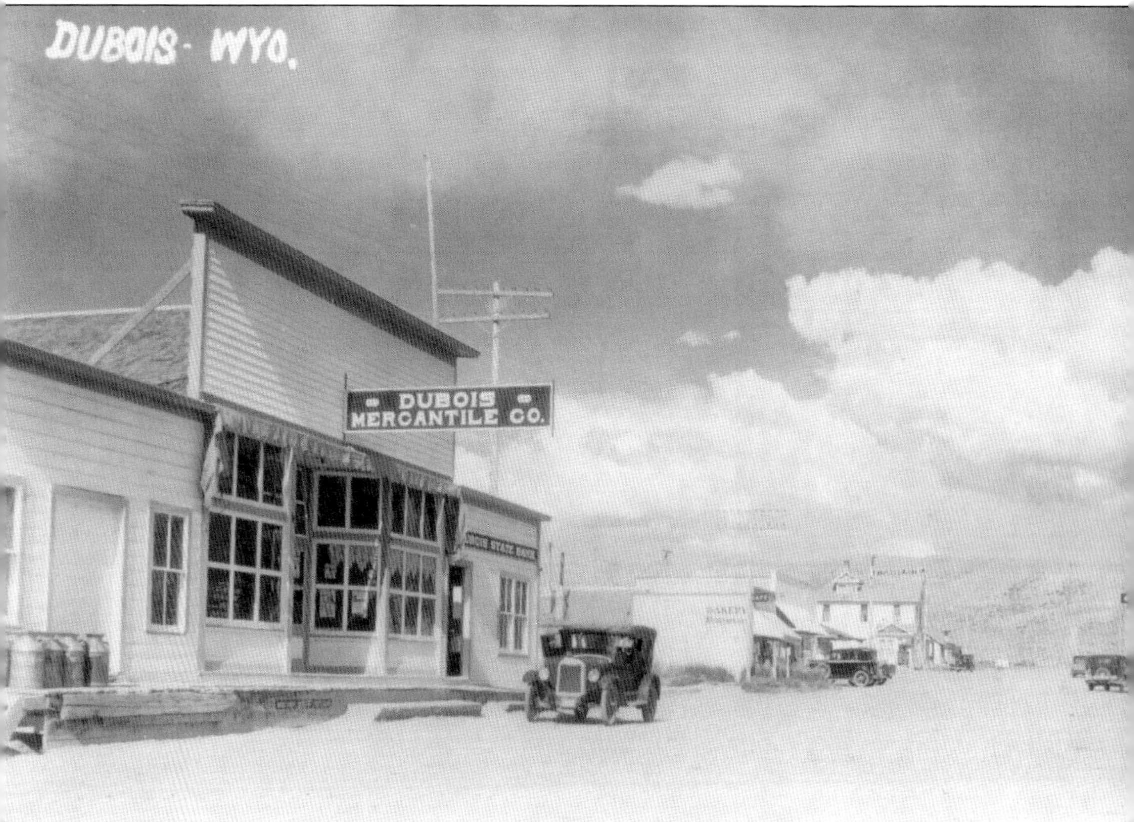

Dubois Mercantile is pictured in 1924. The opening of Dubois Mercantile in 1913 gave F.A. Welty General Merchandise its first competition. Wyoming Tie and Timber Company purchased the business in 1947 after the company's railroad tie–cutting operation in the Dubois area closed.

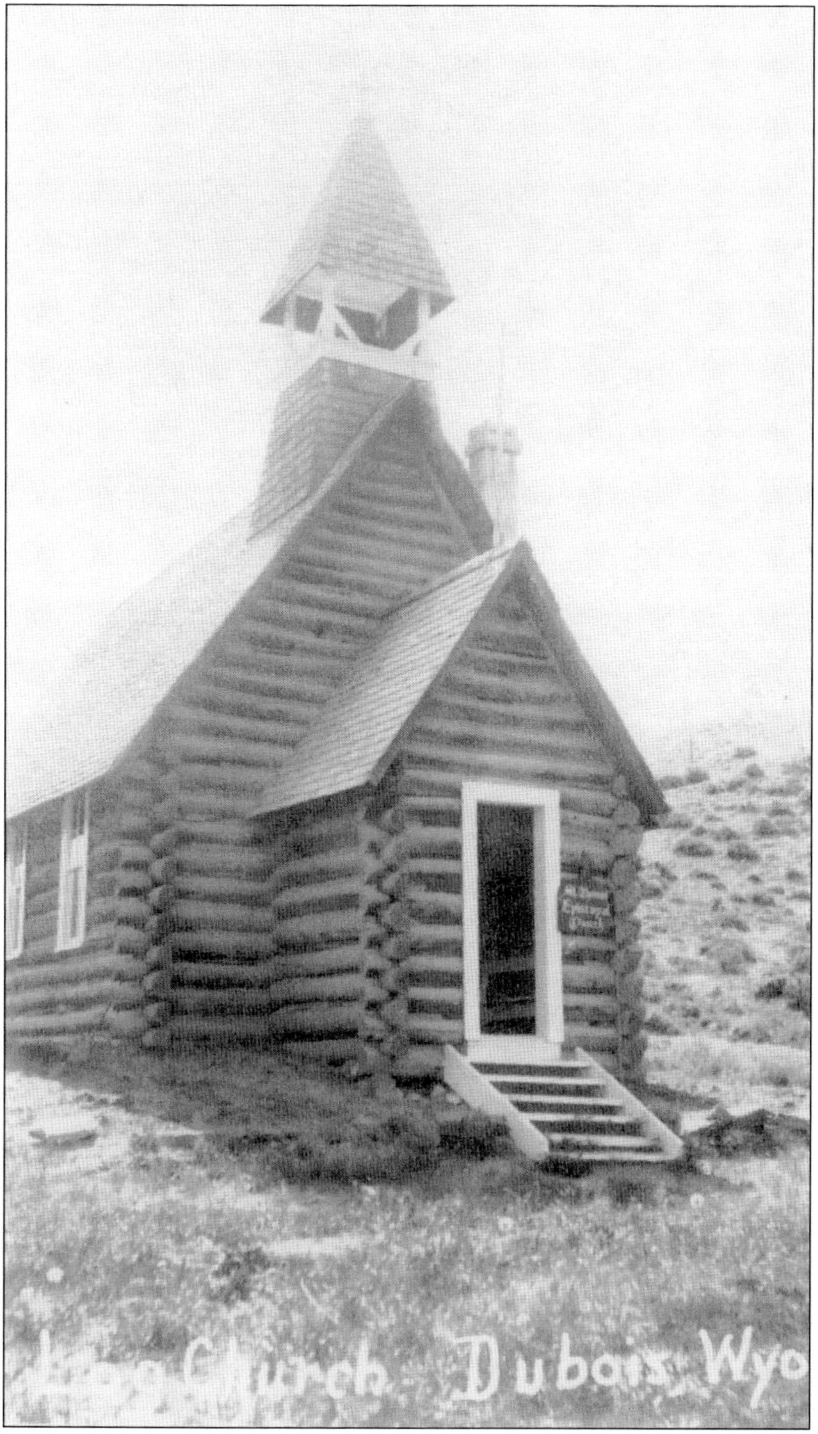

The St. Thomas Episcopal Church congregation constructed the log building pictured in 1910 on two lots donated by Dr. Frances Welty, using volunteer labor and logs donated by Wyoming Tie and Timber Company. The original log church, now with two additions, is still in use today. (Courtesy St. Thomas Episcopal Church.)

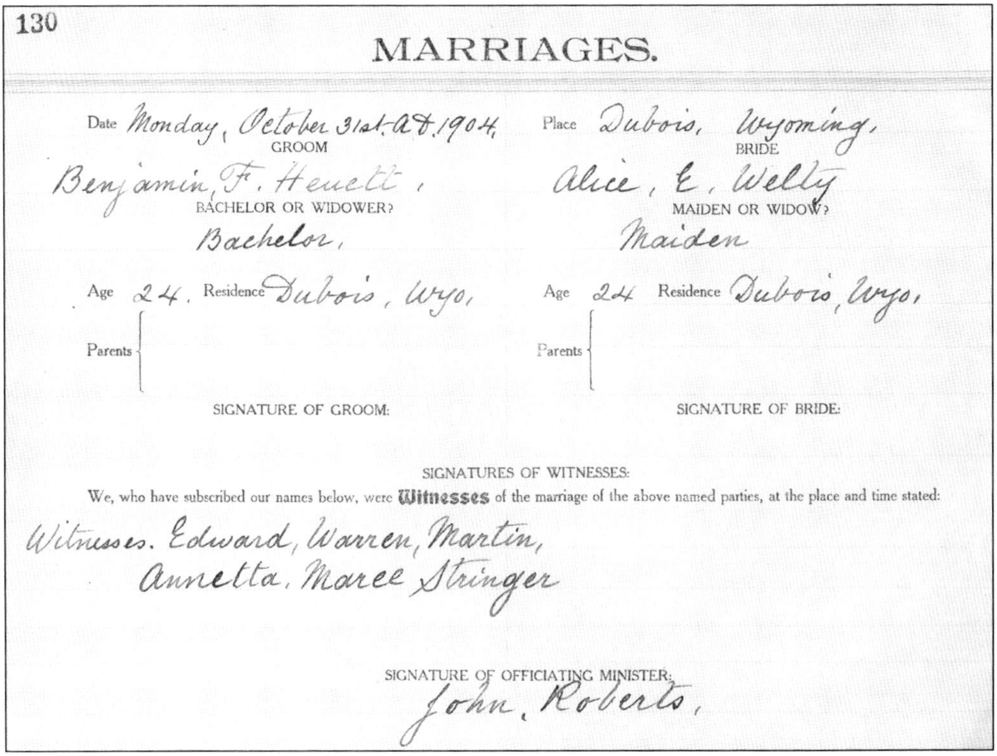

130

MARRIAGES.

Date Monday, October 31st AD 1904. Place Dubois, Wyoming.

GROOM

Benjamin, F. Hewett.

BACHELOR OR WIDOWER?

Bachelor.

Age 24. Residence Dubois, Wyo.

Parents

SIGNATURE OF GROOM:

BRIDE

Alice, E. Welty

MAIDEN OR WIDOW?

Maiden

Age 24 Residence Dubois, Wyo.

Parents

SIGNATURE OF BRIDE:

SIGNATURES OF WITNESSES:

We, who have subscribed our names below, were **Witnesses** of the marriage of the above named parties, at the place and time stated:

Witnesses. Edward, Warren, Martin,
Annetta. Maree Stringer

SIGNATURE OF OFFICIATING MINISTER:

John. Roberts.

The Reverend John Roberts, Episcopal missionary to the Shoshone Indians on the Wind River Reservation, performed a wedding ceremony for Benjamin Hewitt and Alice Welty, daughter of Dr. Frances Welty, in 1904. The marriage certificate is pictured here. Although Reverend Roberts had held services at various locations ins since 1901, it was the first wedding ceremony performed for the young congregation. (Courtesy St. Thomas Episcopal Church.)

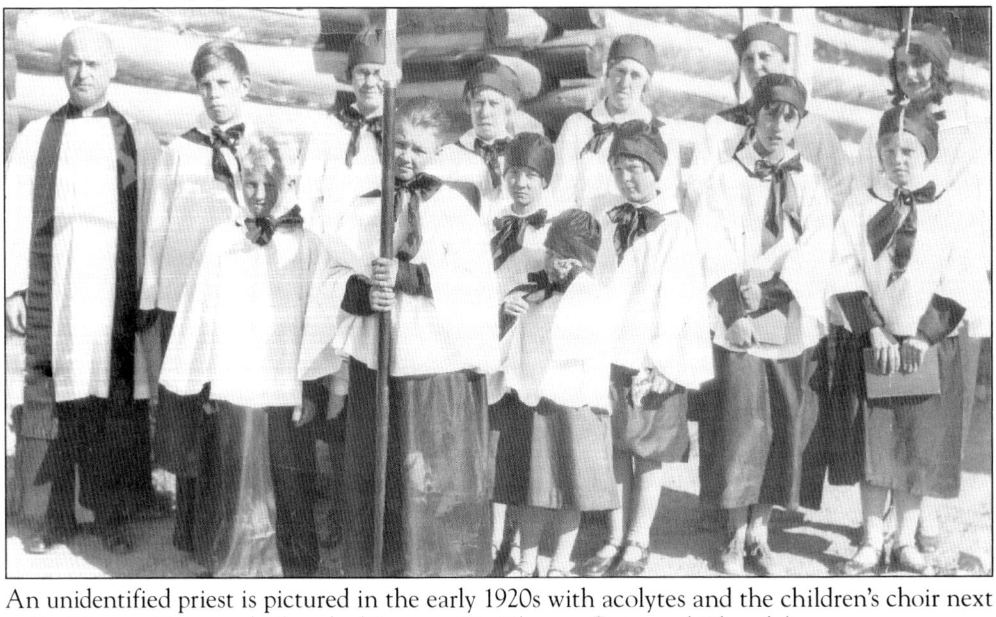

An unidentified priest is pictured in the early 1920s with acolytes and the children's choir next to St. Thomas Episcopal Church. (Courtesy St. Thomas Episcopal Church.)

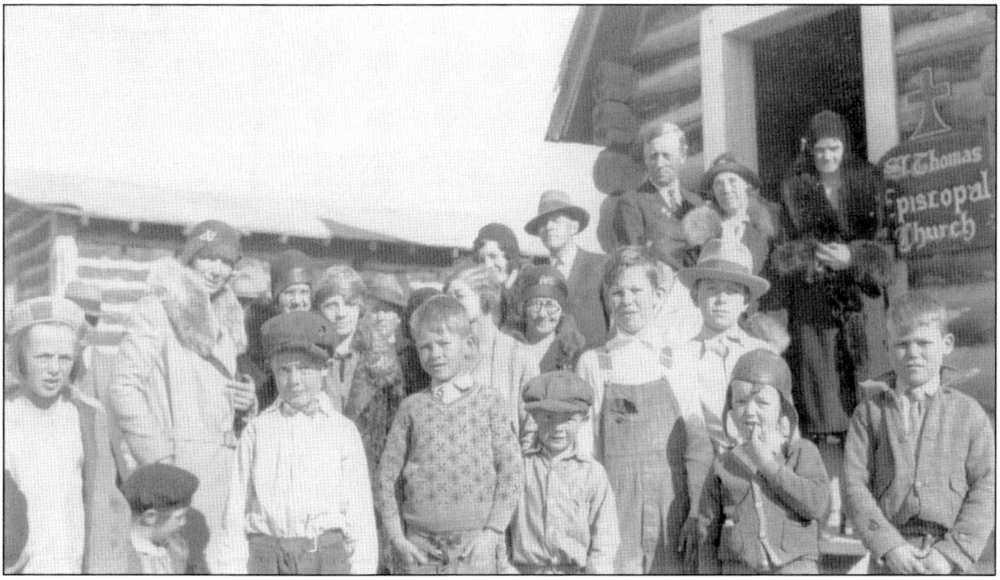

A congregation files out of St. Thomas Episcopal Church's chapel in this early-1920s photograph. (Courtesy St. Thomas Episcopal Church.)

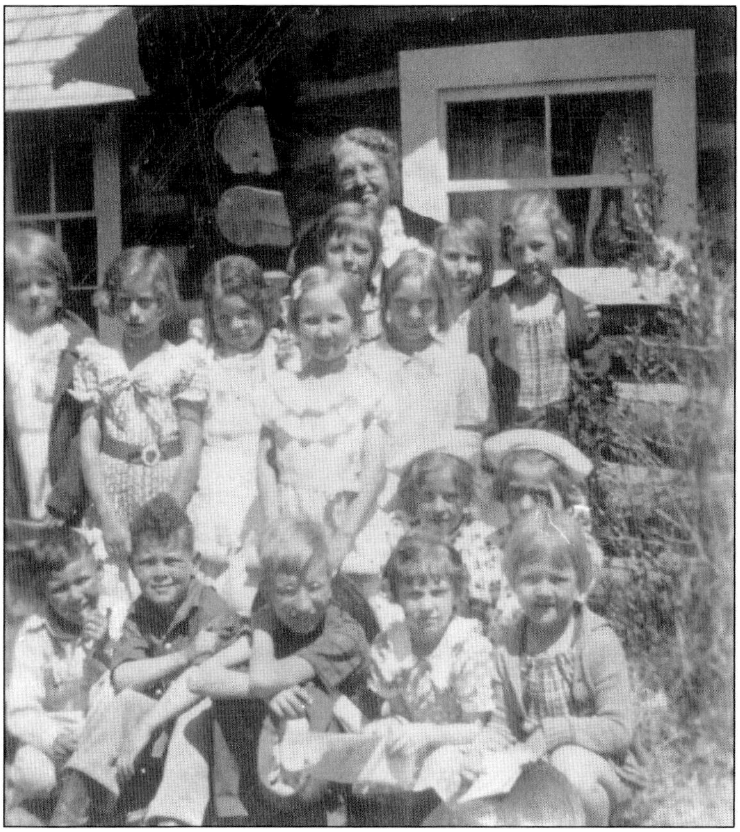

This 1937 photograph shows a St. Thomas Episcopal Church Sunday school class. From left to right are (first row) Glen McMichael, Mike Orr, Les Fossey, Marion McKie, and Junie Hulett; (second row) twins Jean and Ann White; (third row)Anna Fossey, Helen Henthorne, Shirley Redman, Gladys Williamson, and Lydia Ward; (fourth row) Mae Hutchison, Emma Stringer, and Jeanie Hulett. The teacher is not identified. (Courtesy St. Thomas Episcopal Church.)

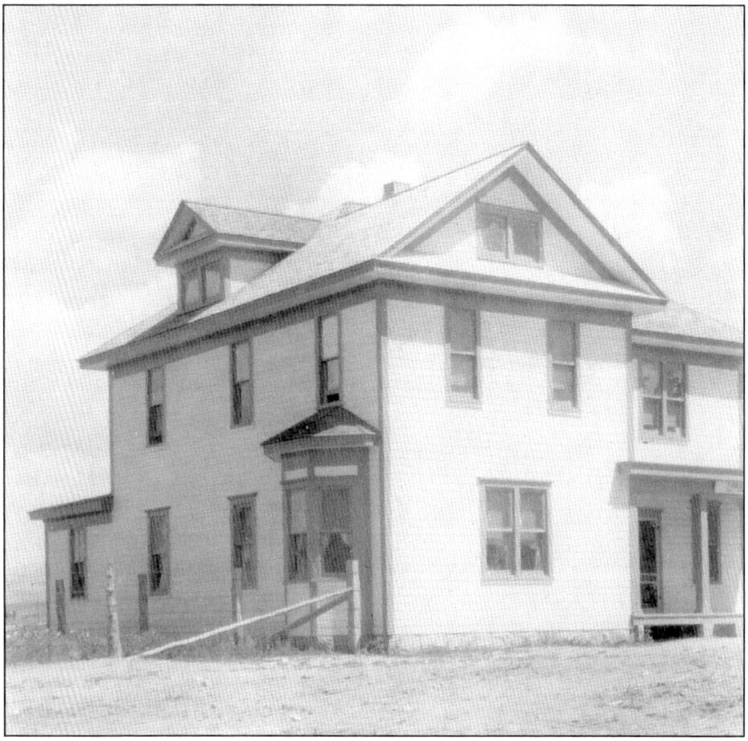

The Stringer Hotel, pictured here in the 1920s, was built in 1913 by Albert and Oscar Stringer. The brothers came to the Dubois area from Oklahoma in 1901 to homestead with brothers Carl and Ernest, their sister Nettie, and their mother, Sarah. Oscar and Albert operated the hotel, while the rest of the family worked on the family homesteads. Nettie also cooked for the hotel. The Stringer family operated the hotel until after World War II.

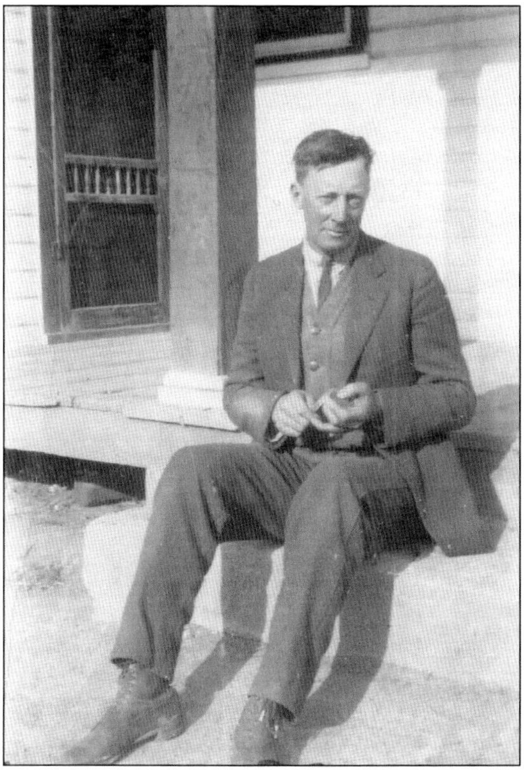

Albert Stringer is pictured on the Stringer Hotel front porch in the 1920s. The hotel was not known for its luxurious accommodations, and its rooms were reputed to be extremely cold in the winter.

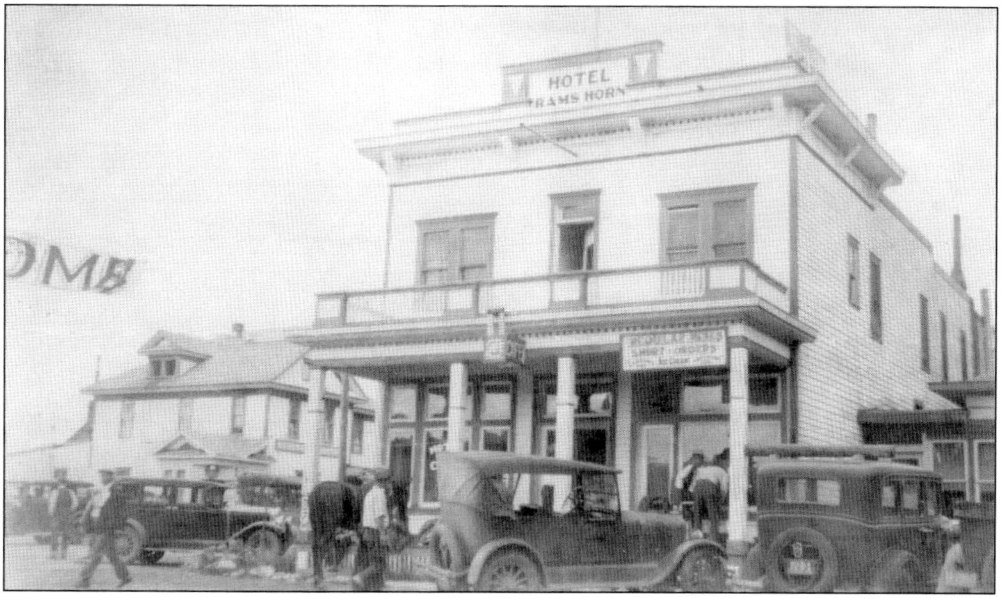

The Ramshorn Hotel was constructed in 1919 by Charles Ezra Shippen. The hotel, luxurious for the time, featured 12 rooms with a bathtub between every two rooms. It also had one full bathroom for the use of all guests. A series of people operated the hotel until it burned in 1935. It was not rebuilt, and the Stringer Hotel took its name.

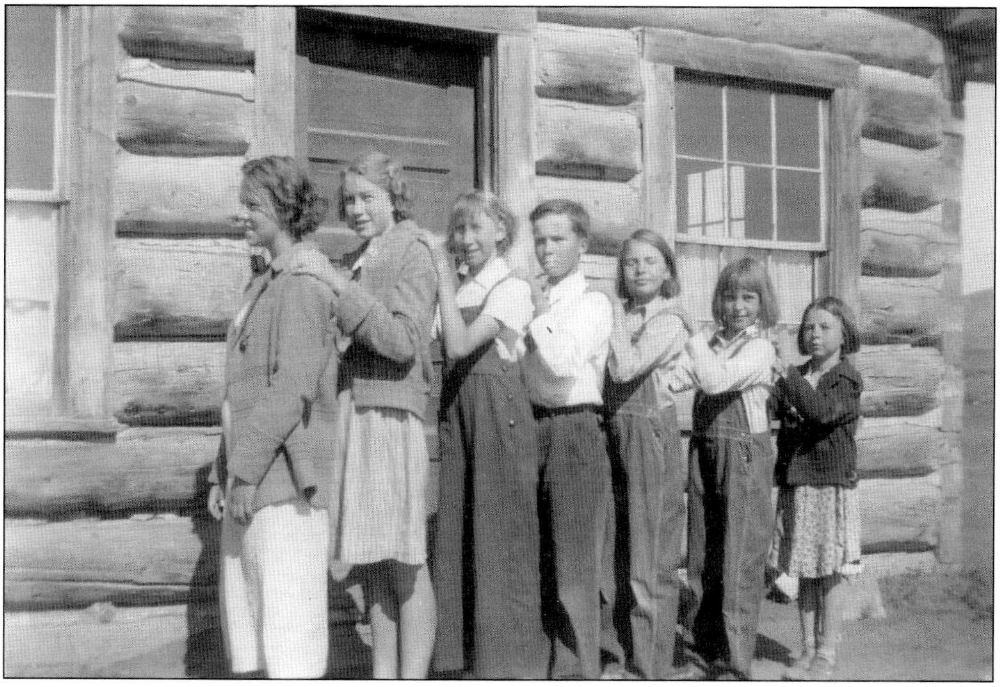

A group of schoolchildren is shown in front of the Green School in 1936. The students pictured behind their teacher are, from left to right, Edith Harrison, Mary Lee Thompson, Kenneth Ward, Marion Thompson, Lydia Ward, and Hazel Ward. The school, two miles west of present-day Dubois, was in operation from 1895 until 1947. It was the first school in the Dubois area, but other settlements on tributaries of the Wind River often had one-teacher schools.

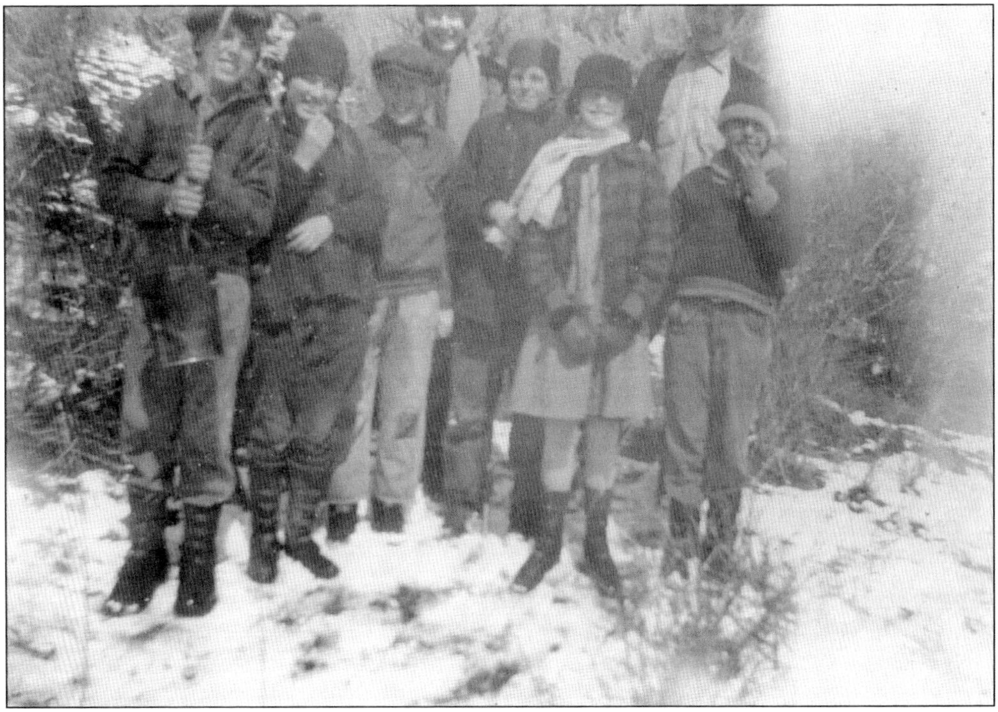

Six unidentified students and two adults are pictured during a winter school outing in the 1930s. Classes were small in early Dubois schools, and teachers could give students extra attention.

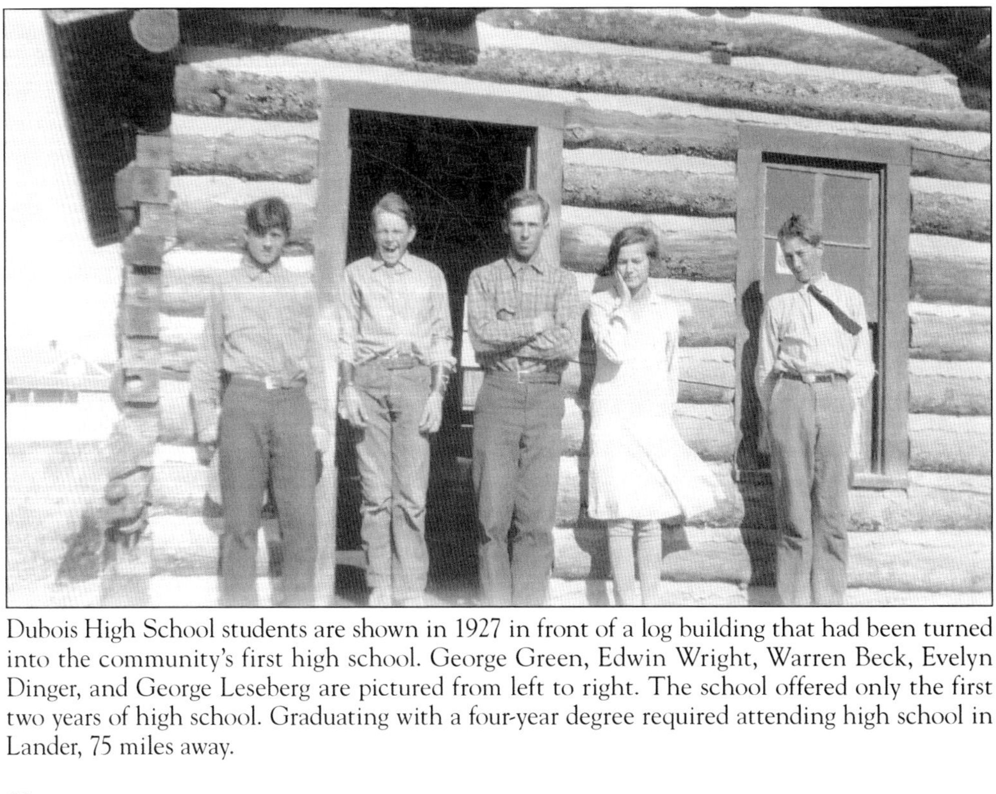

Dubois High School students are shown in 1927 in front of a log building that had been turned into the community's first high school. George Green, Edwin Wright, Warren Beck, Evelyn Dinger, and George Leseberg are pictured from left to right. The school offered only the first two years of high school. Graduating with a four-year degree required attending high school in Lander, 75 miles away.

Alice (Howell) Latta (left) and Alo (Jones) Fossey were teachers at the first Dubois High School in 1927. They are pictured in front of the Dubois Post Office.

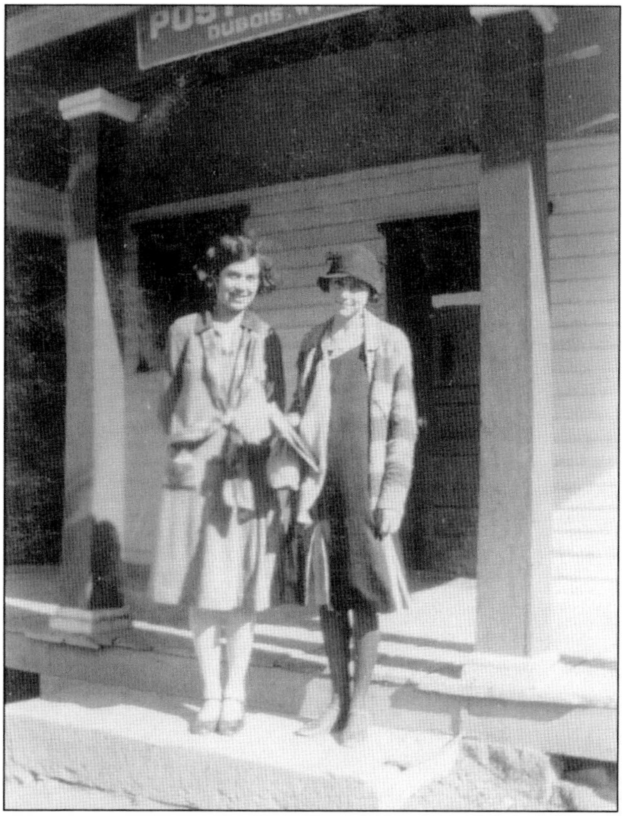

A photograph taken during the 1940–1941 school year shows elementary and high school students and their teachers in front of a log high school building, constructed in 1937. The log structure was once listed in the Guinness Book of Records as the largest log school with a regulation gymnasium.

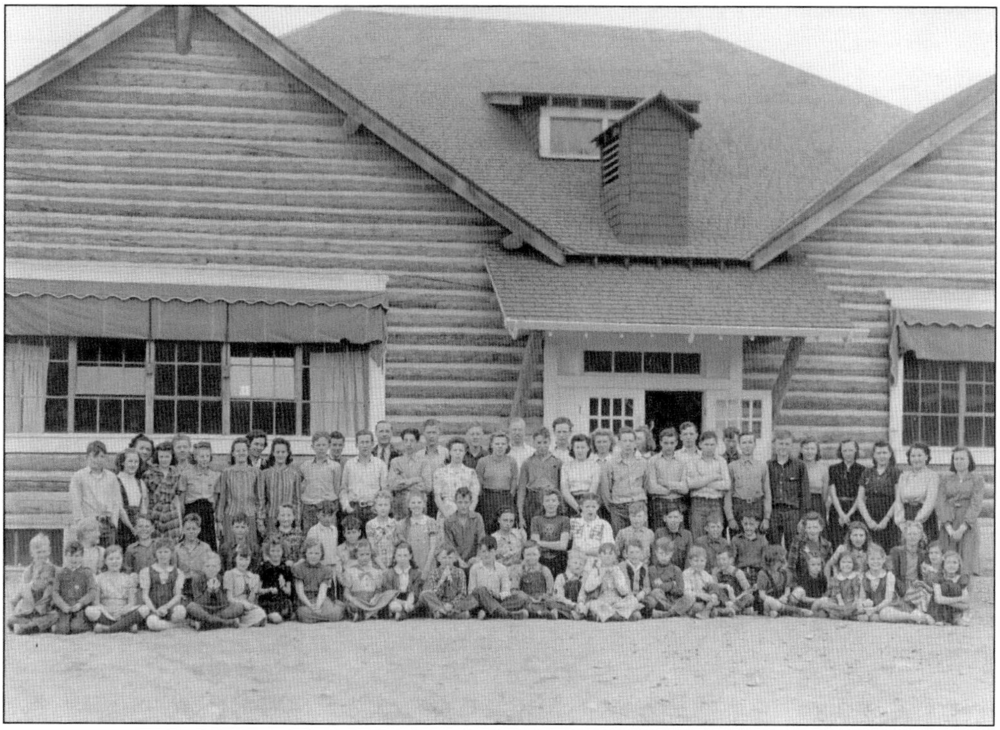

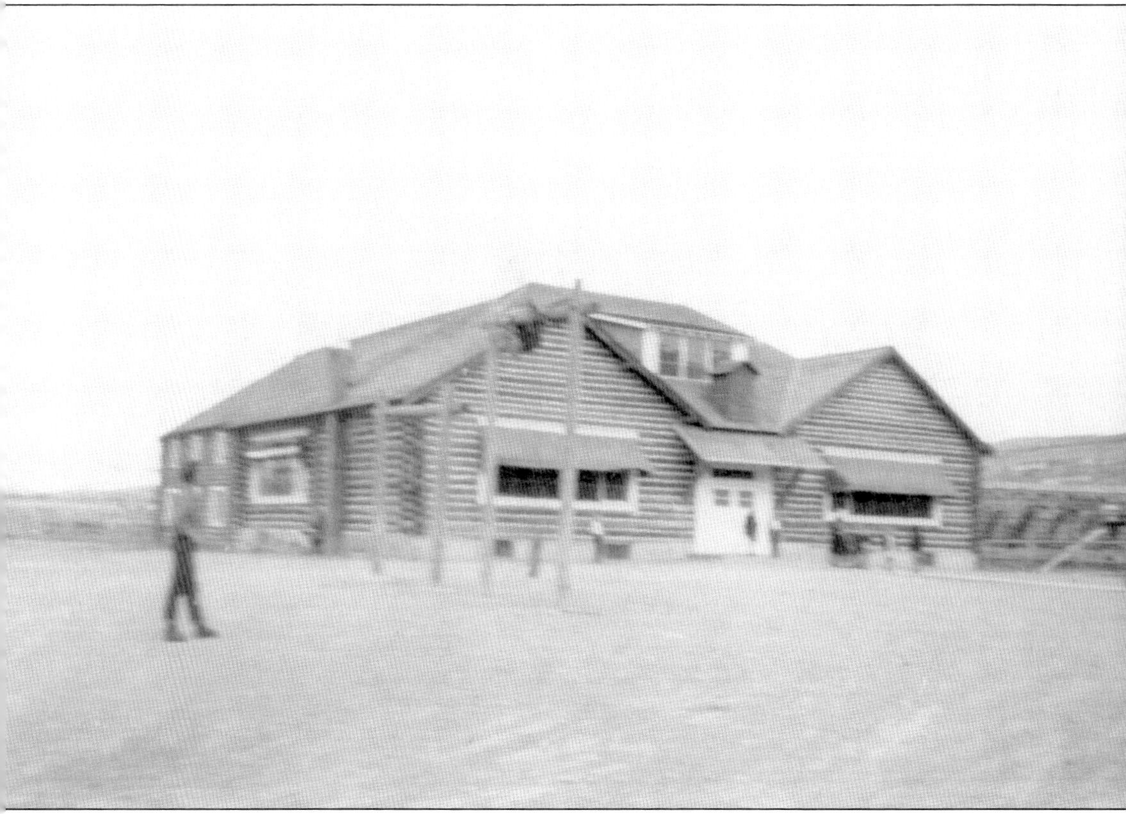

The first Dubois four-year high school is pictured at a distance in 1940 to better show the size of the log building.

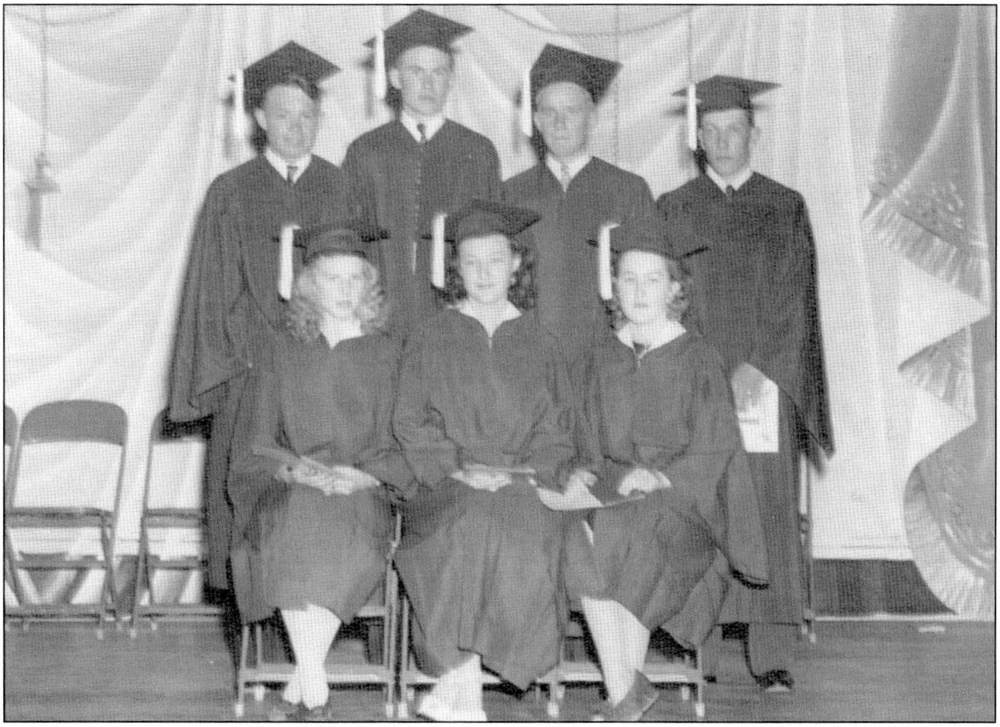

Students in the Dubois High School graduating class of 1944 pose in their caps and gowns. Pictured from left to right are (first row) Wanda Warnock, Jean Hulett, and Belle Morris; (second row) Duane Redman, Claude Werts, Earl Fossey, and Bob Latellier. Students in the class of 1943 were the first to graduate with a diploma for four years of high school. (Courtesy Jean Werts.)

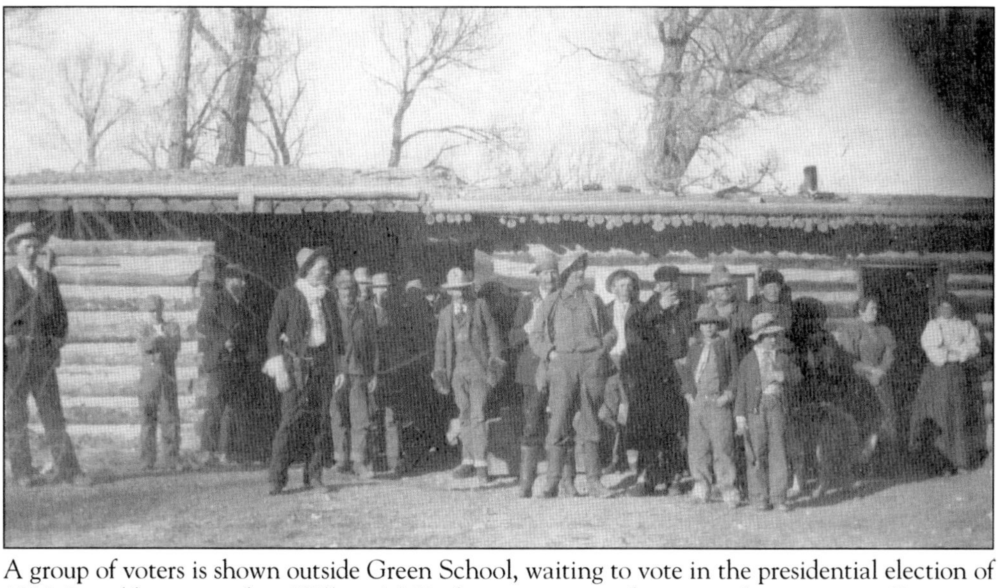

A group of voters is shown outside Green School, waiting to vote in the presidential election of 1900. Republican president William McKinley was running for a second term against Democrat William Jennings Bryan, who had opposed him in 1896 during an intense, hotly debated election campaign. McKinley won again but served only a year before he was assassinated by anarchist Leon Czoisz.

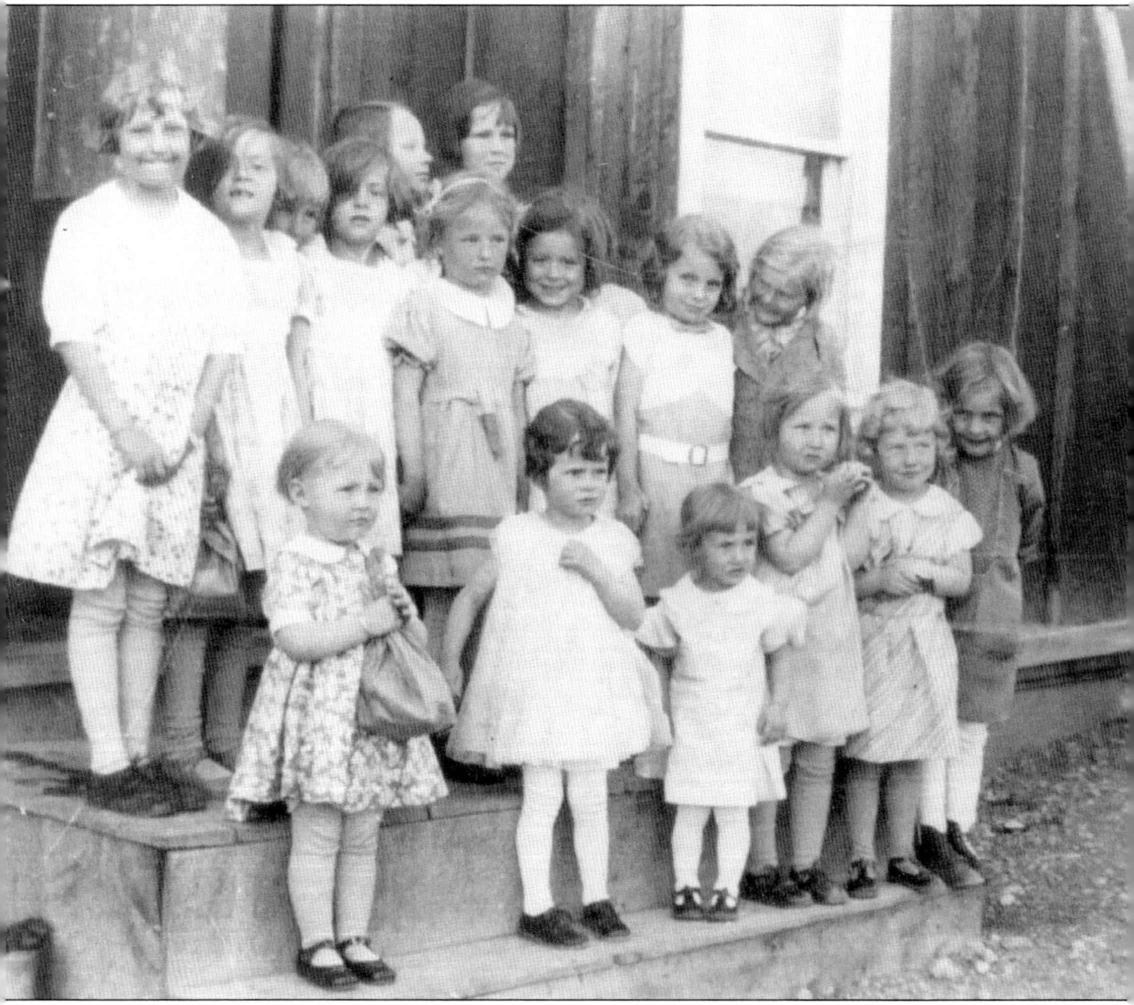

Little girls pose for a photograph in their best spring dresses on Easter Sunday in 1934. Pictured from left to right are (first row) June Hulett, Wanda Hawley, Donna Marie Meckem, Gladys Williamson, Dorothy Lou Meckem, and Mae Hutchison; (second row) Jean Hulett, Jean White, Arlene Scott, Ann White, Anna Fossey, Shirley Redman, Beverly Shoemaker, and Connie Nation; (third row) Violet Meckem and Odette Shippen (Courtesy Jean Werts.)

The interior of the Dubois Community Library is pictured around 1939. The library opened in 1937 in the first Dubois High School building with 688 donated books. Broken windows and a door in the vacant building were repaired with a $40 donation. A chair, table, and heater, as well as all the necessary labor, were donated. Esther Mockler, wife of rancher Frank Mockler, was the driving force behind the community effort to obtain a library.

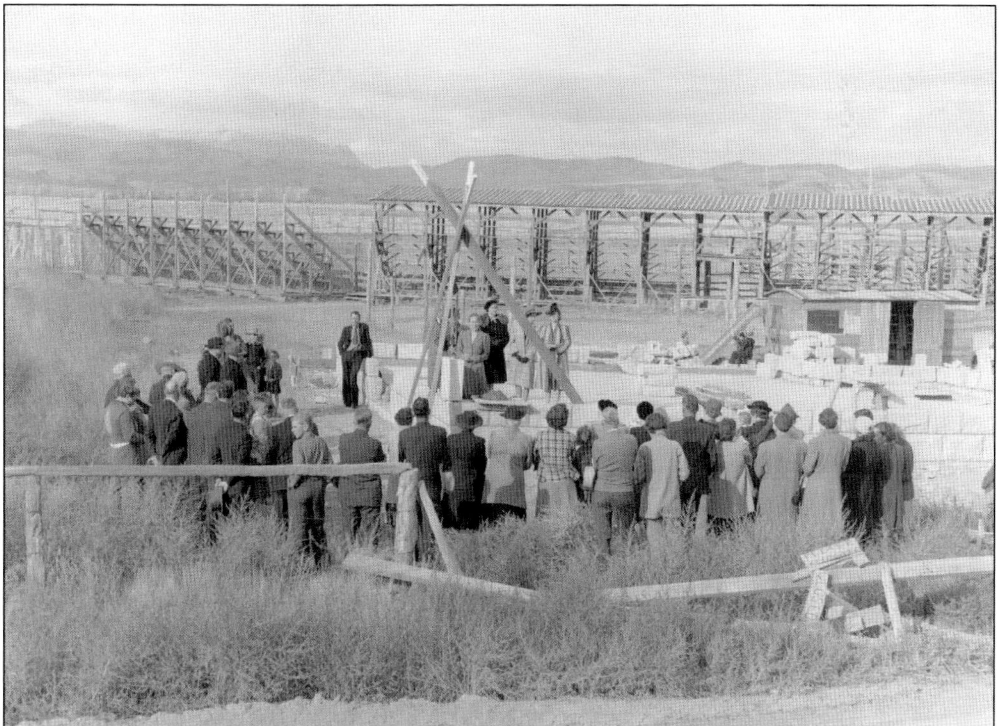

The ground-breaking ceremony for a new library building is shown in this 1941 photograph. Mary Back, one of the first two volunteer librarians, is speaking to the assembled group. The Dubois Community Library grew so much in its first three years of operation, a larger structure became necessary, and Esther Mockler decided it made more sense to construct a new building. After initial skepticism, the recently organized Dubois Library Board had plans drawn up for a new building. Mockler also persuaded the board to use native stone for the construction material, although it was more expensive.

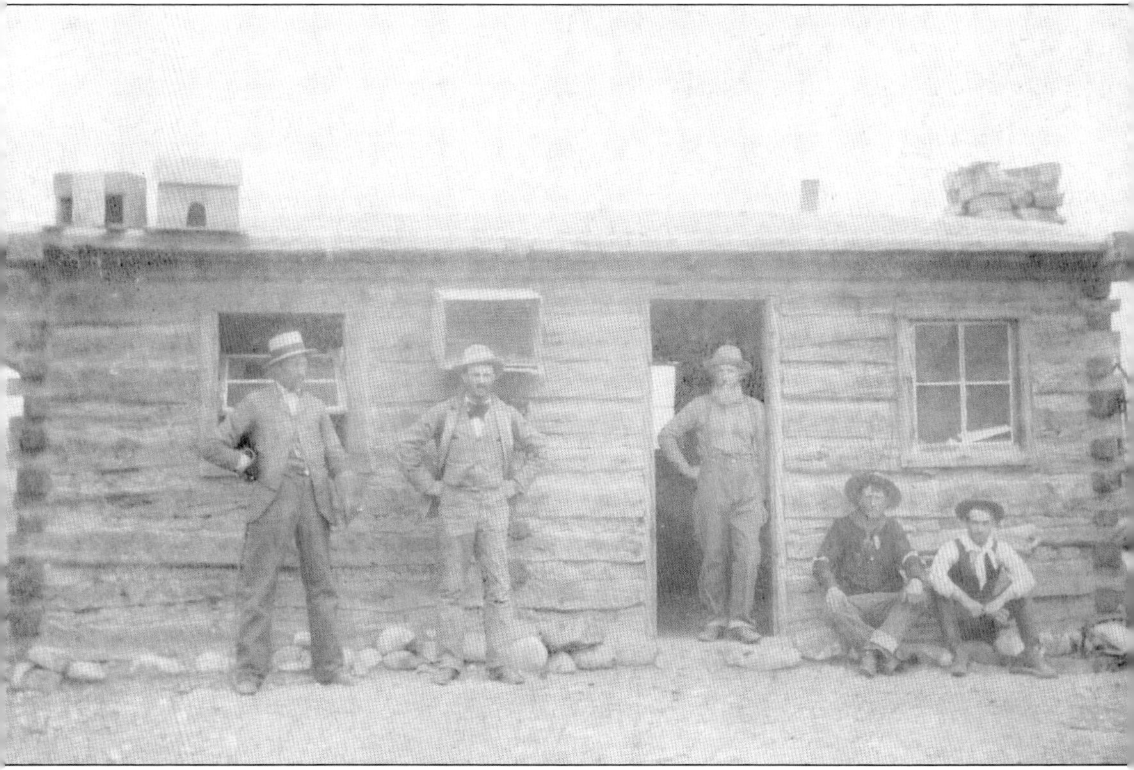

This is the first Dubois post office soon after it was constructed in 1889. The men pictured in front of the building include Eugene Amoretti, far left, and Butch Cassidy, second from right. The other men are unidentified. Cassidy and Al Heiner lived just outside present-day Dubois for a few years in the late 1800s before embarking on their highly publicized crime spree.

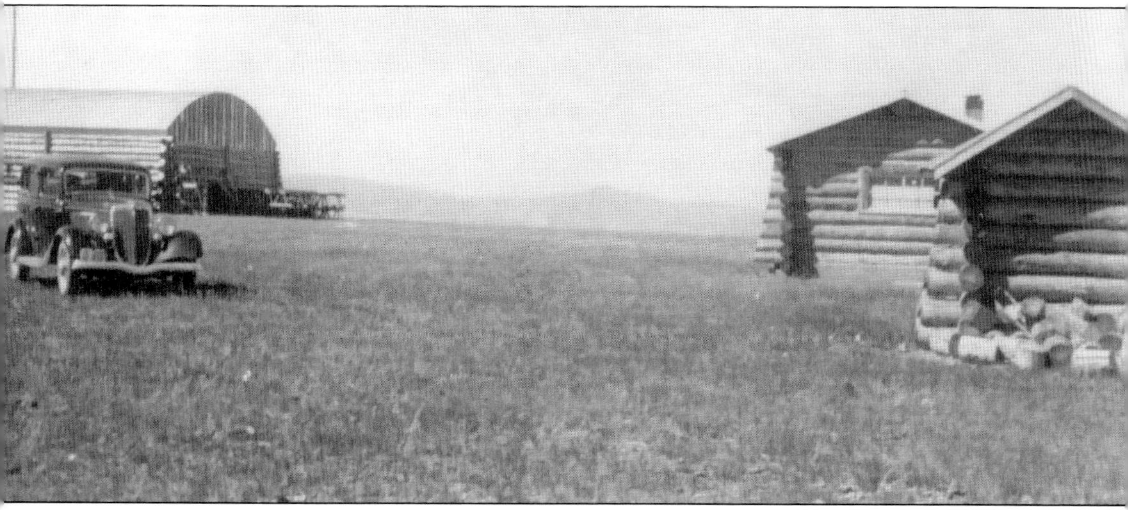

The first Dubois airport was constructed on Table Mountain in 1936 by workers from the Civil Works Administration.

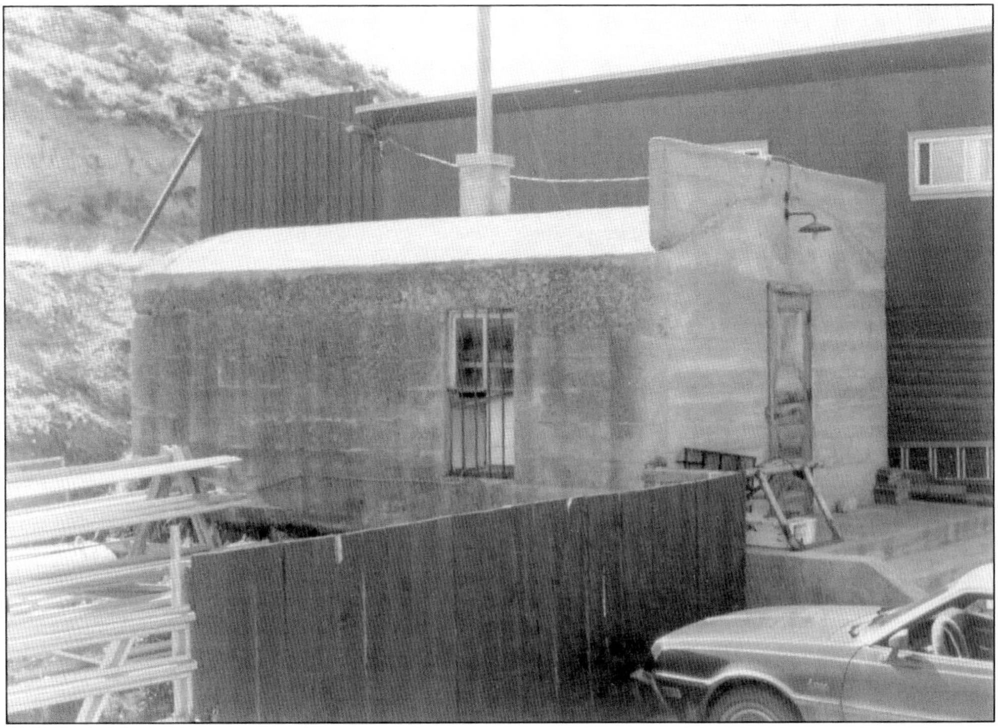

The first Dubois Jail was built in the late 1930s. It was constructed Civil Works Administration workers at a site between St. Thomas Episcopal Church and Circle Electric, the first electric company in the community.

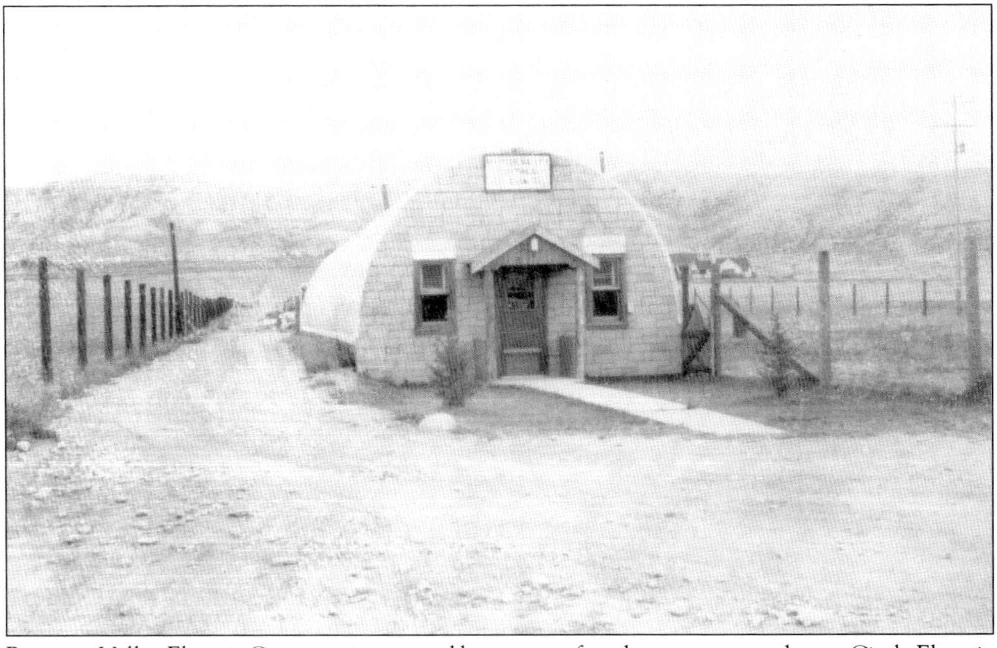

Riverton Valley Electric Company is pictured here soon after the company took over Circle Electric Company in the 1950s. Circle Electric began providing electricity in Dubois in the 1930s with a generator powered by water from Warm Springs Creek.

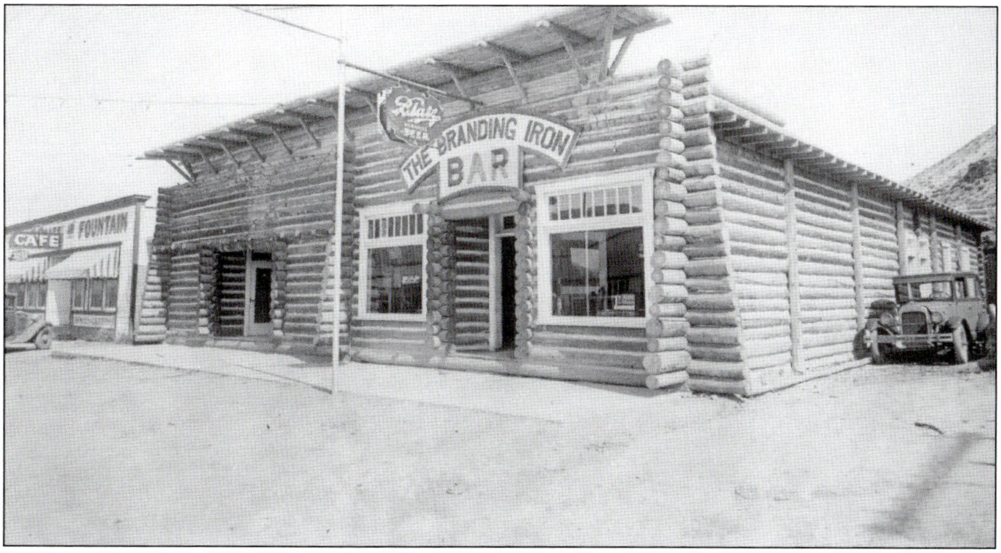

The Branding Iron Bar is pictured in the late 1930s. Les Wright and Tom Hulett constructed the bar in 1934, and it flourished during the 1940s when gambling was legal in Dubois. (Courtesy Jean Werts.)

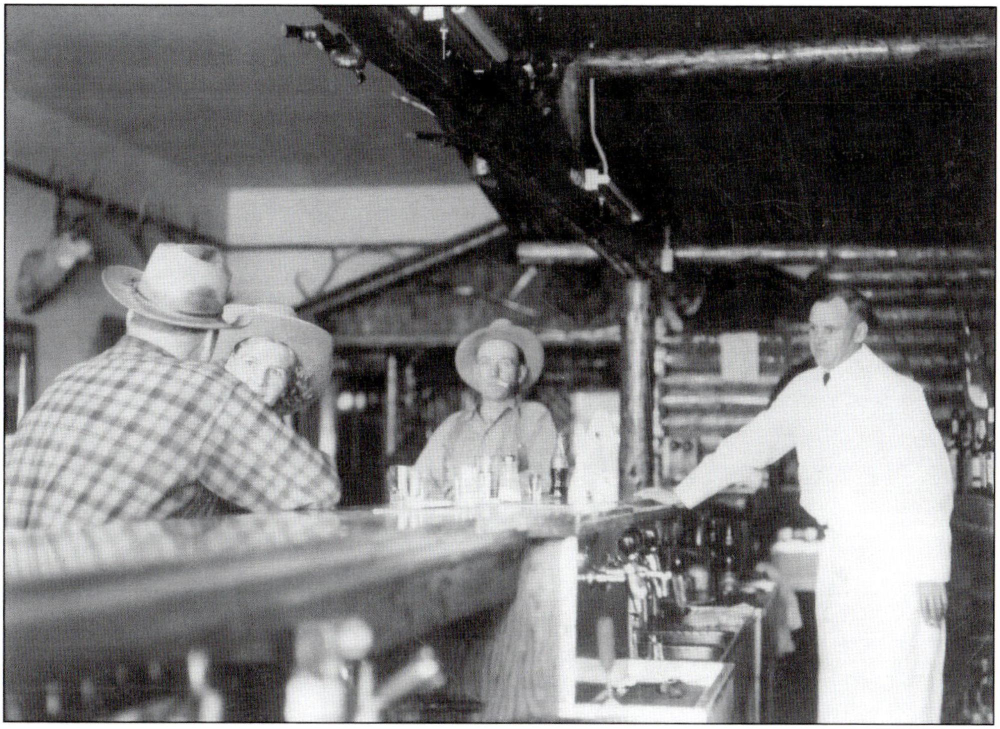
The Branding Iron Bar soon became a center for community activities. In a photograph taken in the 1930s, Tom Hulett is shown manning the bar during an unknown celebration. (Courtesy Jean Werts.)

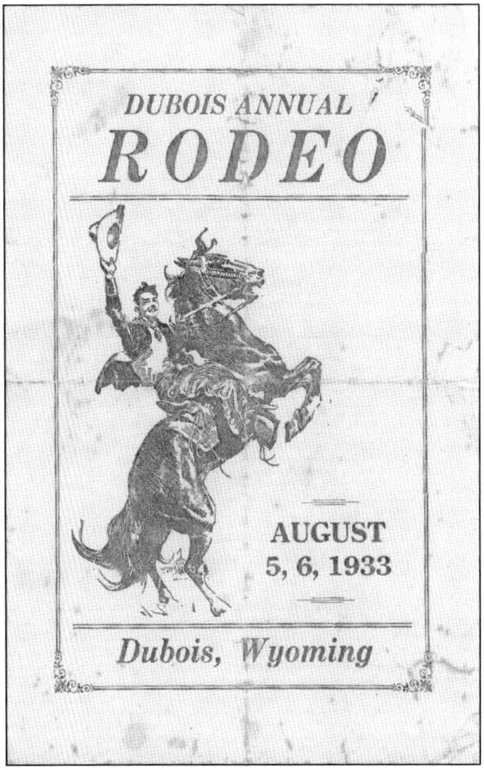

The cover and inside front page of the 1933 Dubois annual rodeo poster illustrates the organization that had developed around rodeos by the 1930s. Local cowboys tested their skills at informal rodeos for years, but the first fully organized rodeo was held in 1921 as part of a celebration for the opening of US Highway 287 across Togwotee Pass.

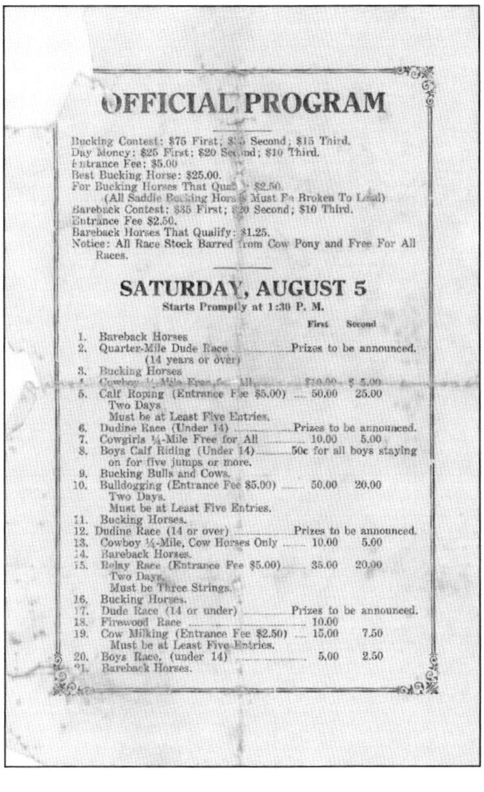

OFFICIAL PROGRAM

Bucking Contest: $75 First; $[illegible] Second; $15 Third.
Day Money: $25 First; $20 Second; $10 Third.
Entrance Fee: $5.00
Best Bucking Horse: $25.00.
For Bucking Horses That Qualify: $2.50.
(All Saddle Bucking Horses Must Be Broken To Lead)
Bareback Contest: $35 First; $20 Second; $10 Third.
Entrance Fee $2.50.
Bareback Horses That Qualify: $1.25.
Notice: All Race Stock Barred from Cow Pony and Free For All Races.

SATURDAY, AUGUST 5

Starts Promptly at 1:30 P. M.

		First	Second
1.	Bareback Horses		
2.	Quarter-Mile Dude Race (14 years or over)	Prizes to be announced.	
3.	Bucking Horses		
4.	Cowboy ¼-Mile Free for All	$10.00	$ 5.00
5.	Calf Roping (Entrance Fee $5.00) Two Days Must be at Least Five Entries.	50.00	25.00
6.	Dudine Race (Under 14)	Prizes to be announced.	
7.	Cowgirls ¼-Mile Free for All	10.00	5.00
8.	Boys Calf Riding (Under 14)	50c for all boys staying on for five jumps or more.	
9.	Bucking Bulls and Cows.		
10.	Bulldogging (Entrance Fee $5.00) Two Days. Must be at Least Five Entries.	50.00	20.00
11.	Bucking Horses.		
12.	Dudine Race (14 or over)	Prizes to be announced.	
13.	Cowboy ¼-Mile, Cow Horses Only	10.00	5.00
14.	Bareback Horses.		
15.	Relay Race (Entrance Fee $5.00) Two Days. Must be Three Strings.	35.00	20.00
16.	Bucking Horses.		
17.	Dude Race (14 or under)	Prizes to be announced.	
18.	Firewood Race	10.00	
19.	Cow Milking (Entrance Fee $2.50) Must be at Least Five Entries.	15.00	7.50
20.	Boys Race, (under 14)	5.00	2.50
21.	Bareback Horses.		

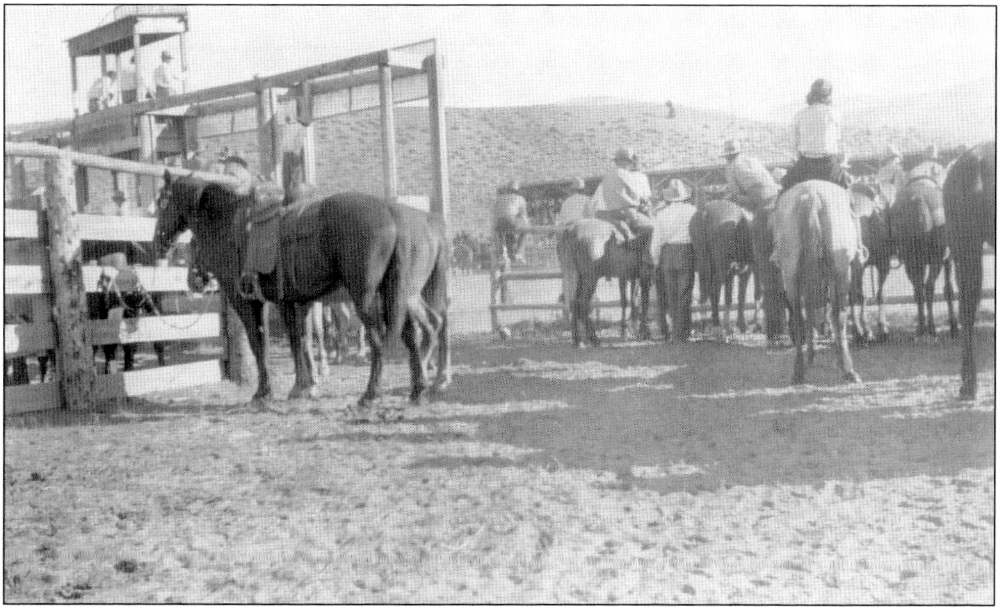

Contestants are shown waiting patiently to compete at the 1933 annual Dubois rodeo. Rodeos were heavily attended by local residents and tourists.

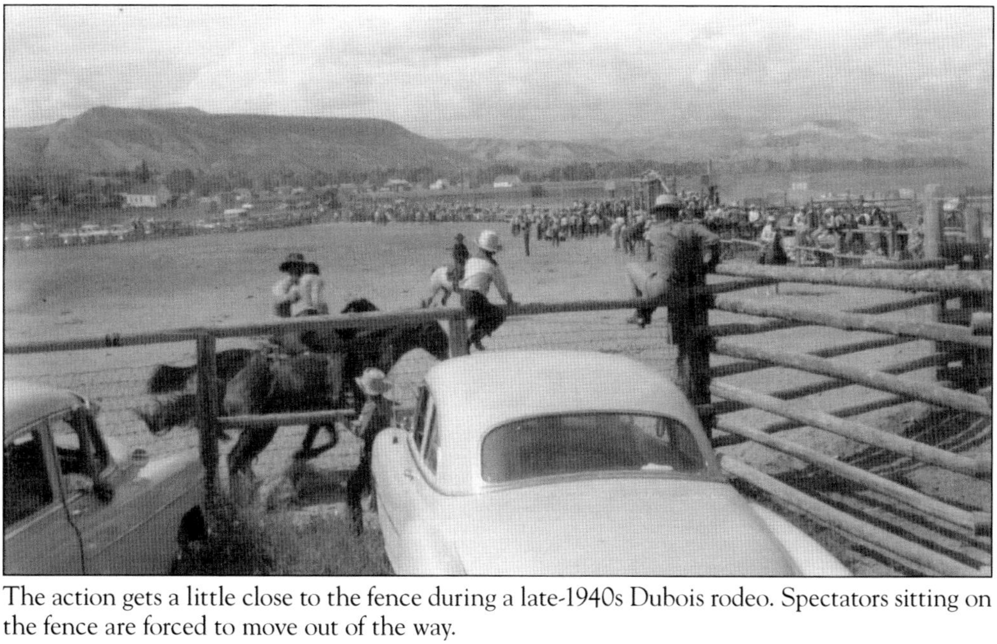

The action gets a little close to the fence during a late-1940s Dubois rodeo. Spectators sitting on the fence are forced to move out of the way.

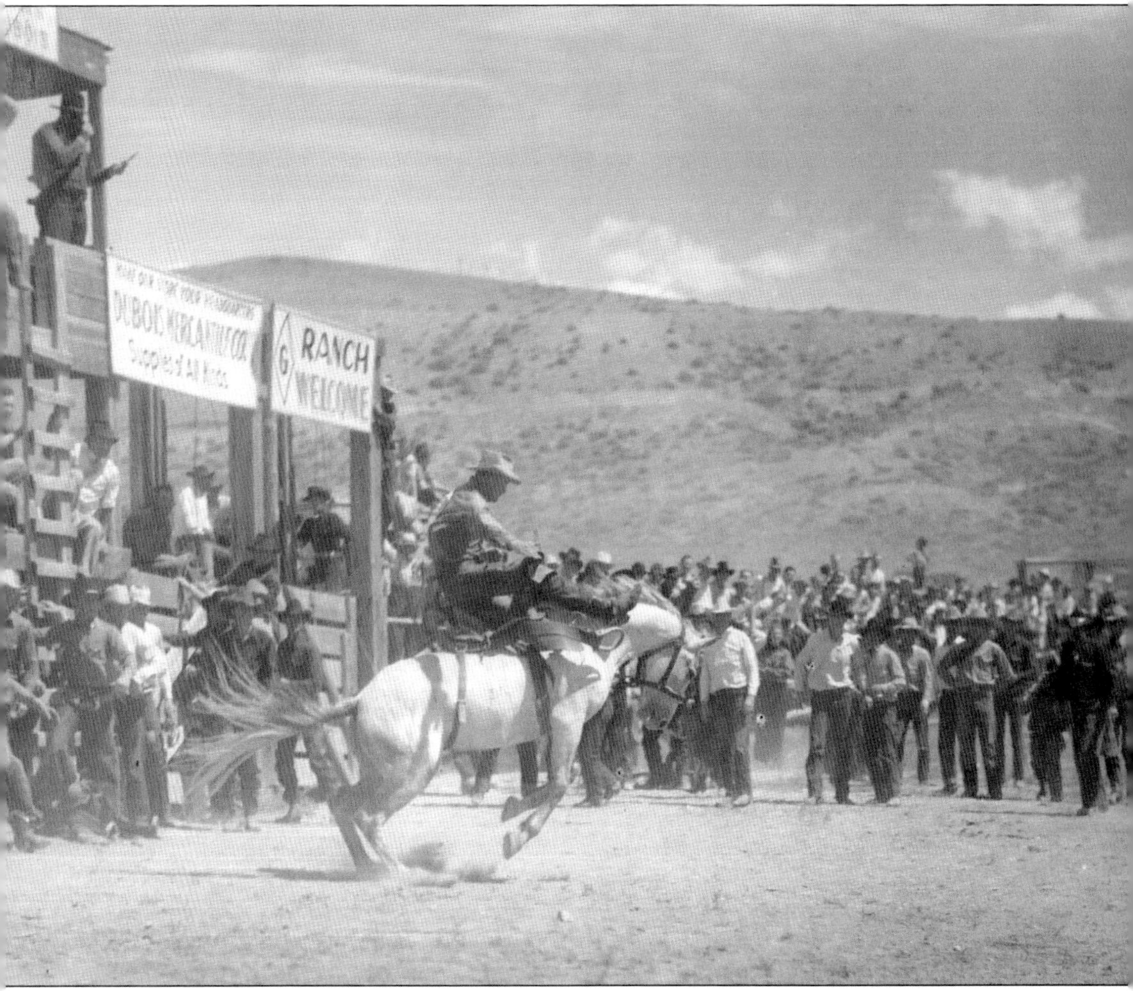

A rider in the saddle bronc competition at the first Dubois rodeo grounds is still hanging on in this 1930s photograph, but his boots are out of the stirrups, readying him to hit the ground running.

Three

The First National Forest

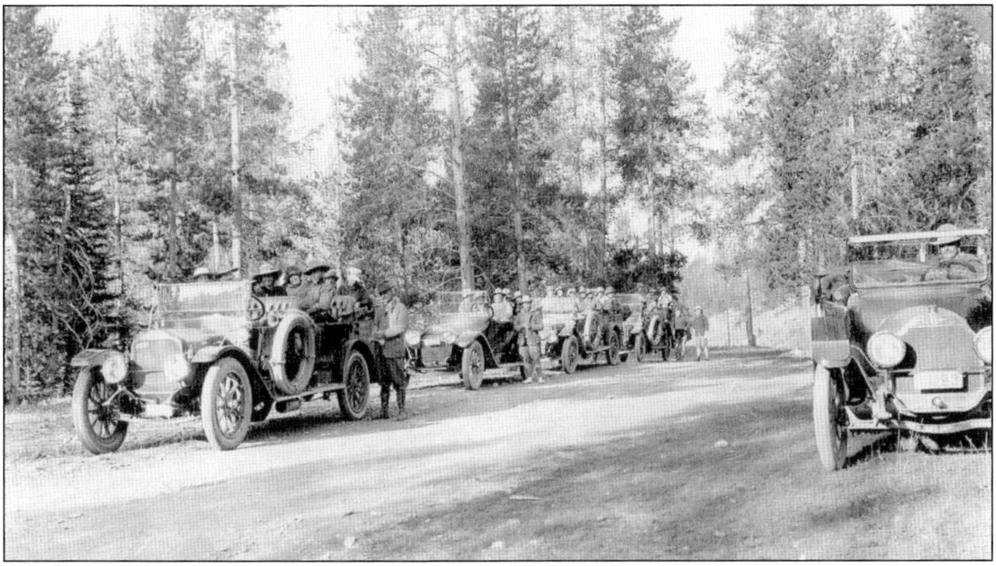

Tourists are shown here in the 1930s stopped along a snow-dusted road and talking to a Washakie National Forest ranger. The growing popularity of automobiles made it possible for average citizens to visit national parks and forests. In the past, only the affluent could afford to travel for pleasure. (Courtesy Shoshone National Forest.)

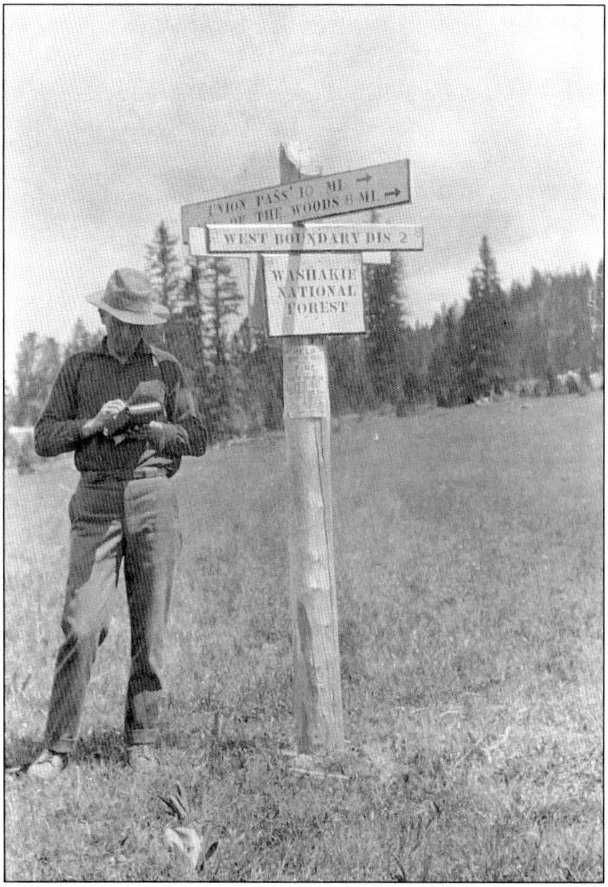

In this 1917 photograph, an unidentified ranger stands next to a sign marking the boundary of the west division of the Washakie National Forest. The west division included national forest lands around Dubois. National forests were new, and final boundaries were still being determined. (Courtesy Shoshone National Forest.)

In this 1917 image, a ranger rides through a new snowfall with signs to erect in the Washakie National Forest. Bonneville National Forest became Washakie National Forest on July 1, 1917. In 1945, the Washakie National Forest merged with the Shoshone National Forest. (Courtesy Shoshone National Forest.)

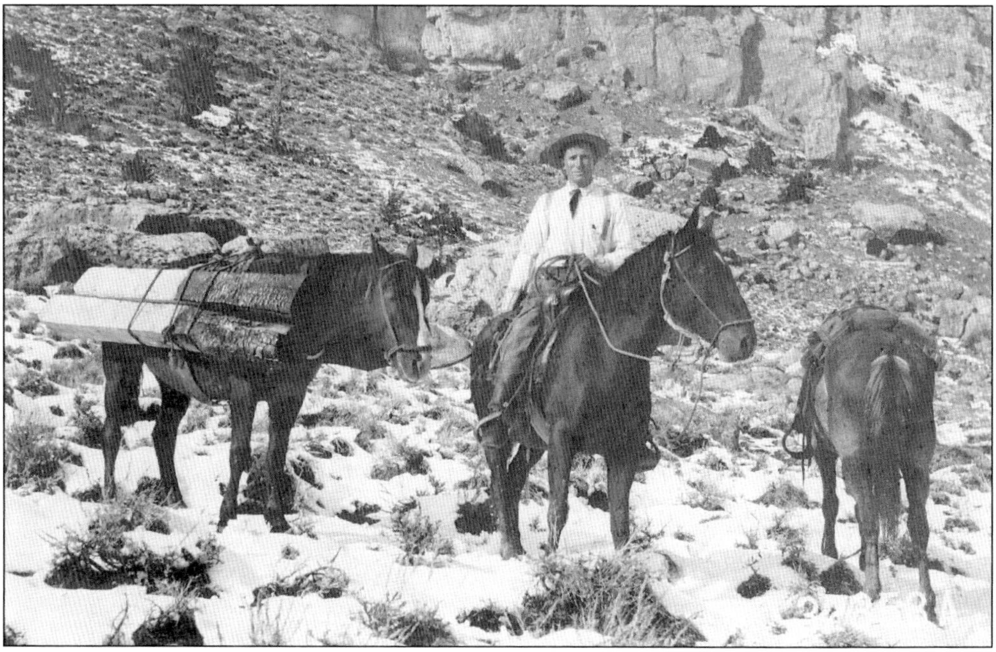

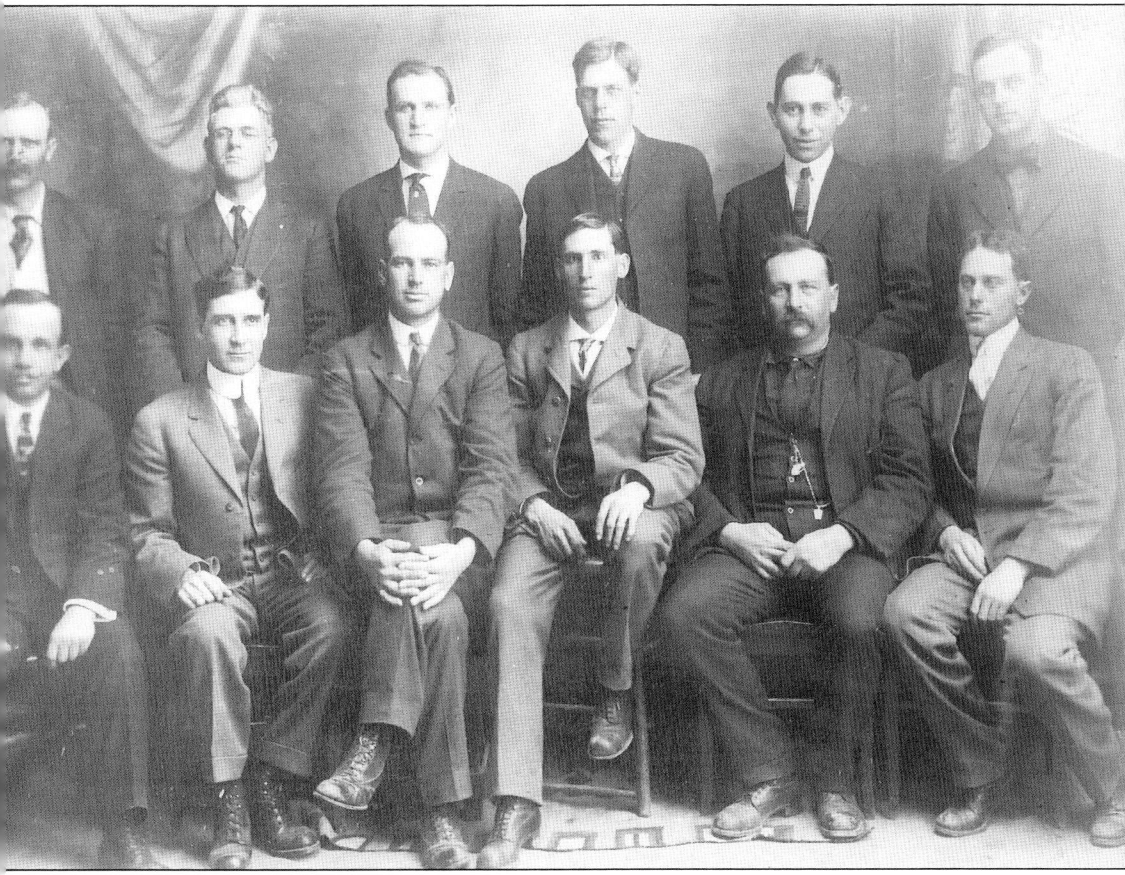

A 1912 photograph shows a meeting of unidentified Bonneville National Forest rangers and supervisors looking a little uncomfortable in suits and ties. The Bonneville National Forest was created in 1911 from Timberland Reserves that had been set aside in 1891 to protect Yellowstone National Park, the nation's first national park. (Courtesy Shoshone National Forest.)

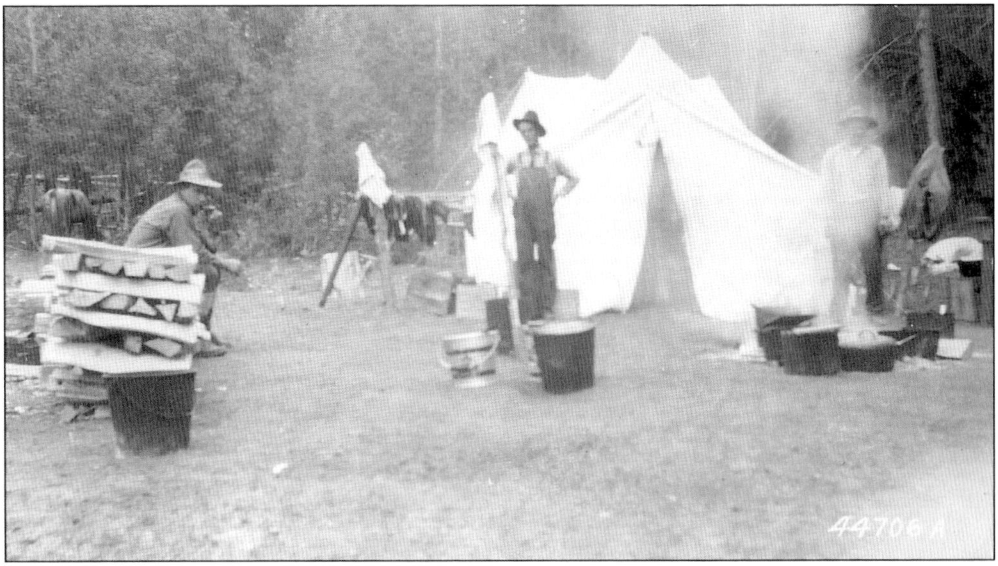

A group of forest rangers meets in the Bonneville National Forest in the early 1900s before it became the Washakie National Forest. The man pictured wearing bib overalls is likely the camp cook overseeing the meal, cooking in Dutch ovens over an open fire. (Courtesy Shoshone National Forest.)

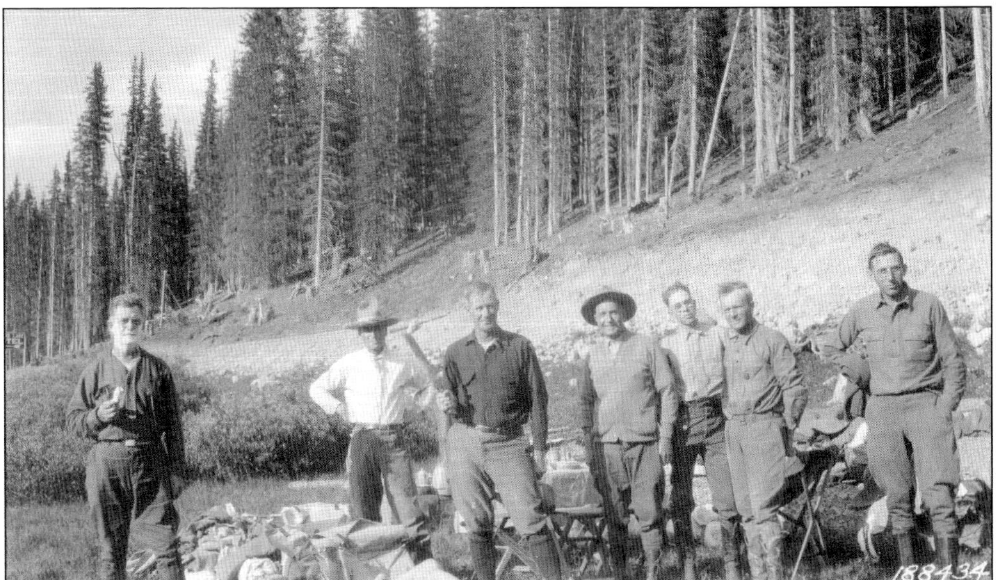

US Forest Service foresters cook breakfast during a meeting at Brooks Lake in the Washakie National Forest in 1924. Some of the foresters in the photograph are wearing pistols. Today's national forest employees, other than law enforcement, are not allowed to wear guns.

A fire tower stands guard over the Washakie National Forest in an early-1920s photograph. Fire towers were placed at strategic locations throughout the national forest. (Courtesy Shoshone National Forest.)

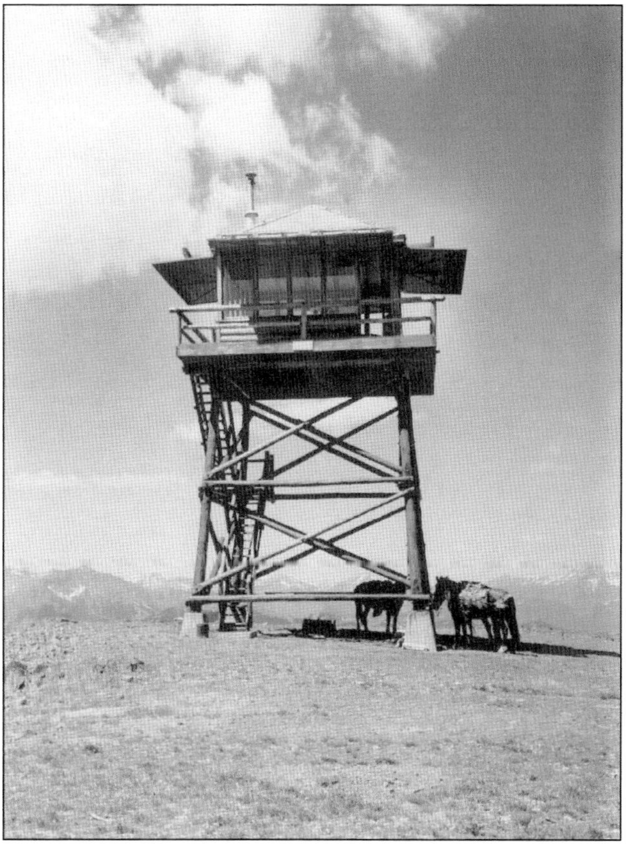

From the earliest days of the US Forest Service, fighting fires was one of its accepted functions. A group of 12 unidentified Washakie National Forest fire fighters poses on its way to a fire in the forest near Dubois.

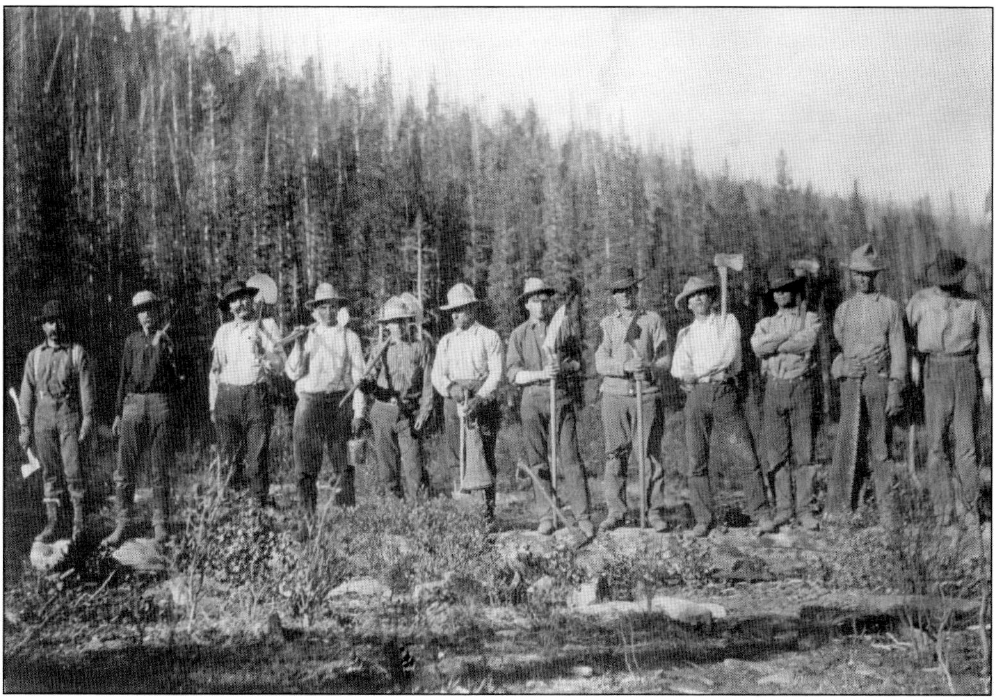

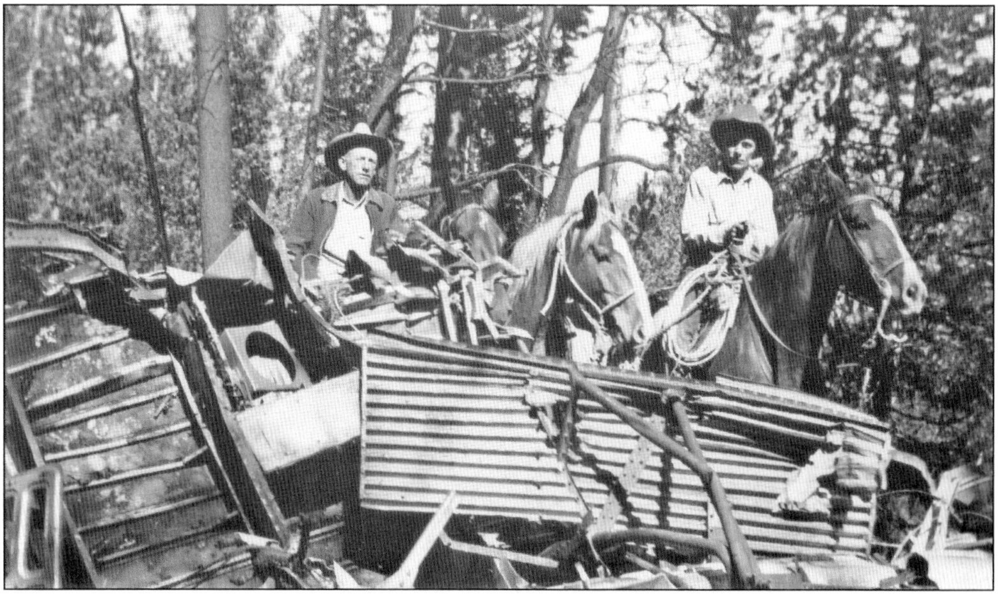

Dubois residents Ben Weeks (left) and Les Shoemaker are shown in 1947 with a US Forest Service crew, packing out wreckage from a bomber crash at a rugged site in the Wind River Mountains. The bomber was on a training mission from an airbase in Pocatello, Idaho, and all 11 airmen were killed when it crashed. Over the years, many locals have worked for the national forest in various capacities.

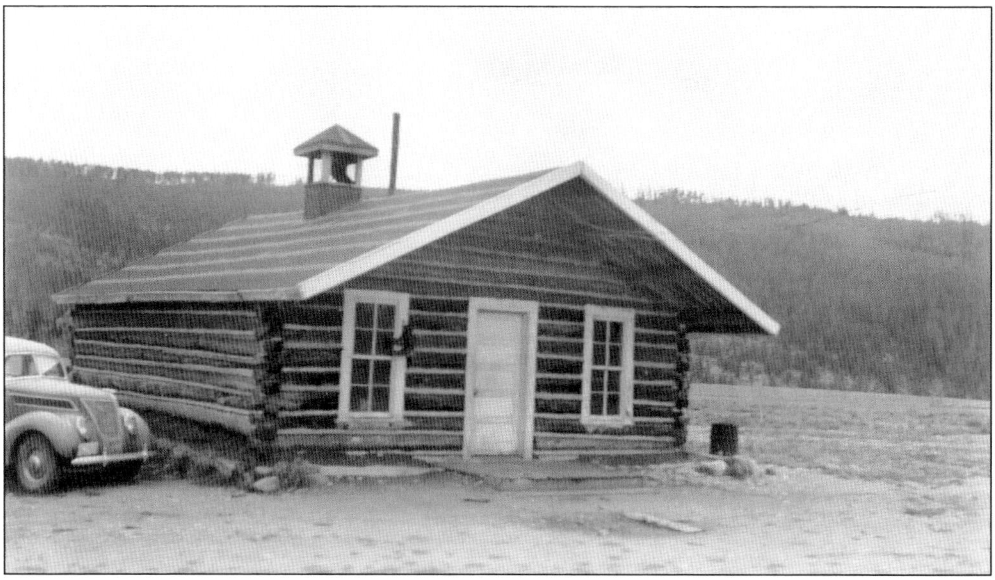

A Washakie National Forest ranger station at Wyoming Tie and Timber Company's West Dunoir headquarters camp is pictured in 1920. Ranger stations were placed at or near headquarters camps so that rangers could supervise the company's tie-cutting activities. (Courtesy Shoshone National Forest.)

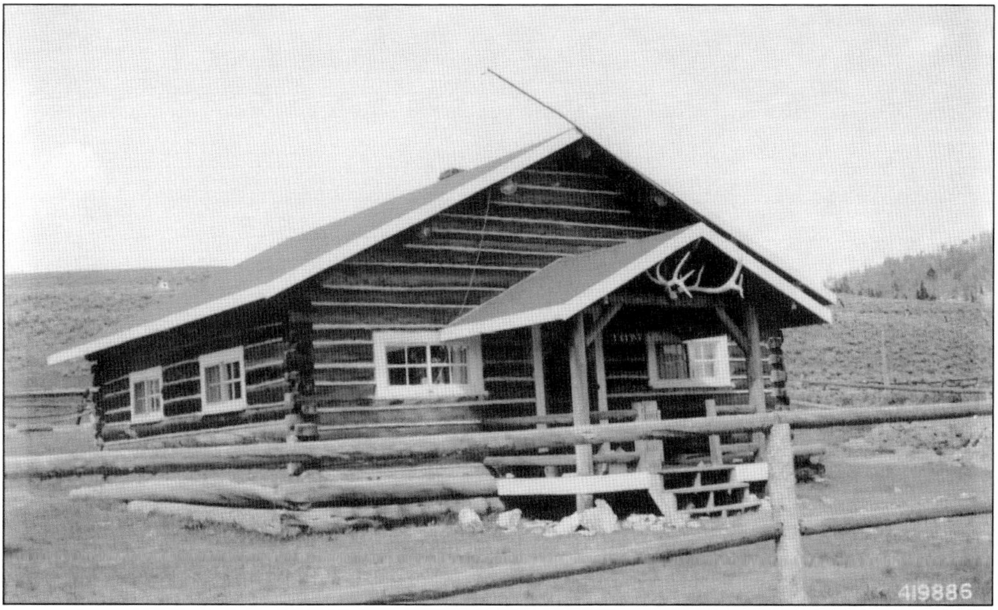

Rangers and their families lived at ranger stations scattered throughout the national forest. The Sheridan Creek Ranger Station, pictured in 1921, was located at Wyoming Tie and Timber Company's headquarters in the Wind River Mountains west of Dubois. (Courtesy Shoshone National Forest.)

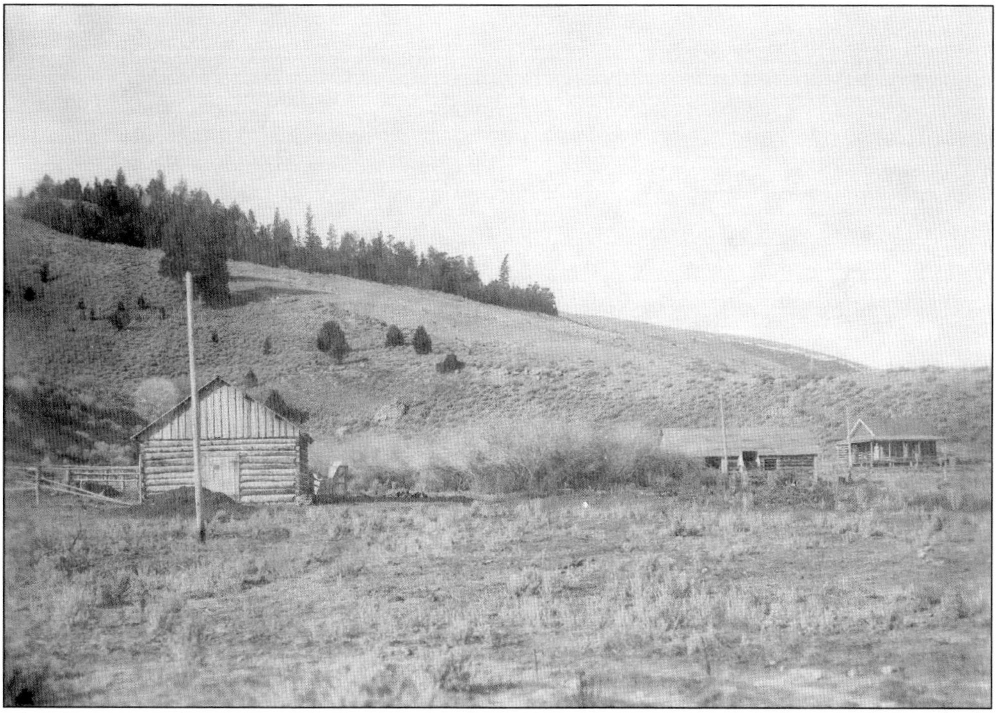

The Geyser Creek Ranger Station, located about five miles west of present-day Dubois, is seen here in 1912. Ranger Wilber Goodson and his wife, Cleo, lived there when this photograph was taken.

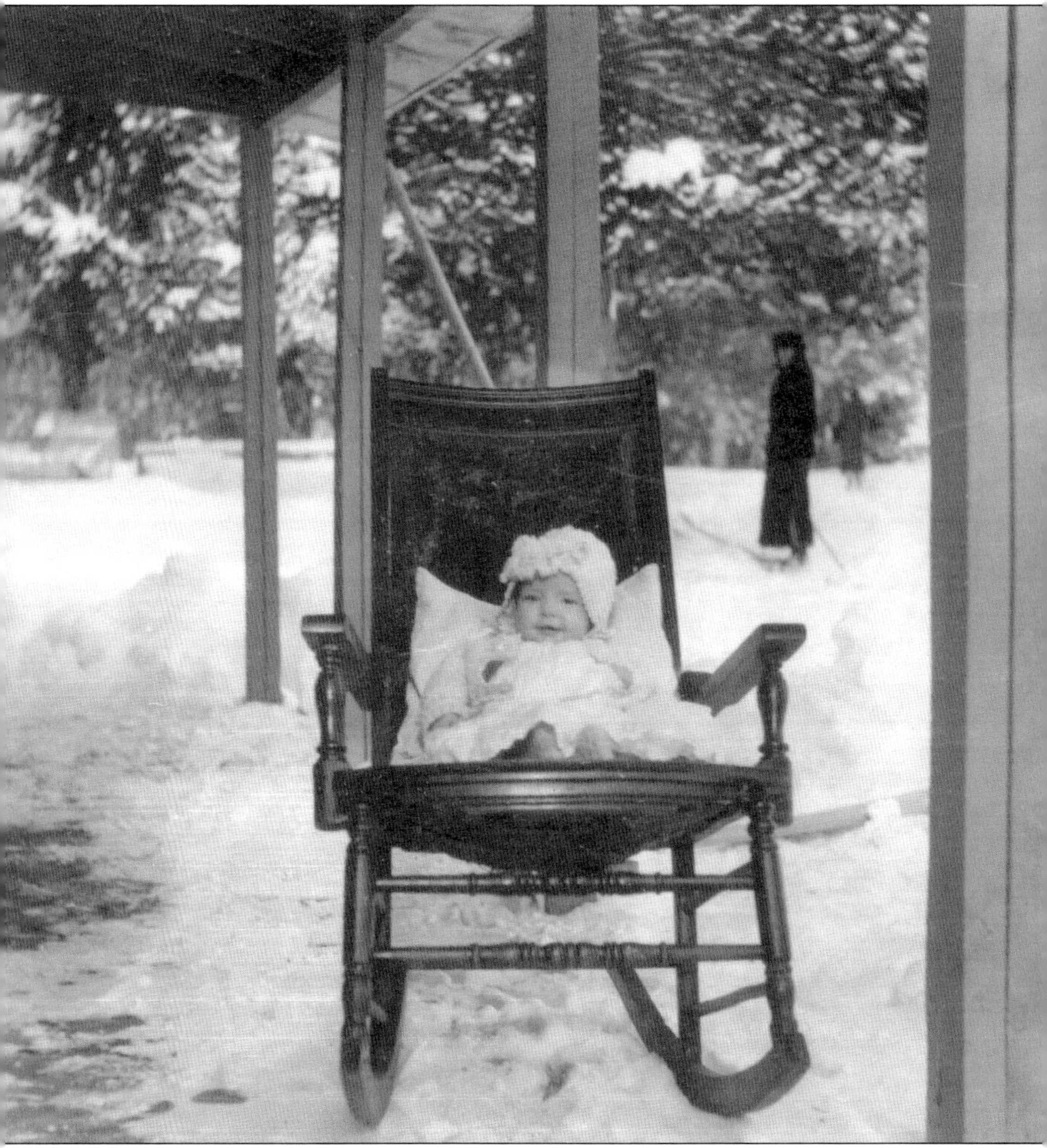

Doris Clark, infant daughter of Washakie National Forest ranger Cay Clark and his wife, Lydia, is pictured in a sunny spot in front of the Sheridan Creek Ranger Station where her parents lived. In the 1930s, Clark was stationed near the Wyoming Tie and Timber Company headquarters camp to supervise tie cutting. He died of influenza two years after Doris was born.

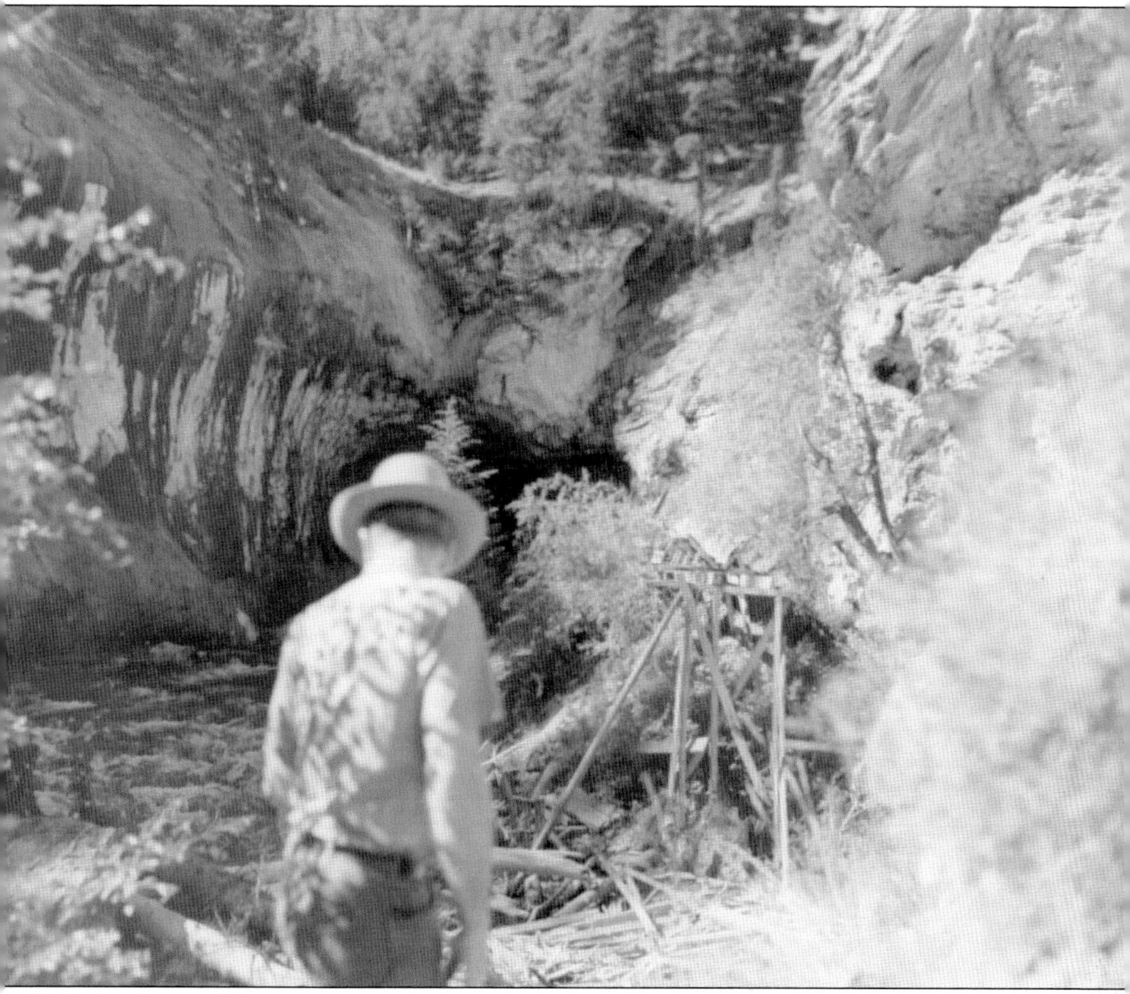

Washakie National Forest supervisor John Lavin is pictured in the early 1920s inspecting a bridge on Warm Springs Creek west of Dubois. (Courtesy Shoshone National Forest.)

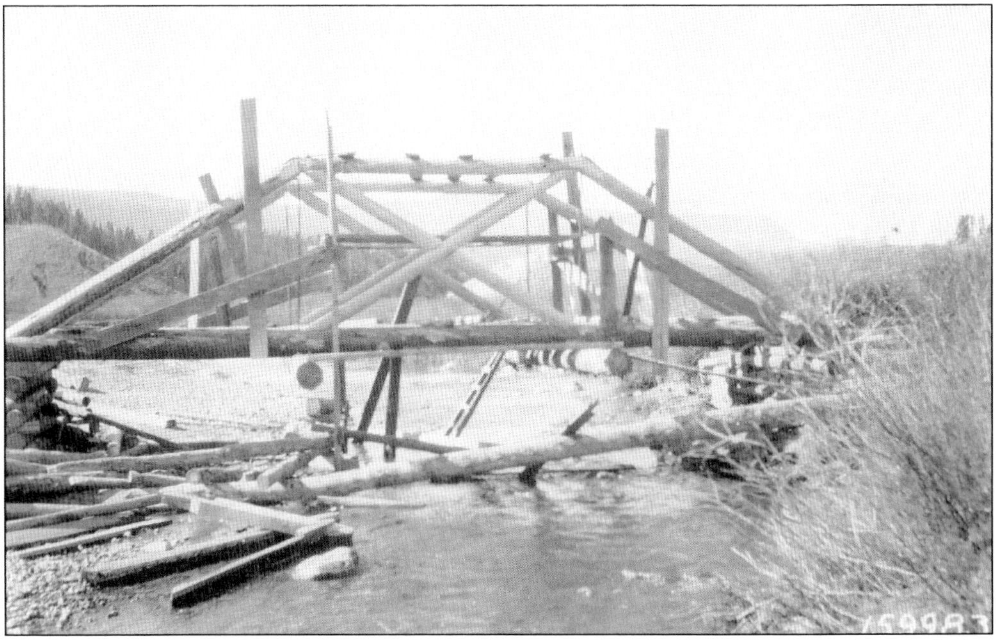

A 1920s photograph shows construction of a bridge across Sheridan Creek in the Washakie National Forest west of Dubois. The bridge provided access for Wyoming Tie and Timber Company tie-cutting activities in the national forest. (Courtesy Shoshone National Forest.)

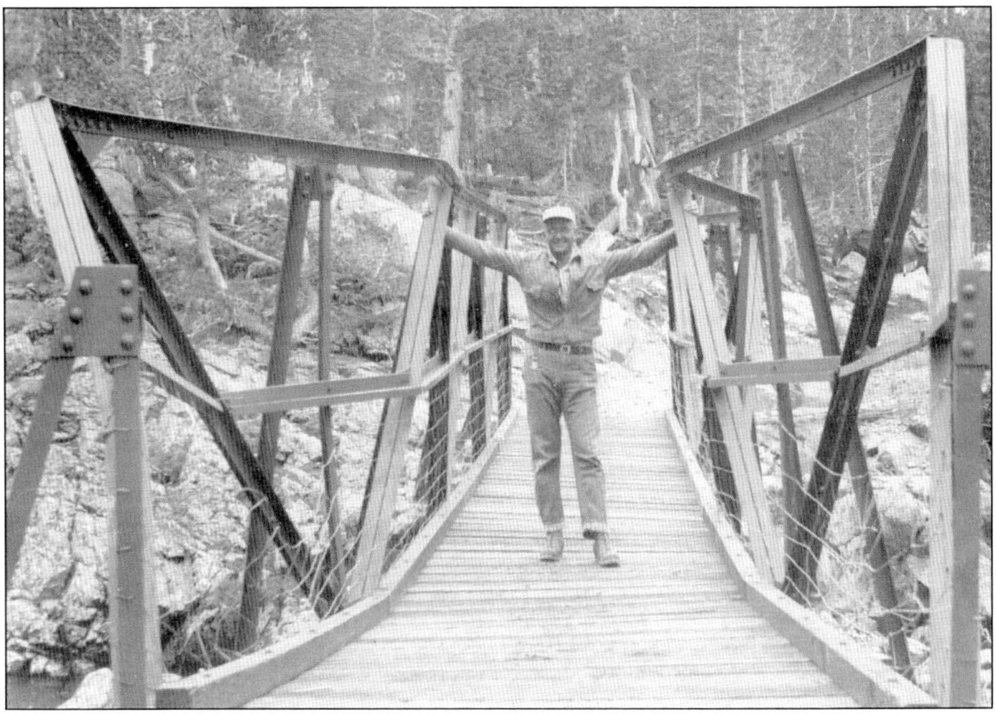

An unidentified Washakie National Forest ranger inspects the width of a bridge in 1920. (Courtesy Shoshone National Forest.)

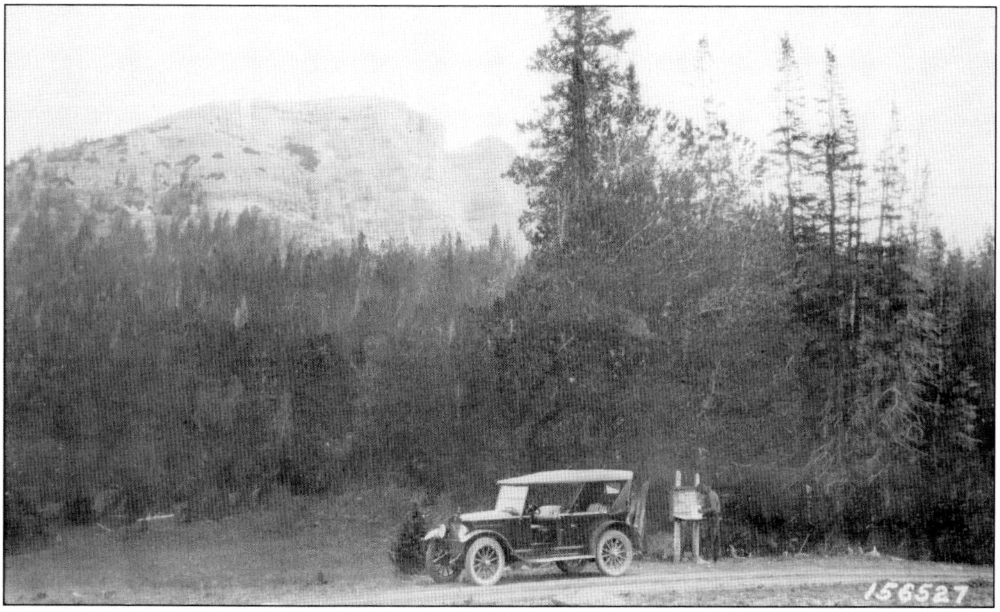

A 1920s photograph shows a man signing a visitor register at the boundary between the Washakie and the Teton National Forests. (Courtesy Shoshone National Forest.)

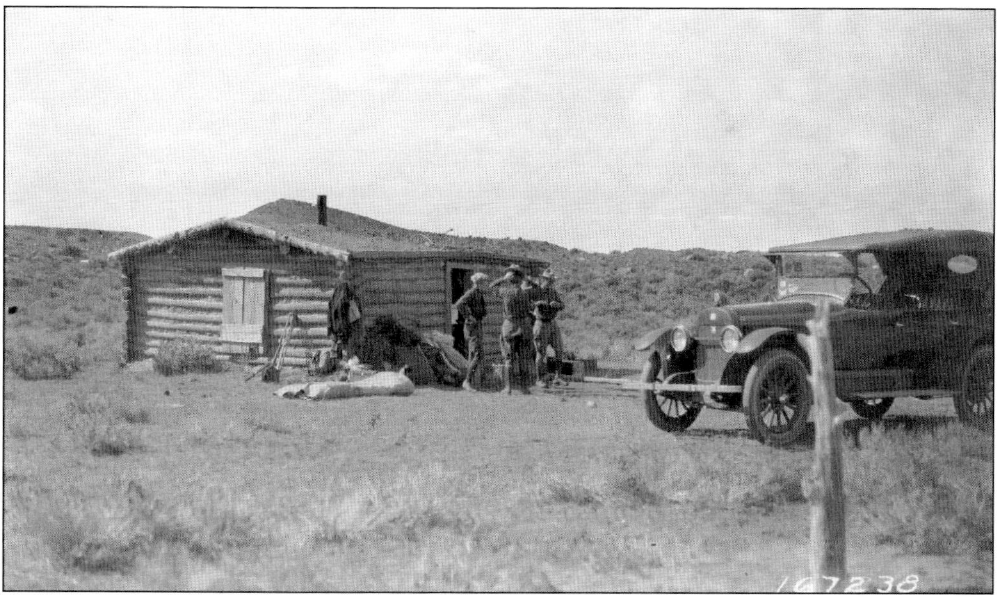

Some things have not changed all that much in the national forest. In this 1920s photograph, two men ask a ranger for information or directions at one of the Washakie National Forest ranger stations. (Courtesy Shoshone National Forest.)

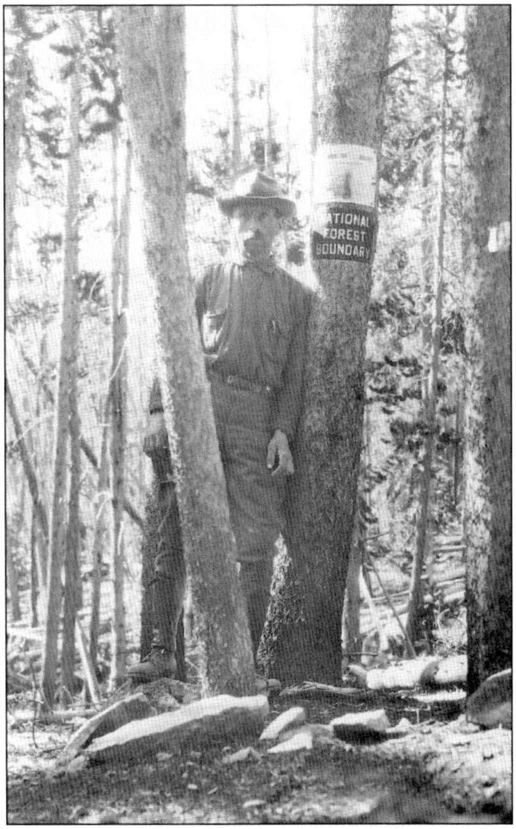

An unidentified man is shown next to a bear warning sign at the Washakie National Forest boundary in the 1920s. Bears were a problem for tourists in those years, as they sometimes are today. (Courtesy Shoshone National Forest.)

A Washakie National Forest ranger is pictured inspecting a picnic table and sign in 1924. Many of the current duties for forest rangers were established during the early years of the US Forest Service. (Courtesy Shoshone National Forest.)

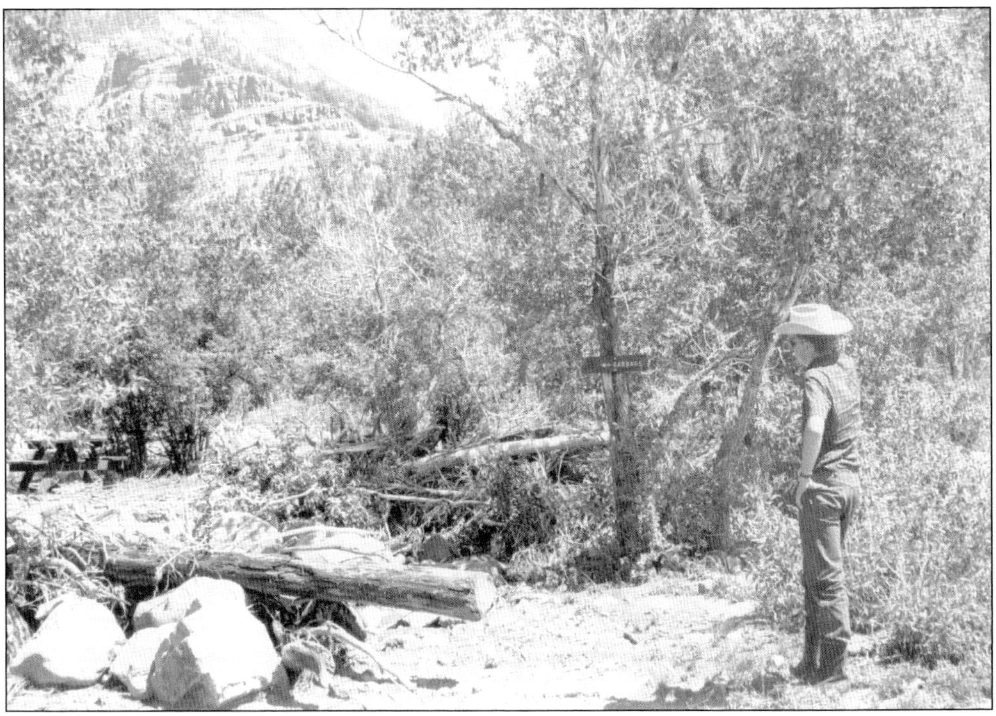

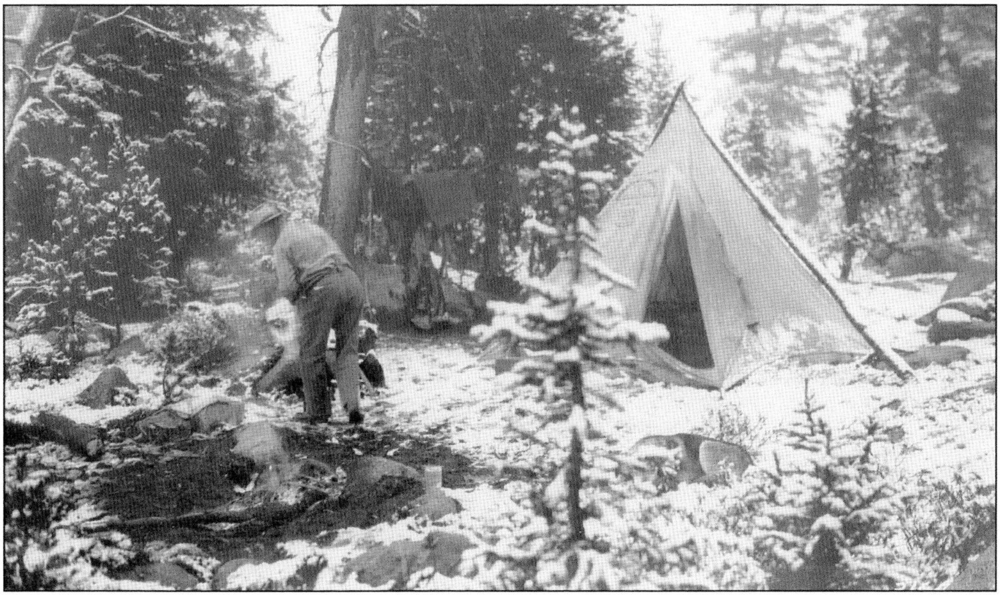

Trail maintenance in the Washakie National Forest could be dangerous at times. Charles E. Thomas is shown in 1933 setting up a tent along the Little Wind River on the southern end of the forest to protect him from an unexpected snowstorm. (Courtesy Shoshone National Forest.)

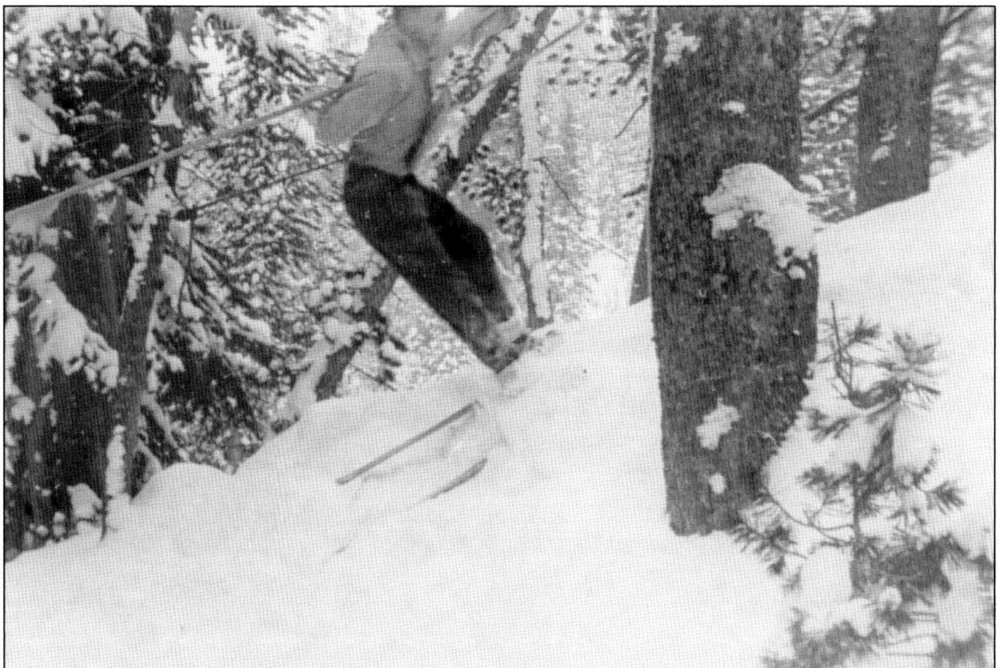

Life was not all work for Washakie National Forest district ranger Clarence S. Thornock. He is pictured in 1942 riding a rope tow up a tree-studded slope in the Togwotee Pass area, located northwest of Dubois. (Courtesy Shoshone National Forest.)

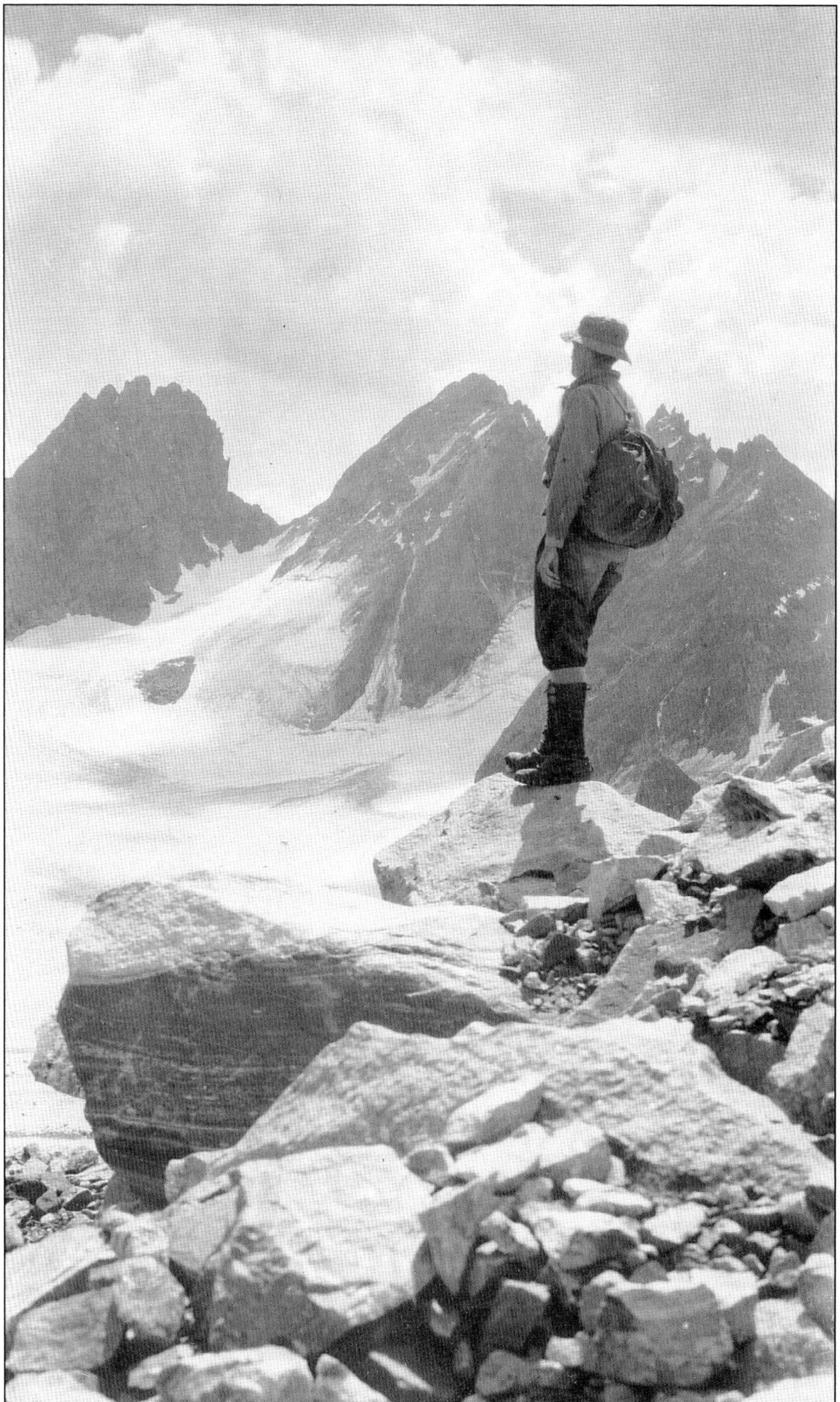

An unidentified man is pictured in 1924 on Gannett Ridge approaching Gannett Peak in the Wind River Mountains. Gannett Peak is the highest point in Wyoming at an elevation of 13,809 feet. (Courtesy Shoshone National Forest.)

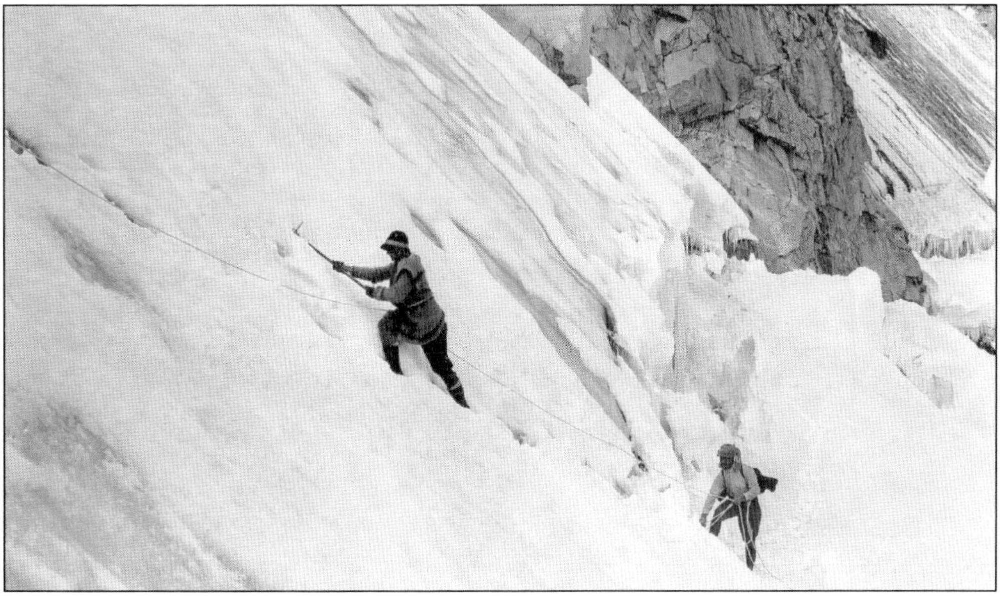

Two men are pictured ice climbing on Gannett Glacier in 1924. Gannett Glacier in the Wind River Mountains is the largest single glacier in the American Rockies. One of the primary trails to Gannett Peak and Gannett Glacier begins 10 miles south of Dubois. (Courtesy Shoshone National Forest.)

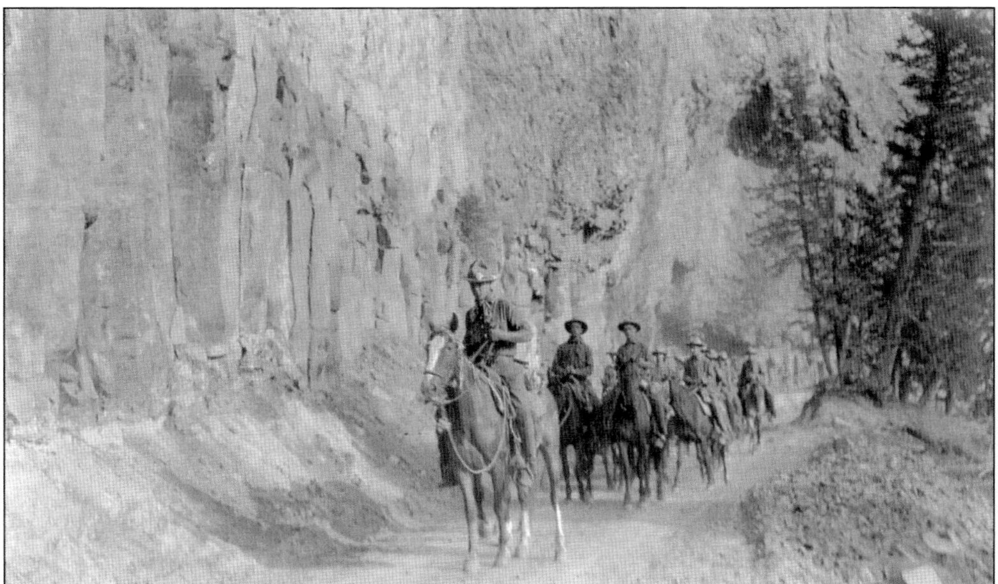

Charlie Moore leads a Ramshorn Ranch boys' camp trip along a road near Tower Falls in Yellowstone National Park around 1910.

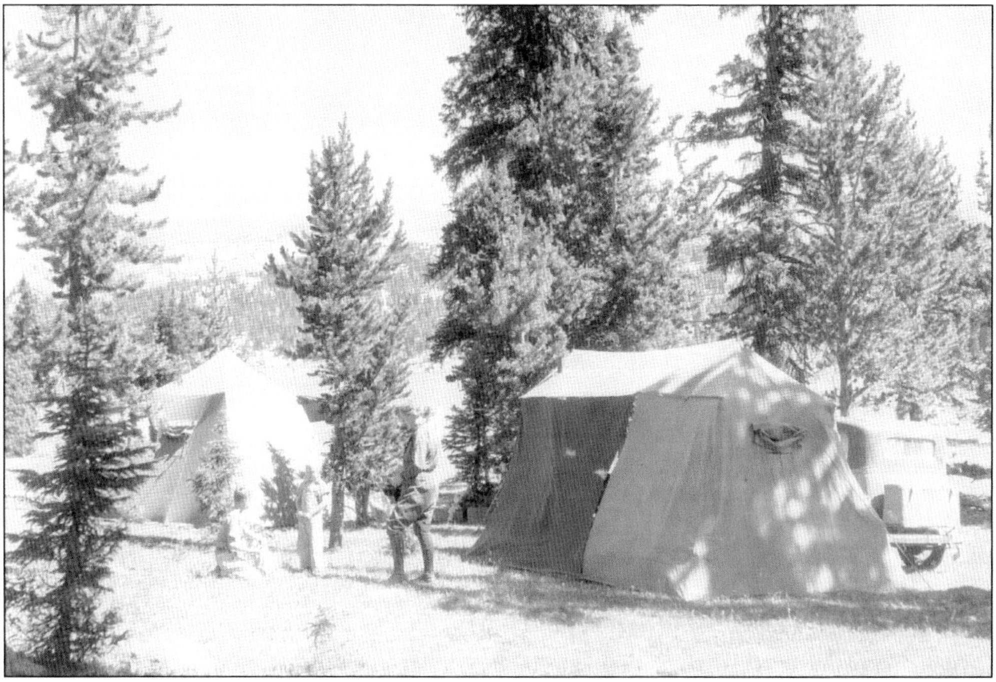

Campers are pictured at a Washakie National Forest camp ground in the early 1920s. Automobiles made it possible for the average citizen to enjoy national forests. (Courtesy Shoshone National Forest.)

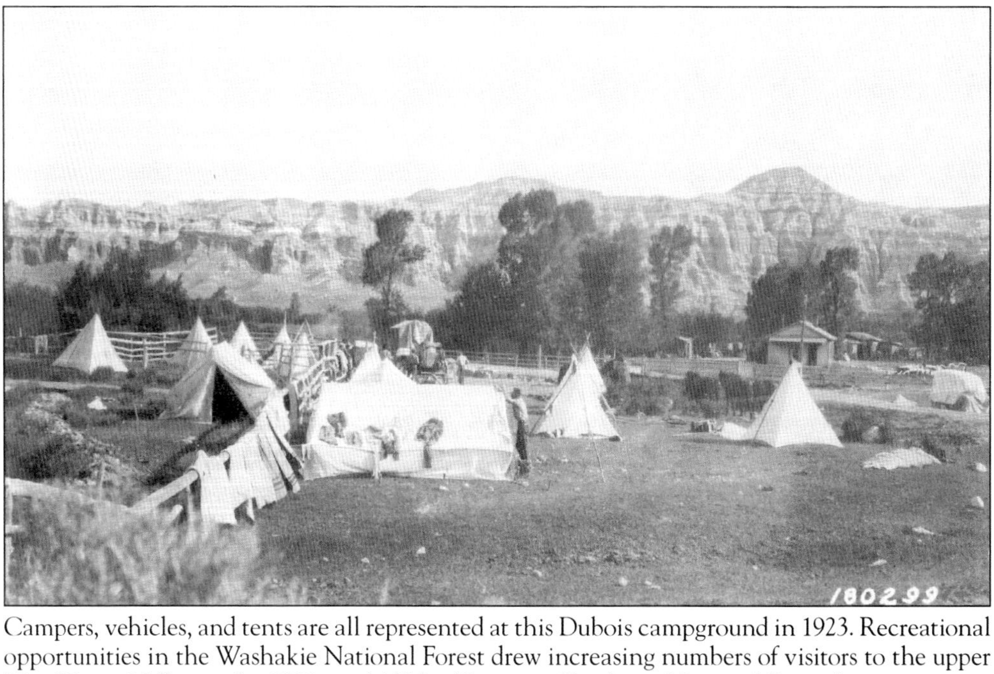

Campers, vehicles, and tents are all represented at this Dubois campground in 1923. Recreational opportunities in the Washakie National Forest drew increasing numbers of visitors to the upper Wind River Valley in the 1920s and 1930s. (Courtesy Shoshone National Forest.)

Four

Making the Most of What You Have

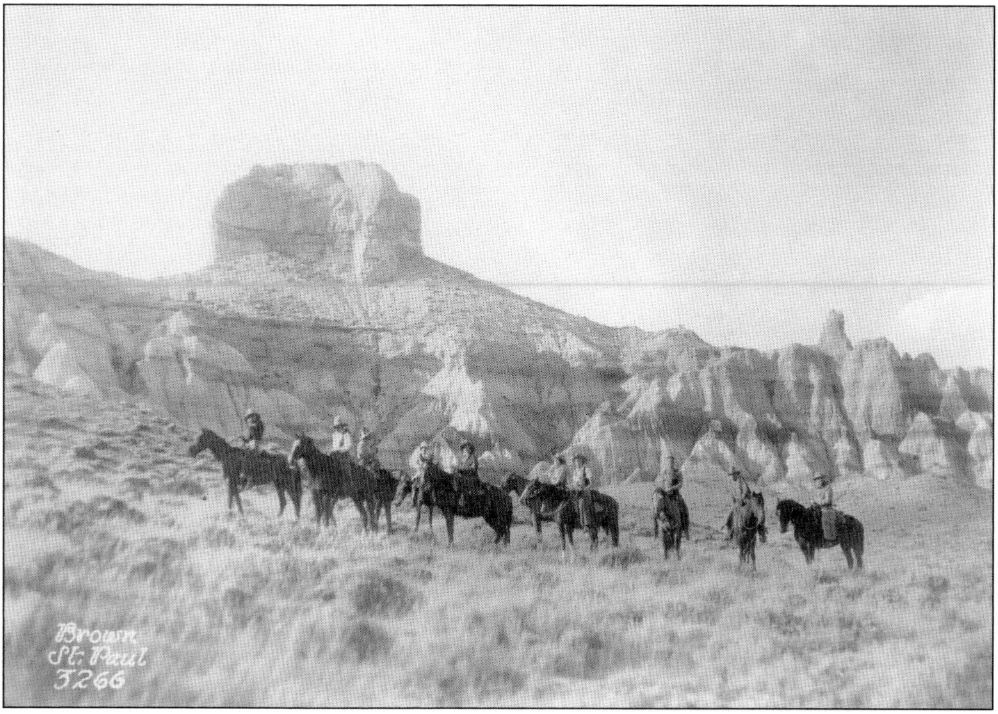

CM Ranch dudes (guests) enjoy a ride through the candy-colored formations of the Dubois badlands in the early 1930s. Charles C. "Charlie" Moore, owner of CM Ranch, was one of the first people in Wyoming to capitalize on the nation's fascination with the West that had been fueled by Yellowstone National Park's growing popularity. Charlie and his brother J.K. "Jimmy" Moore Jr. grew up on the Wind River Reservation, where their father ran the trading post. The Moore brothers spoke fluent Shoshone and Arapaho.

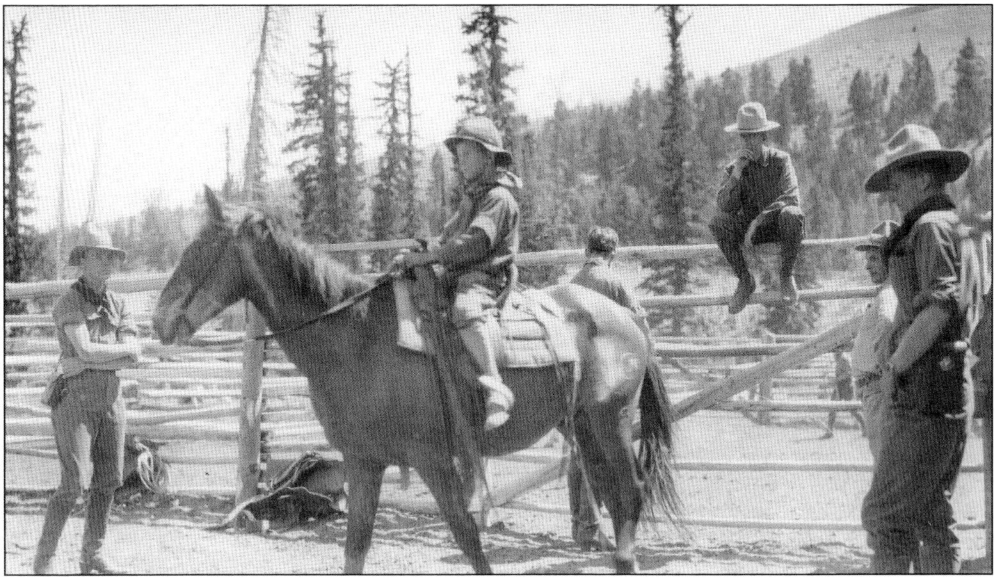

Boys from Charlie Moore's ranch camp learn to ride around 1910. Moore began operating the camp in the Dunoir Valley, a tributary of the Wind River, in 1907. Boys attending the camp were sent by families he met while attending Cheltenham Military Academy in Philadelphia, Pennsylvania. In addition to his other talents, Moore was an excellent rider who rode with Buffalo Bill's Wild West Show when he was a very young man. He went on to earn a law degree from the University of Michigan in Ann Arbor in 1906.

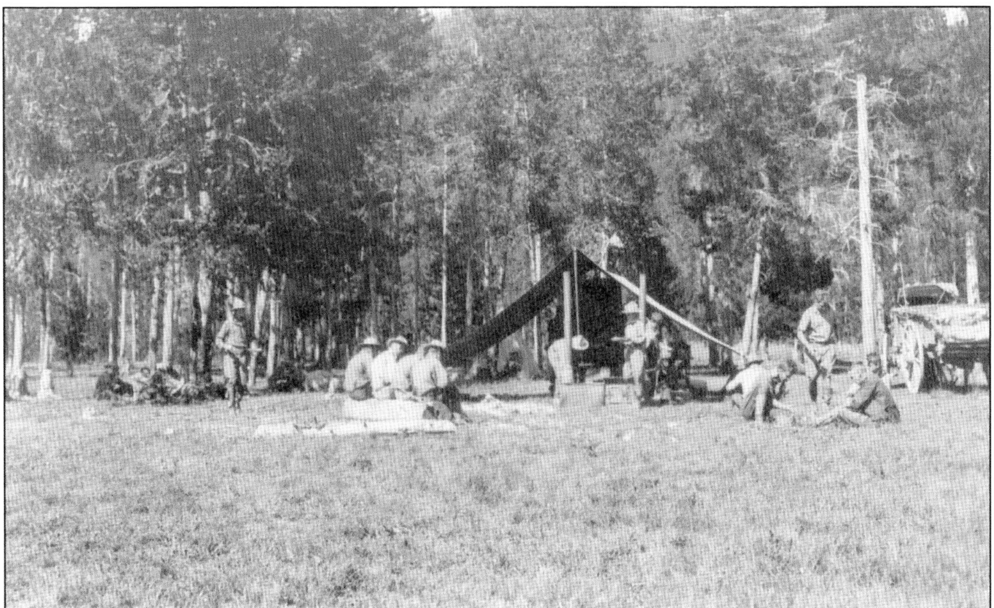

Boys from Charlie Moore's Ramshorn Ranch Camp are shown setting up an alpine camp in the Wind River Mountains around 1909.

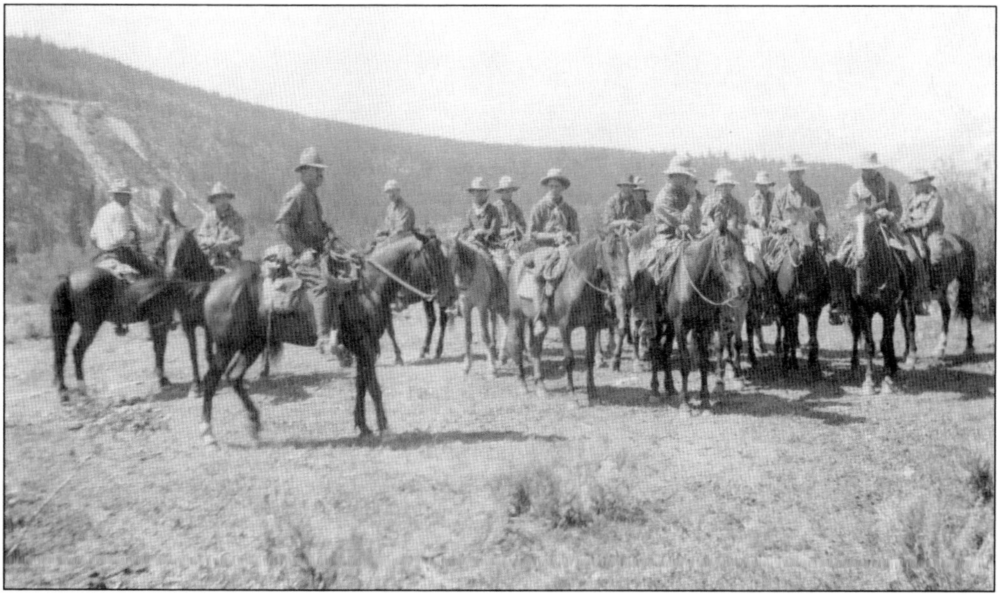

Charlie Moore's Ramshorn Ranch Camp boys are lined up ready to hit the trail to Lava Mountain in the Absaroka Mountains northwest of Dubois.

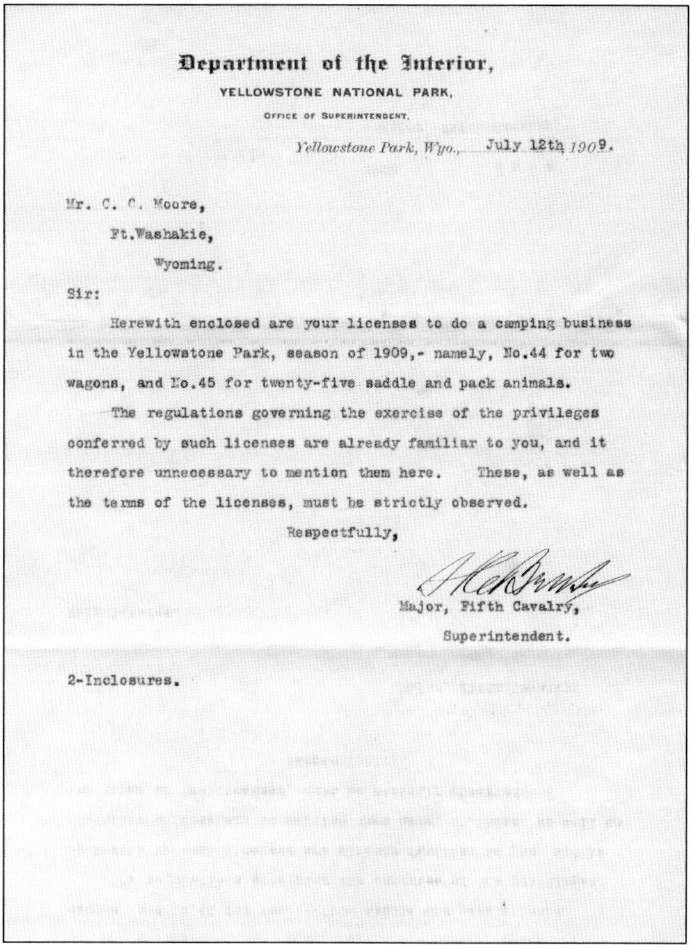

Department of the Interior,
YELLOWSTONE NATIONAL PARK,
OFFICE OF SUPERINTENDENT.

Yellowstone Park, Wyo., July 12th 1909.

Mr. C. C. Moore,
Ft.Washakie,
Wyoming.

Sir:

Herewith enclosed are your licenses to do a camping business in the Yellowstone Park, season of 1909,- namely, No.44 for two wagons, and No.45 for twenty-five saddle and pack animals.

The regulations governing the exercise of the privileges conferred by such licenses are already familiar to you, and it therefore unnecessary to mention them here. These, as well as the terms of the licenses, must be strictly observed.

Respectfully,

Major, Fifth Cavalry,
Superintendent.

2-Inclosures.

A copy of a July 12, 1909, letter accompanying Charlie's permit to operate a camping business in Yellowstone during the 1909 summer season is pictured here. The park was operated by the military at the time, and a major in the 5th US Calvary served as park superintendent.

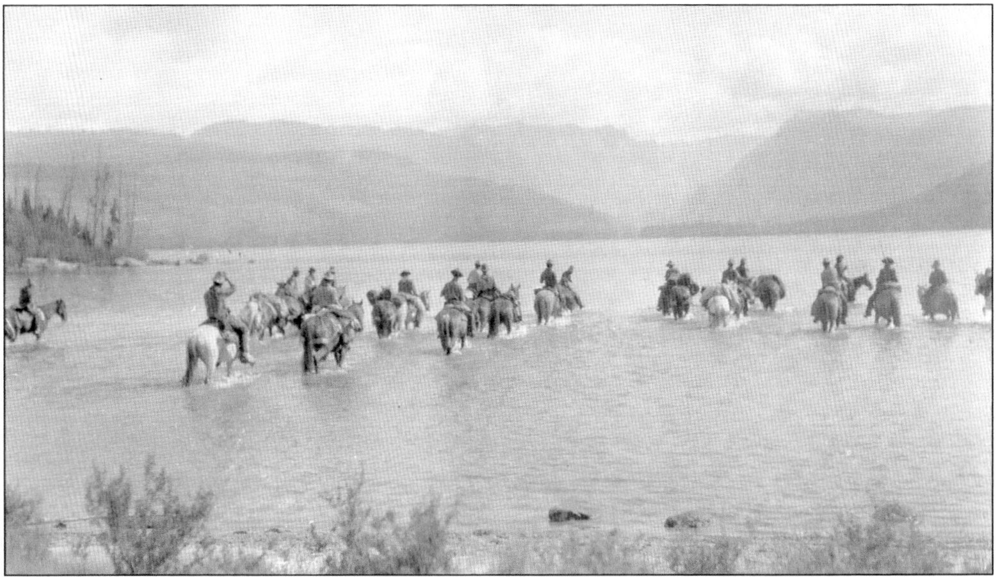

Members of Charlie Moore's Ramshorn Ranch Camp crew water their horses in Yellowstone Lake.

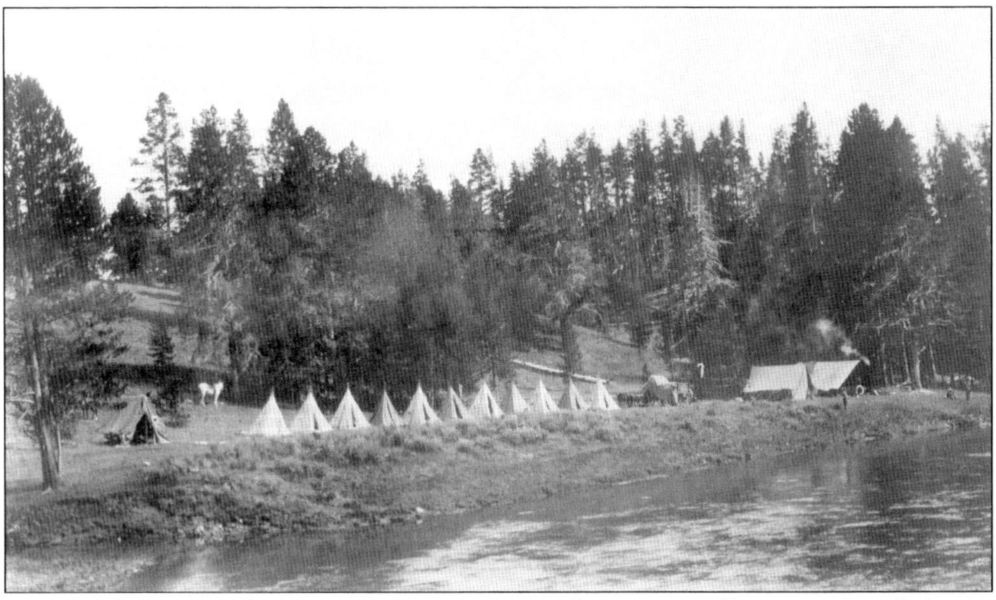

Tents for the boys at Charlie Moore's Ramshorn Ranch Camp are all set up and ready for the night at a Yellowstone River site in Yellowstone National Park.

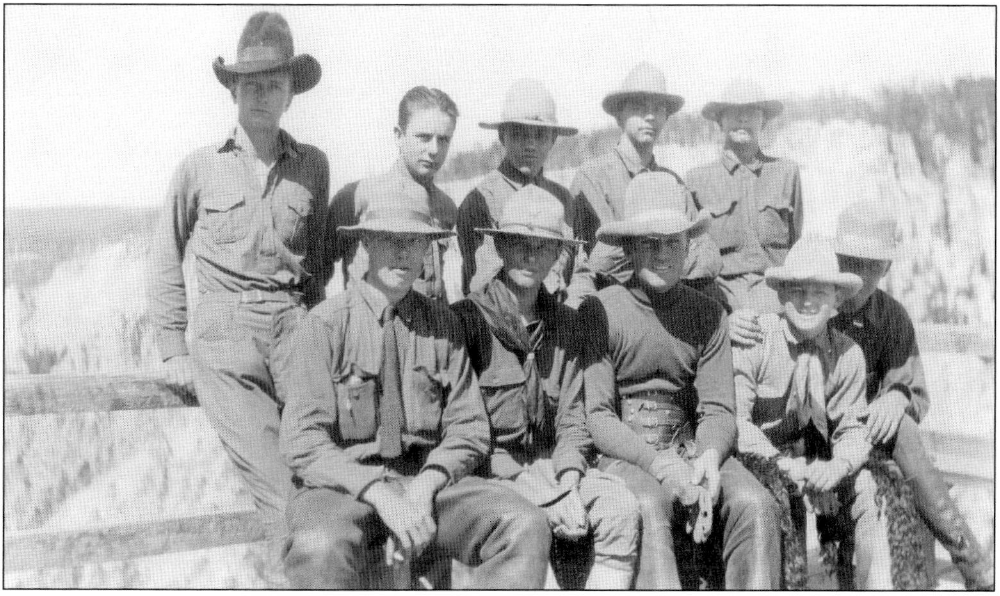

Charlie Moore's ranch camp boys pose at Artists' Point in Yellowstone National Park.

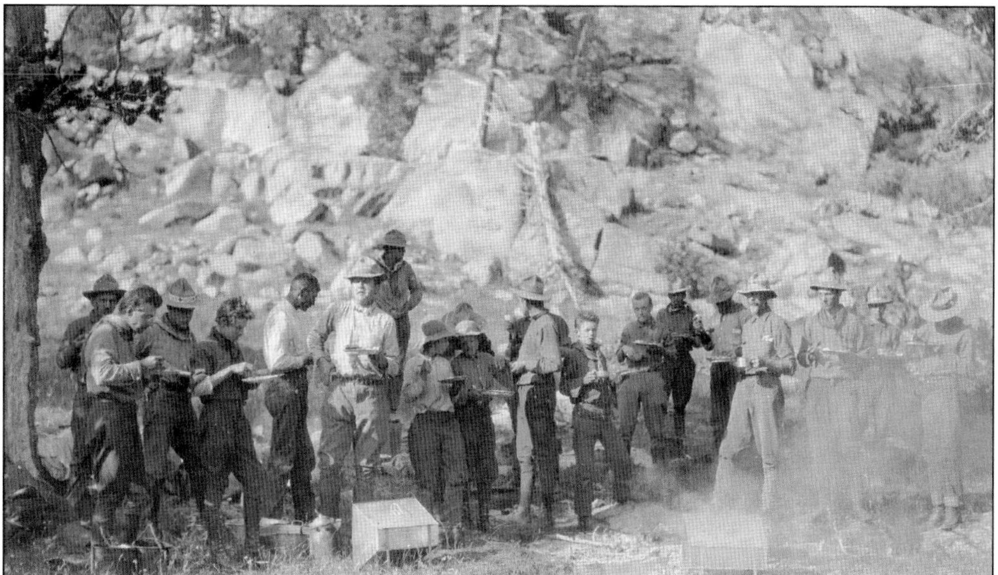

Boys from Charlie Moore's Ramshorn Ranch eat lunch along the trail during a 1909 Yellowstone trip. Moore's Ramshorn Ranch burned in 1919. He purchased the Elwood S. Wilson homestead on Jakey's Fork of the Wind River in 1920 and resumed business as the CM Ranch.

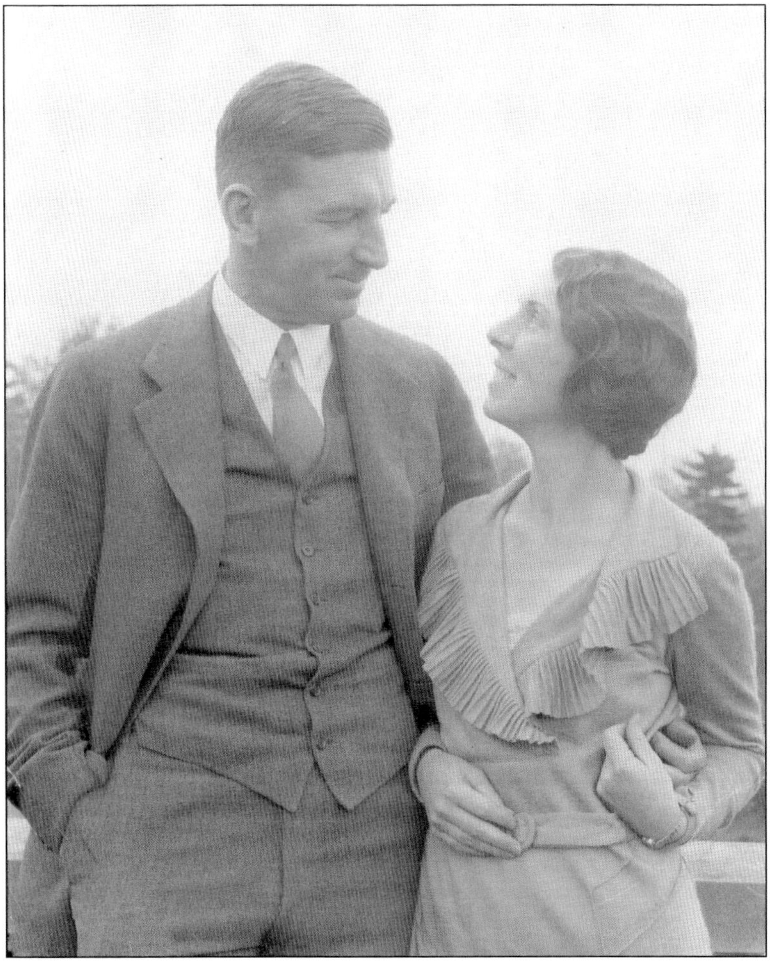

Charlie Moore and his second wife, Marion Laidlaw Moore, are shown on their wedding day in 1927. They operated the CM Ranch together until 1952 when they sold the business to Les and Alice Shoemaker.

Marion Moore feeds a horse and colt at the CM Ranch in the late 1930s. Marion Moore shared Charlie Moore's love of the West and enjoyed their lives at the CM Ranch.

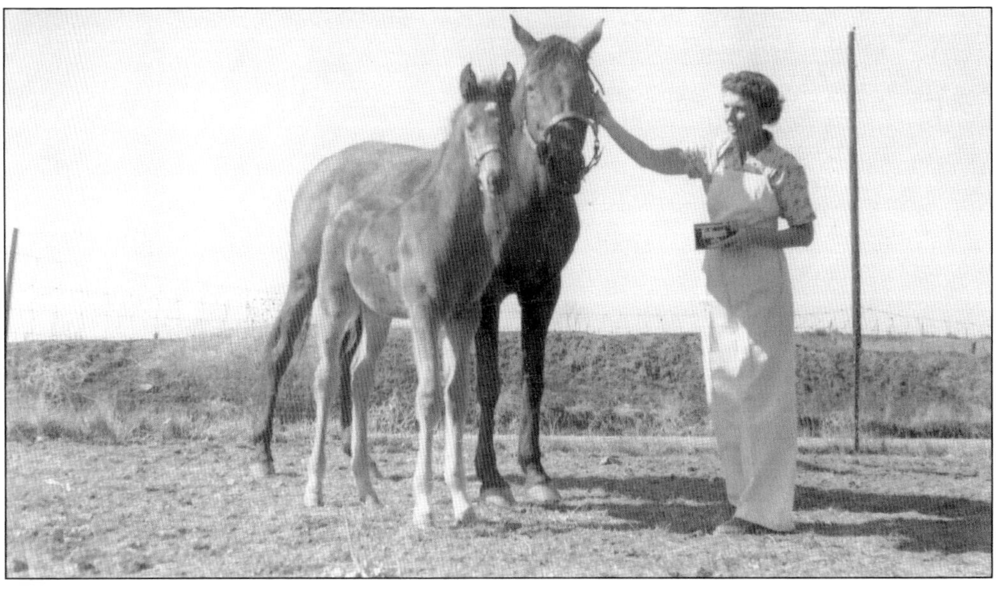

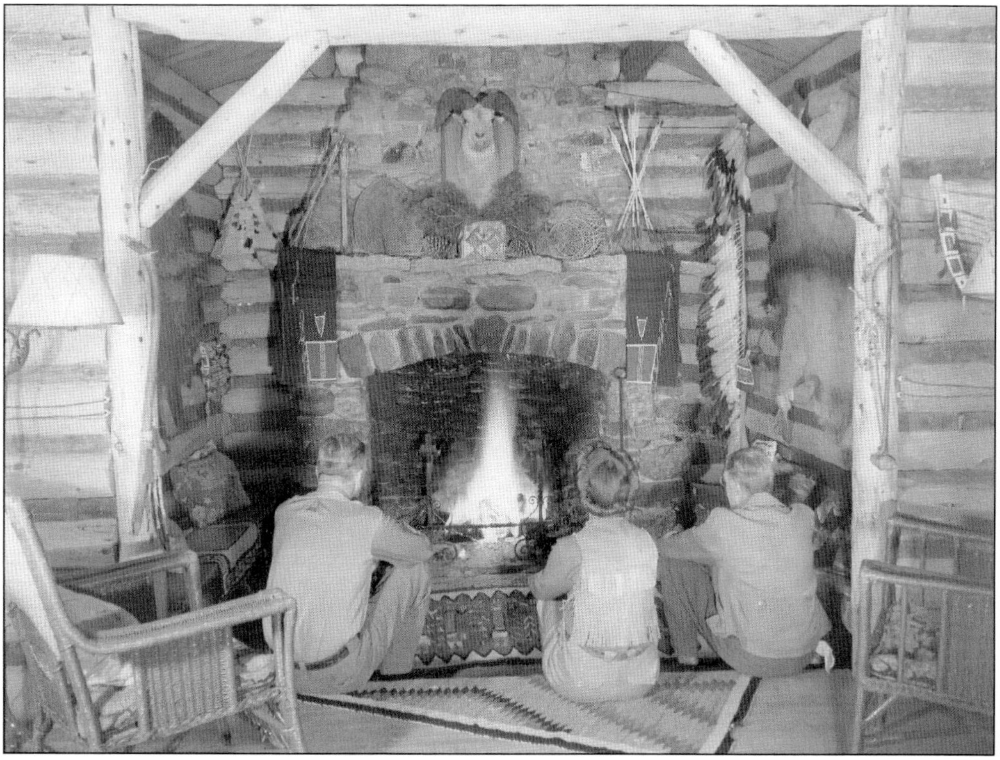

Charlie and Marion Moore and a guest relax in front to a fireplace in the lodge at CM Ranch. The ranch was later purchased by Les and Alice Shoemaker and acquired by the Kemmerer family in 1997. It remains in operation today. Jay Kemmerer and his sisters Betty and Connie frequently visited the CM Ranch as children.

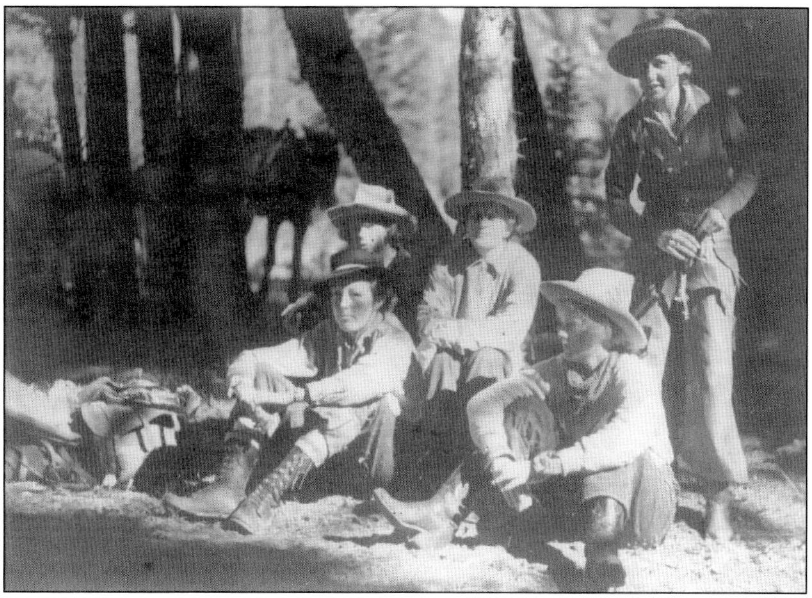

CM Ranch guests are shown taking a break along the trail in the 1930s. Charlie Moore wanted his guests to experience the West he knew and loved.

HE CODY (Wyo.), ENTERPRISE WEDNESDAY, OCT. 8, 1969

Charlie Moore-Wyo.'s Oldest Dude Ranck

There were many fond collections of the early days in yoming, and his life as one of e original "dude" ranchers hen Charles C. Moore came to dy with his wife Marion to new their many old quaintances and visit the newly panded Buffalo Bill Historical nter.

"Charlie," as his many friends ow him, is the original owner the CM Ranch near Dubois d at a spry and active 89 is the dest known living dude rancher. e sold his ranch and retired in 52 and, with his wife, now ads a pleasant life summering in yoming and Colorado and intering in Thousand Palms, alif. While here they were ests of their old friends, Paul d Eloise Stock.

And it is no wonder that his sit to the Center brought back emories for Charlie knew ederic Remington and was a ersonal friend of Charles ussell . . . and of course there as the time when he rode the inois circuit with Col. W. F. ody in 1900.

Born 10 years before yoming became a state at Fort ashakie on Feb. 3, 1880, oore lived and grew up at the rt with the dreams that all oys have of cowboys, Indians d soldiers made more vivid nce he was living in their midst. he Indians were his constant mpanions and he soon learned e languages of the Shoshoni, rapahoe, Sioux and Cheyenne. e knew Red Cloud and took are of Chief Washakie when he as dying.

Charlie's father had been a age in the U.S. Senate before oming west to Montana in 1874 here he became a post trader at ort Stanhope and later Fort ashakie.

Given the job of delivering 35

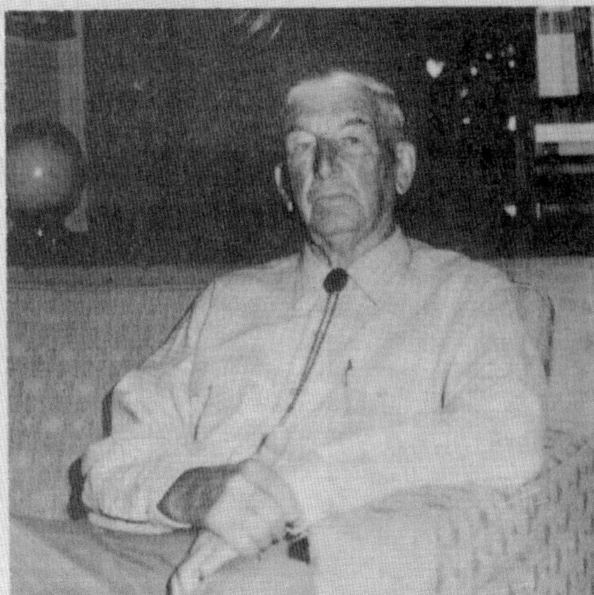

head of his father's "outlaw" horses to the Buffalo Bill Wild West Show in Chicago, he first met the famous showman. He recalls that when the Colonel saw one of the horses being saddled for a ride in the arena, he remarked, "That's an old deadhead." Charlie replied, "Better put a good man on him." The outcome was havoc i the arena as the "deadhead" scattered all of Annie Oakley's guns and dashed into the grandstand from which he had to be forcibly removed.

He liked the show and obtained his parents permission to stay on. The Colonel offered him $60 a month and a medical guarantee to pay all doctor bills if he was injured. Thus he toured during 1900 through Illinois with the always moving extravaganza.

But when offered the opportunity of touring Europe, his parents finally balked, so he missed the chance to make the grand tour with the show.

Instead it was back to school for Charlie, from which he emerged with a degree in law from the University of M After graduation he can to Wyoming to practice Cheyenne.

Meanwhile in 1904, th Ranch near Sheridan ha taking paying guest developing the idea emerged into the Dude industry. Charlie sa potential of this idea, an acquired his ranch, star development of a boys The idea spread and soon popular on many of the ranches.

Many of the boy's expressed the desire to their sons and also en interest and activities inh western ranch life, so h evolved into a full-fledg ranch operation.

He has been active Dude Ranchers' Associa is a Past President, su Cody's Larry Larom position. He also serv terms in the Wy Legislature.

Looking 20 years than his 89 years, Charl active and although maintains his interest in and the West. Well kr many Codyites, his nie Ron Bell resides here, he his best to his many frie

Charlie Moore is honored for his years as a Wyoming outfitter in a 1969 news article from the *Cody Enterprise* in Cody, Wyoming. Charlie was 89 and had been retired when the article was published. Charlie and Marion divided their time between Colorado, Wyoming, and California until Charlie's death in 1971 at age 91.

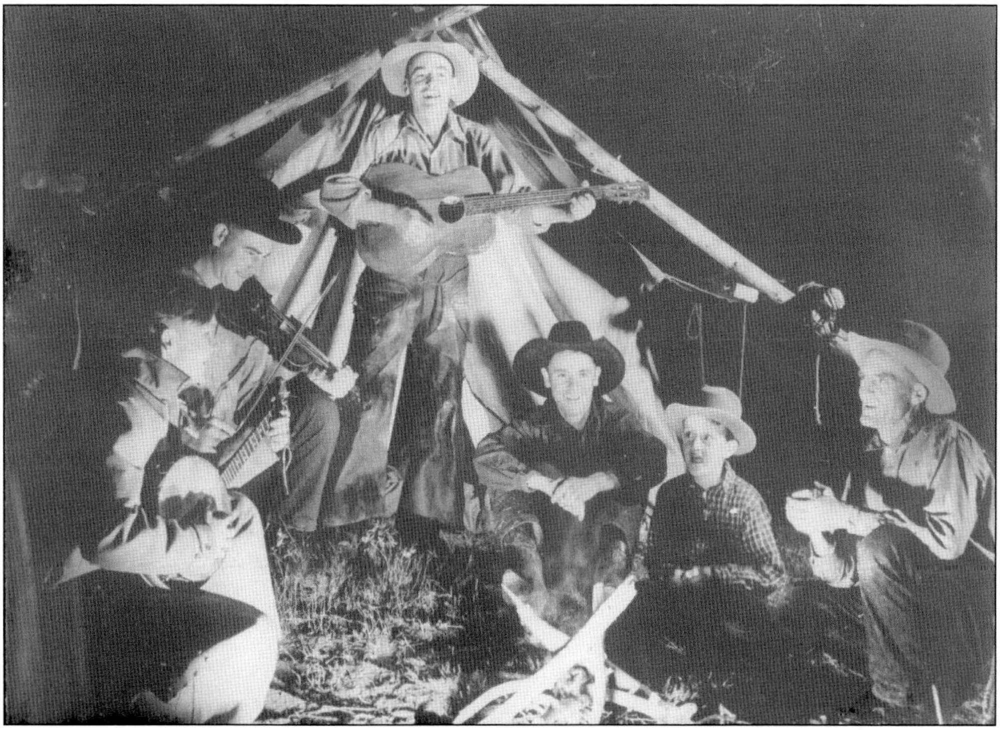

Guests at the T Cross Ranch enjoy a campfire song in the 1930s. The ranch, originally known as the Hermitage, was constructed in 1918 by Henry M. "Dutch" Seipt and his wife, Ora, on a former homestead in the Absaroka Mountains within the Washakie National Forest. The young couple and their two small children lived in a tent on the property while they were building cabins for themselves and guests.

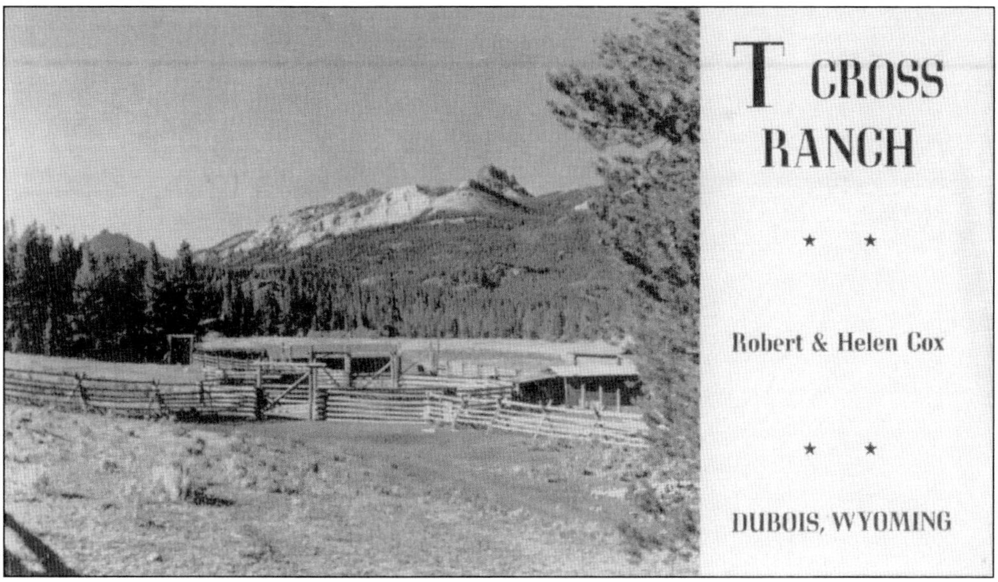

This 1942 brochure cover was designed by Bob and Helen Cox to entice visitors to their guest ranch. The Coxes purchased the Hermitage from Dutch and Ora Seipt in 1929 and renamed it the T Cross Ranch.

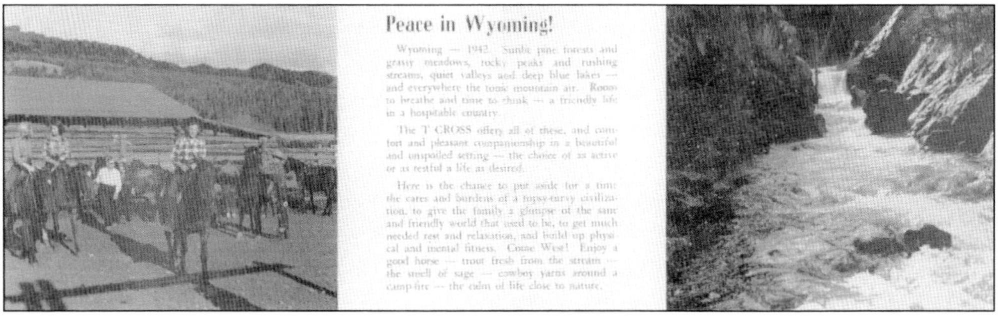

Peace in Wyoming!

Wyoming — 1942. Sunlit pine forests and grassy meadows, rocky peaks and rushing streams, quiet valleys and deep blue lakes — and everywhere the tonic mountain air. Room to breathe and time to think — a friendly life in a hospitable country.

The T CROSS offers all of these, and comfort and pleasant companionship in a beautiful and unspoiled setting — the choice of as active or as restful a life as desired.

Here is the chance to put aside for a time the cares and burdens of a topsy-turvy civilization, to give the family a glimpse of the sane and friendly world that used to be, to get much needed rest and relaxation, and build up physical and mental fitness. Come West! Enjoy a good horse — trout fresh from the stream — the smell of sage — cowboy yarns around a camp-fire — the calm of life close to nature.

The inside page of the 1942 brochure promised guests peace and tranquility at the T Cross Ranch and featured more enticing photographs of its wilderness setting.

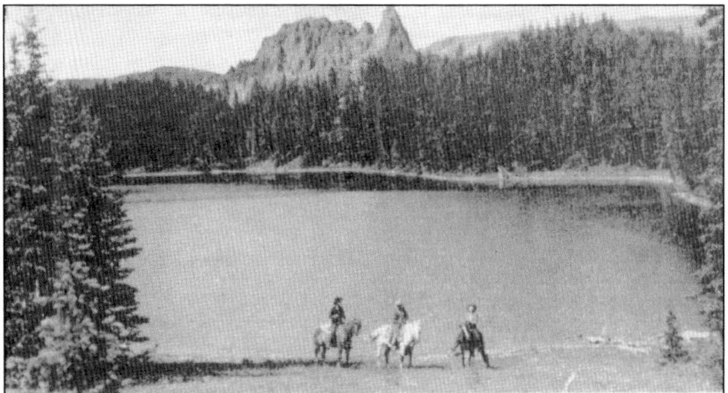

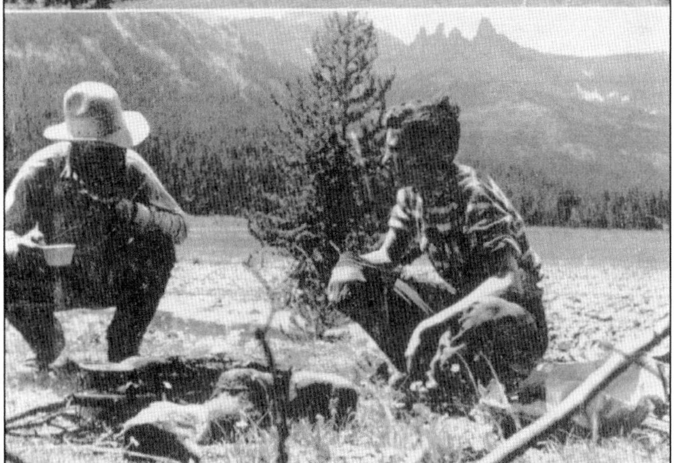

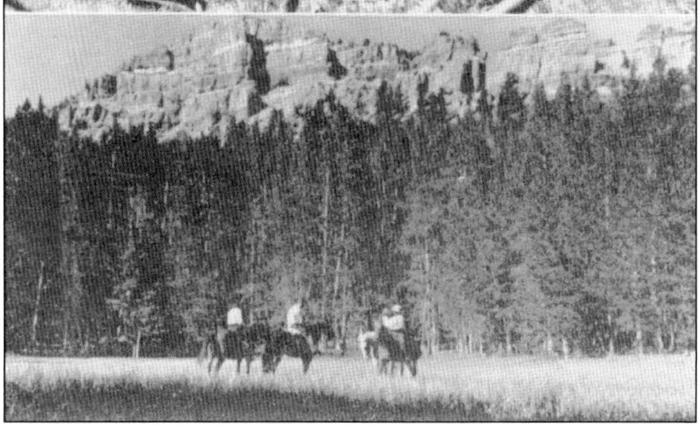

The 1942 T Cross Ranch brochure allowed photographs to illustrate what visitors would experience during their stay at the ranch. The Cox family sold the T Cross to Emily Stevens, and Stevens later sold the ranch to Ken and Garey Neal. It is managed today by the Neal's daughter Gretchen and her husband, Mark Cardall.

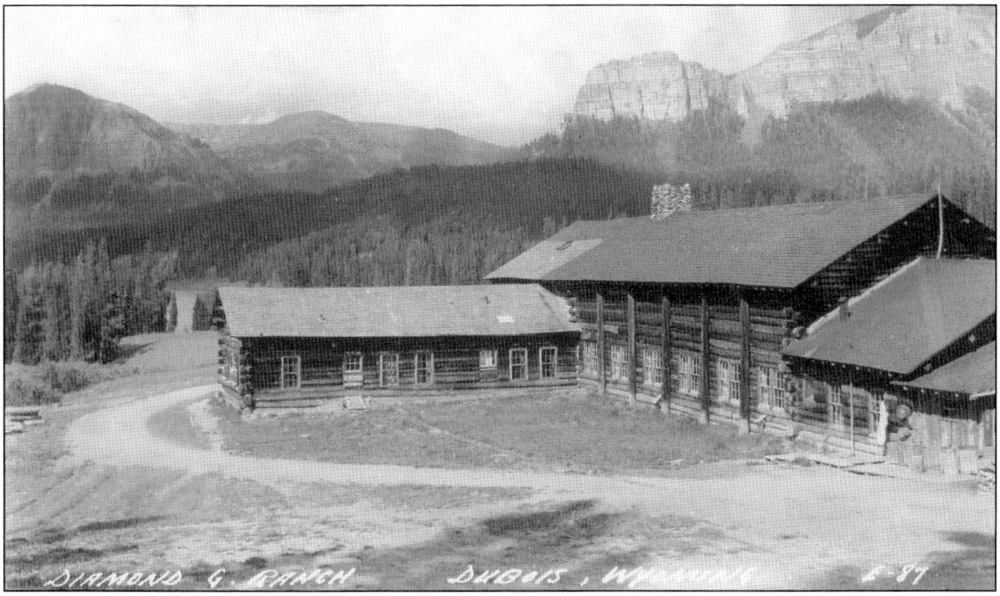

Brooks Lake Lodge, shown in 1934, was constructed in 1922 by Eugene Amoretti Jr. of Lander at Brooks Lake in the Absaroka Mountains within the Washakie National Forest. Amoretti named the lodge Amoretti Hotel and intended it as an overnight stop for Yellowstone National Park bus tours; however, the distances between stops (30 miles from Dubois and 60 miles from the park) made Amoretti's plan impractical. Jim Gratiot, a shareholder from Chicago, took over the lodge around 1927, renamed it Diamond G Ranch, and operated it as a guest ranch. Foster Scott was Gratiot's manager and later owned the Diamond G.

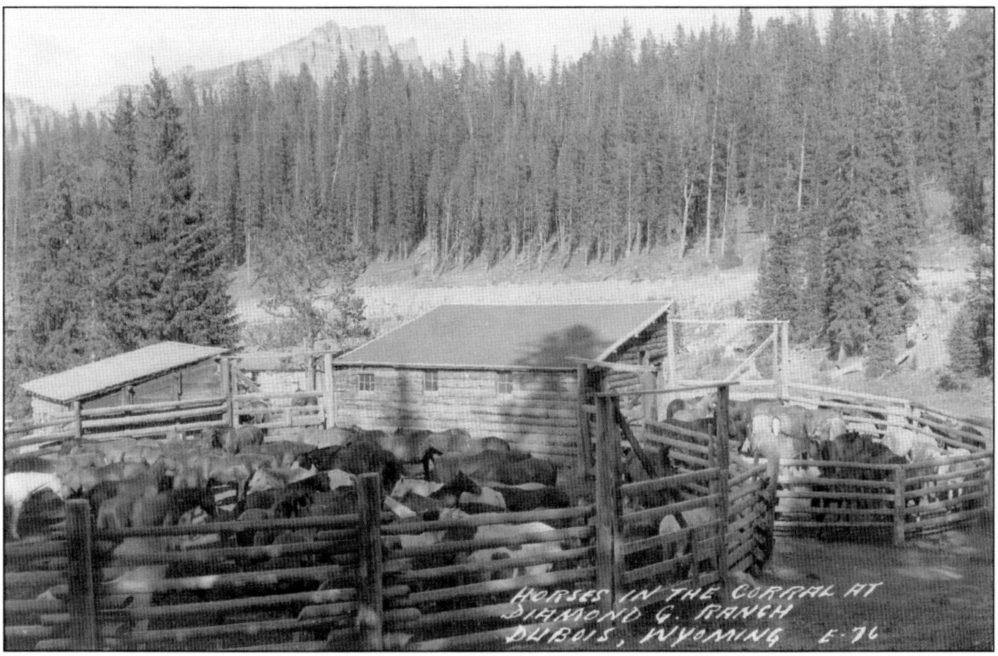

Horses are pictured in the corral at Diamond G Ranch in the 1930s. When the Diamond G Ranch was acquired by new owners in 1953, it became Brooks Lake Lodge. Improved and expanded by a series of owners, today's Brooks Lake Lodge is a luxury lodge owned by Max Chapman Jr.

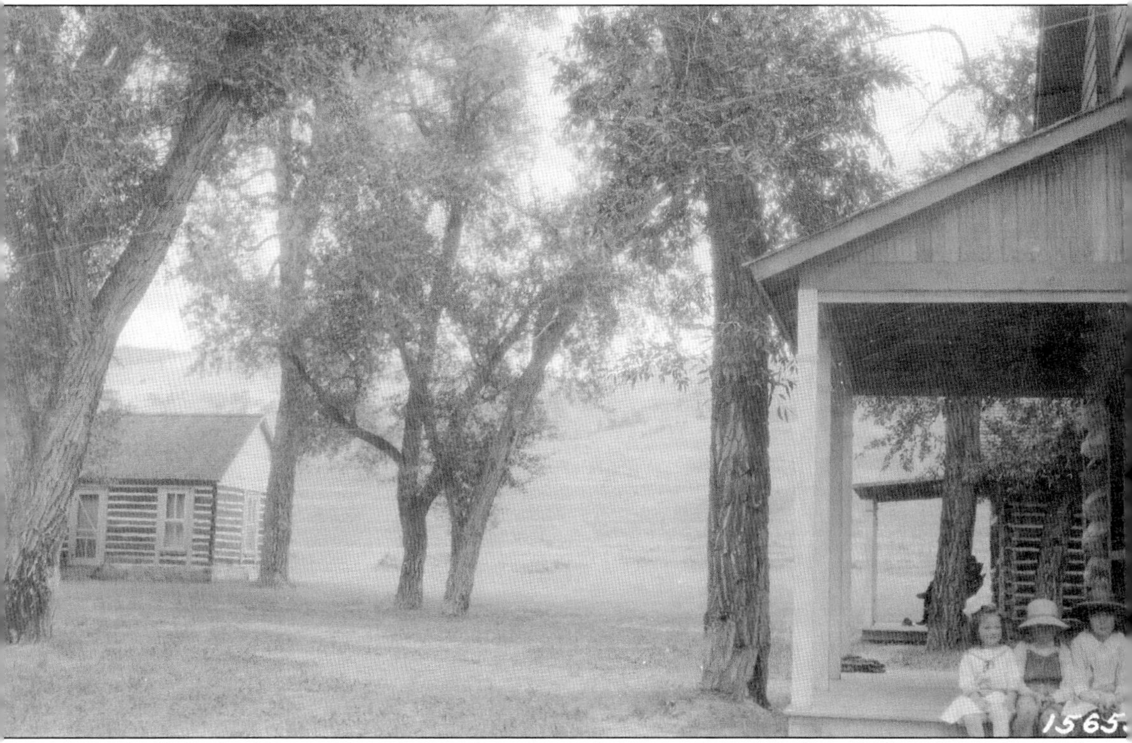

The lodge building at the EA Ranch is pictured in the 1930s with three little girls on the porch. Eugene Amoretti Jr., original owner of Brooks Lake Lodge, purchased the property from outlaws Butch Cassidy and Al Heiner in the early 1900s. The EA Ranch, located about eight miles northeast of Dubois, was one of the early guest ranches that took its visitors to Yellowstone National Park.

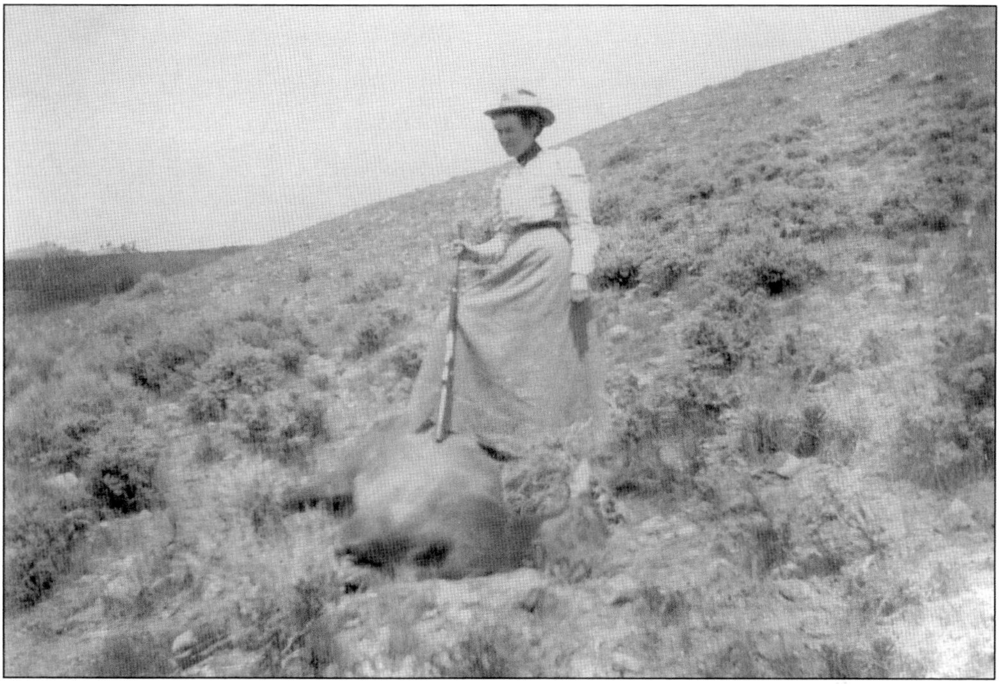

Eloise Amoretti, the wife of Eugene Amoretti, is shown at the Amoretti Ranch in the early 1900s. The Amoretti Ranch later became the EA Ranch. The Amoretti Ranch was one of the early guest ranches. It took guests to Yellowstone National Park in a touring car.

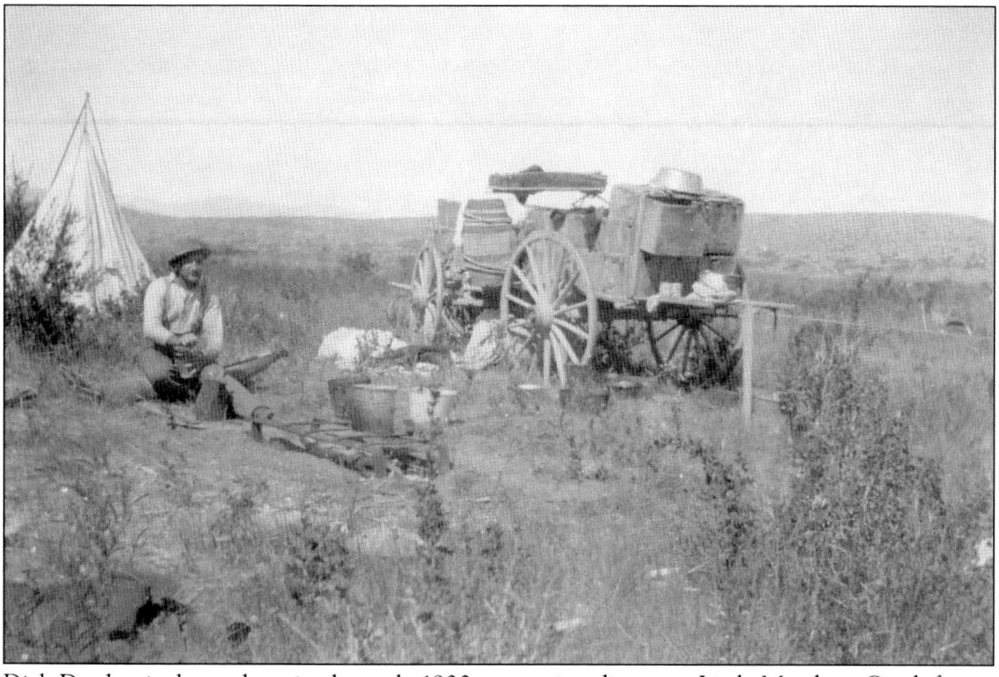

Dick Dryden is shown here in the early 1900s preparing dinner at Little Meadows Creek for an Amoretti Ranch (EA Ranch) cattle drive.

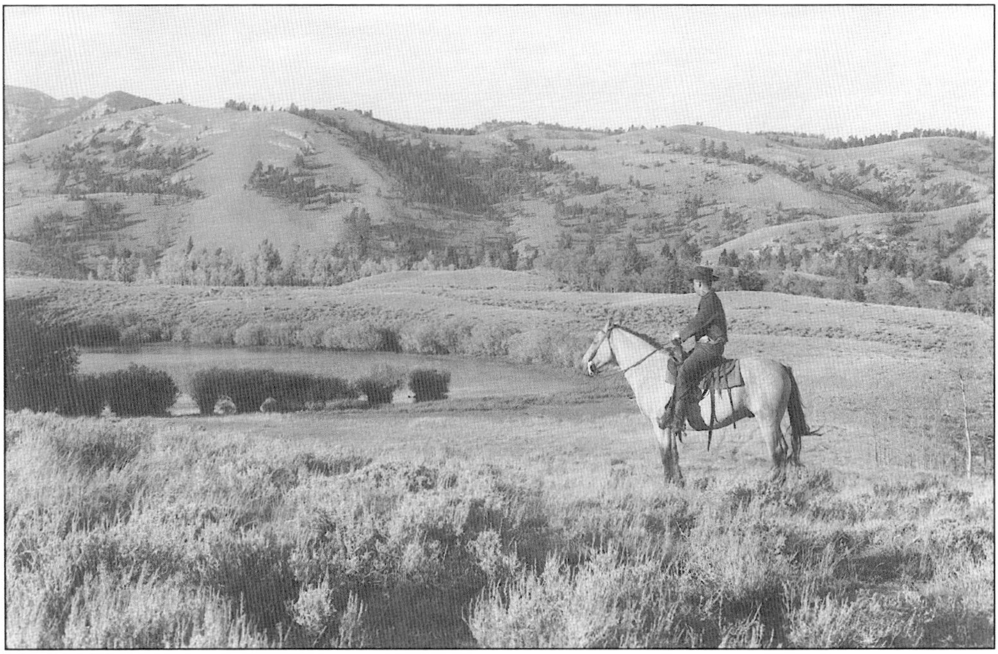

George Peck is pictured in the 1930s at a high meadow overlooking EA Ranch. Peck married Eugene Amoretti's daughter Eloise, and they managed the ranch together. The EA was acquired in the late 1980s by Renny and Tracey Burke, who operated it as a working ranch that accepted paying guests. The current owners have returned the ranch to private use.

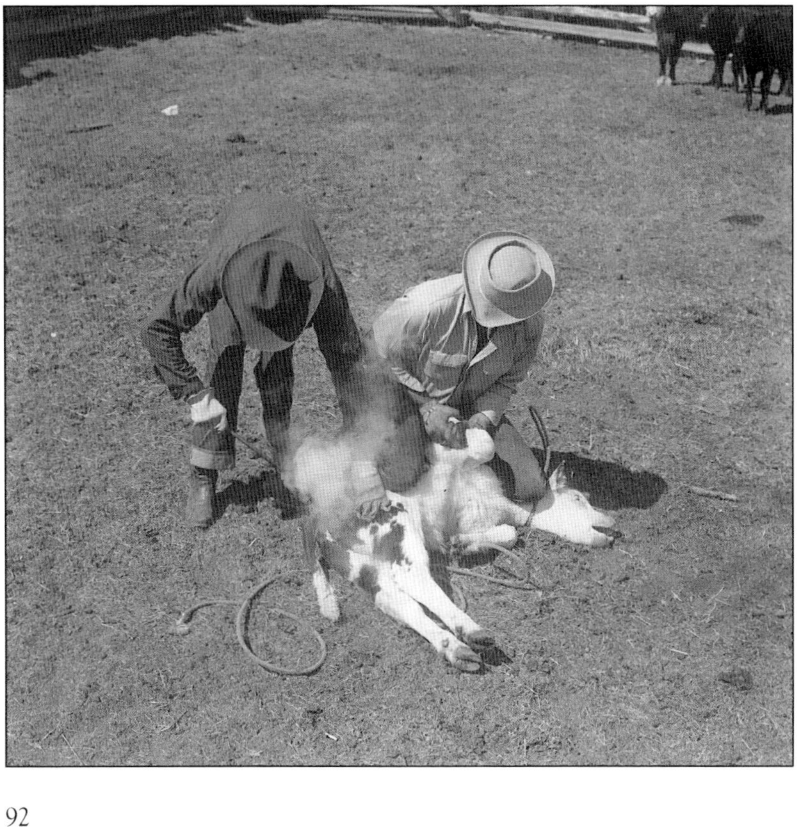

Branding time, pictured in the 1930s, gave EA Ranch guests an opportunity to experience the daily life of a working ranch and help with chores.

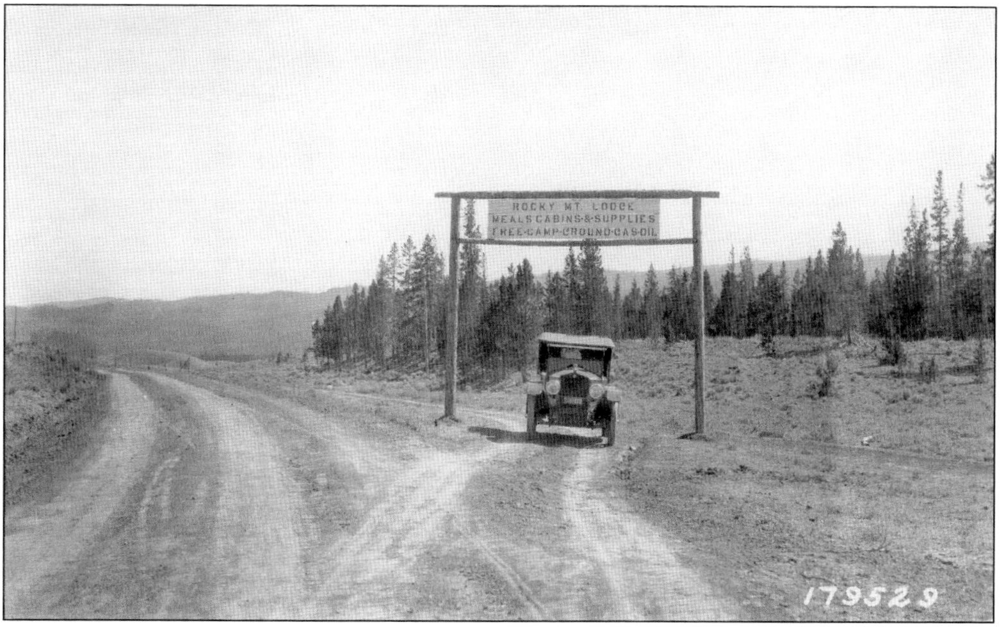

An automobile in the 1920s is parked along US Highway 287 beneath a Rocky Mountain Lodge sign.

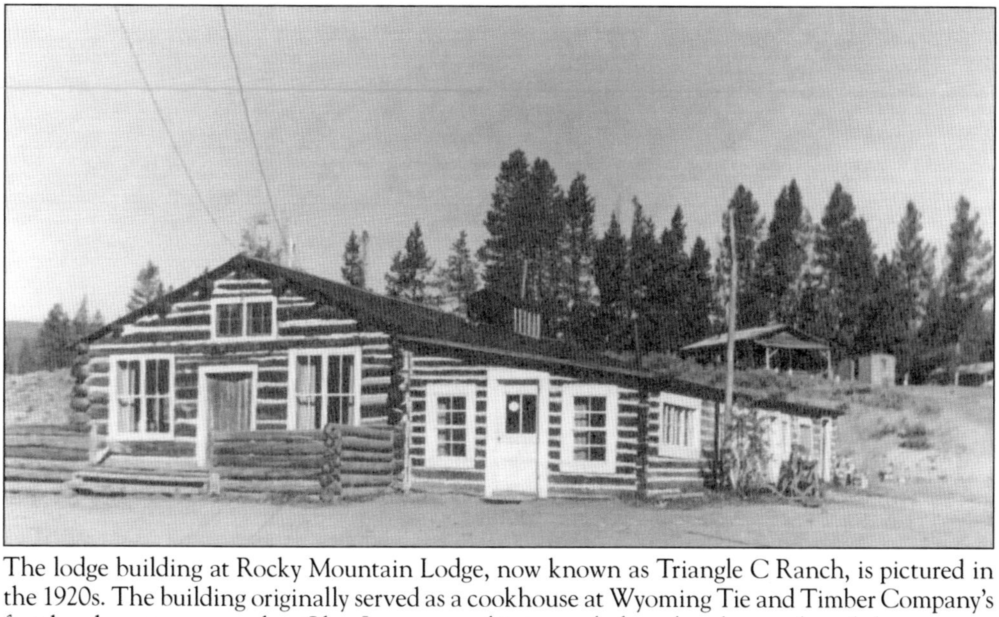

The lodge building at Rocky Mountain Lodge, now known as Triangle C Ranch, is pictured in the 1920s. The building originally served as a cookhouse at Wyoming Tie and Timber Company's first headquarters camp, but Glen Jones turned it into a lodge when he purchased the property along US Highway 287, west of Dubois, in 1922. Jones and his sons Kenneth and Robert mainly used Rocky Mountain Lodge for outfitting hunters but also accepted overnight guests.

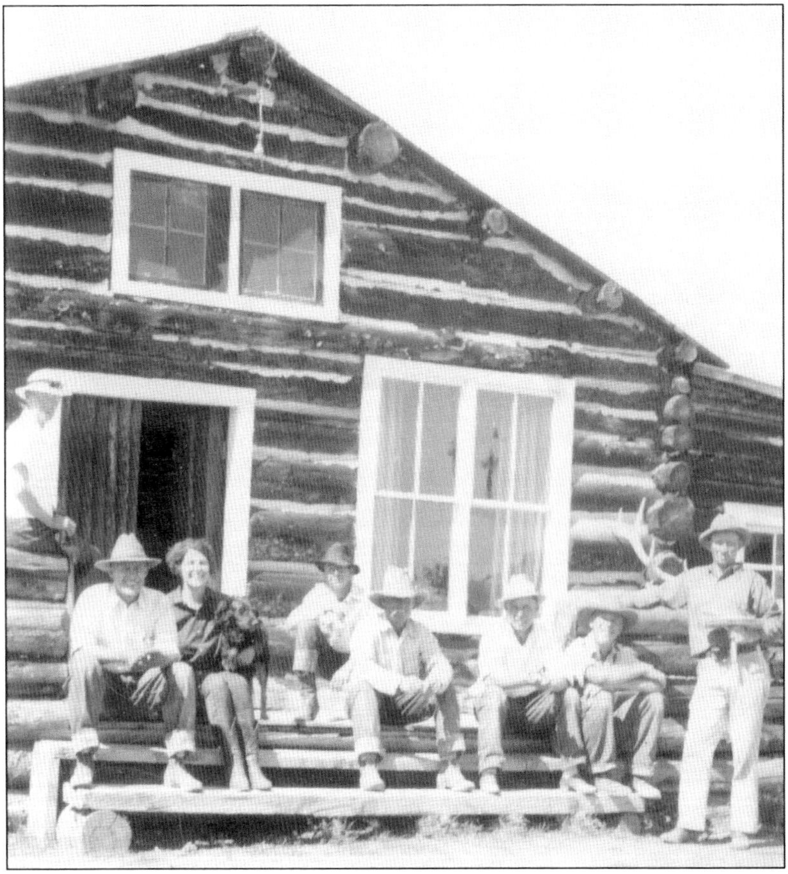

The new lodge building at Triangle C Ranch was constructed in 1933 by Casper dentist Dr. C.H. Carpenter. Glen Jones sold Rocky Mountain Lodge, by then renamed Jumbo Bar JF Ranch, to Carpenter in 1932.

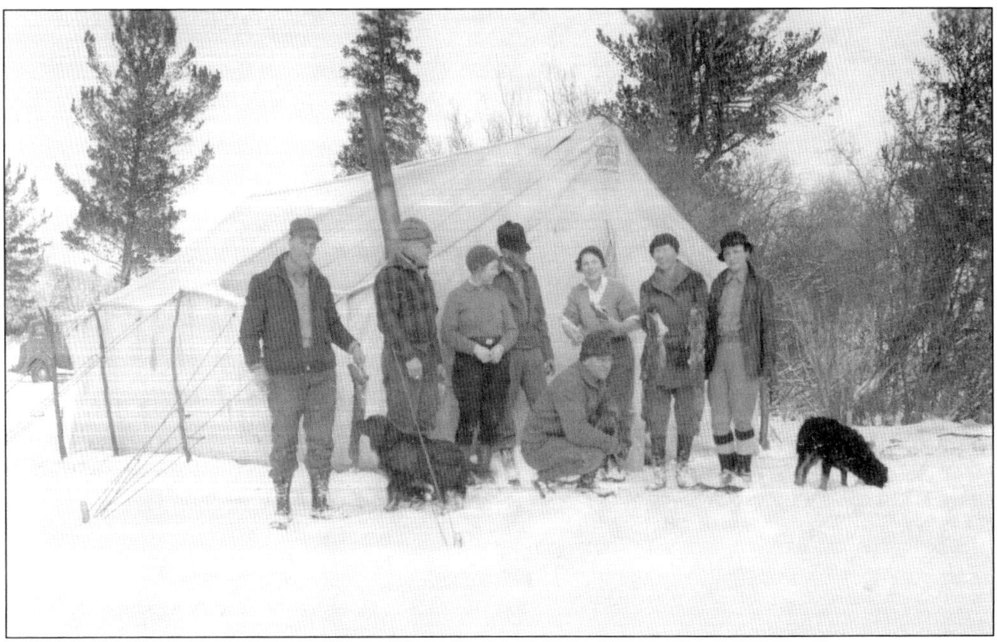

A Rocky Mountain Lodge (Triangle C) fishing camp is pictured in the snow in the early 1920s.

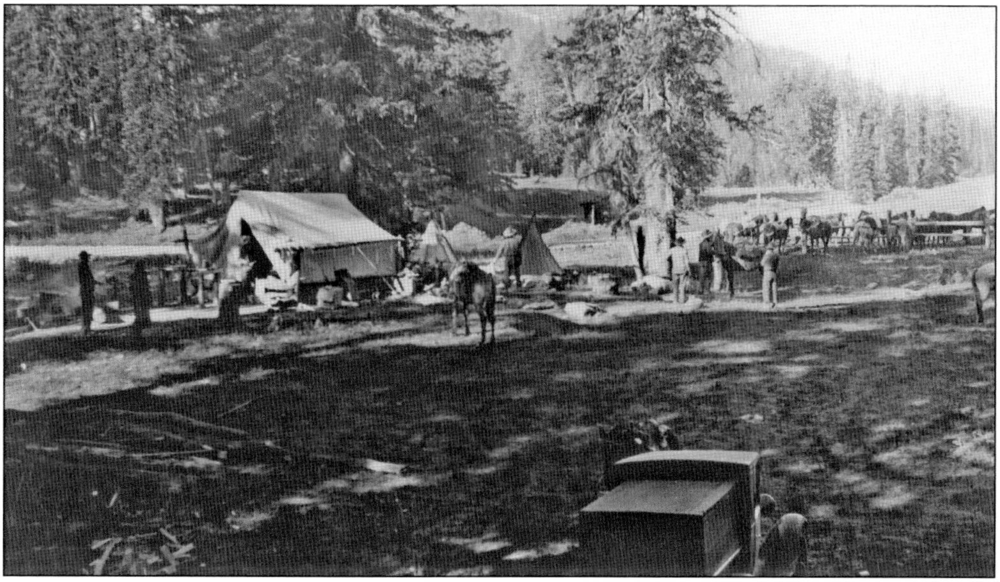

This late-1930s photograph shows a teen camp run by Dr. C.H. Carpenter after he took over operation of the former Rocky Mountain Lodge in 1932. Carpenter had a new lodge built and renamed the ranch the Triangle C.

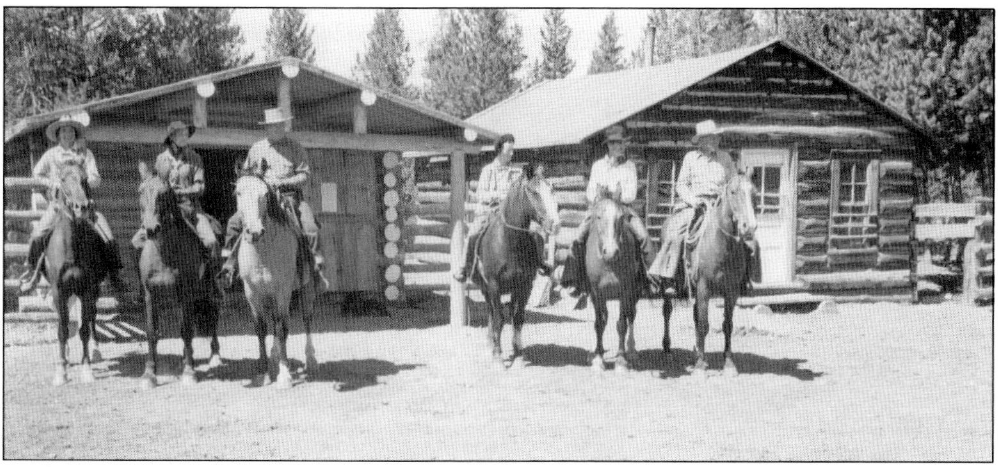

In a late-1930s photograph, Triangle C Ranch guests are ready to begin their morning ride. Triangle C Ranch was operated by a series of owners after 1942. Today, it is run by the Garnick family.

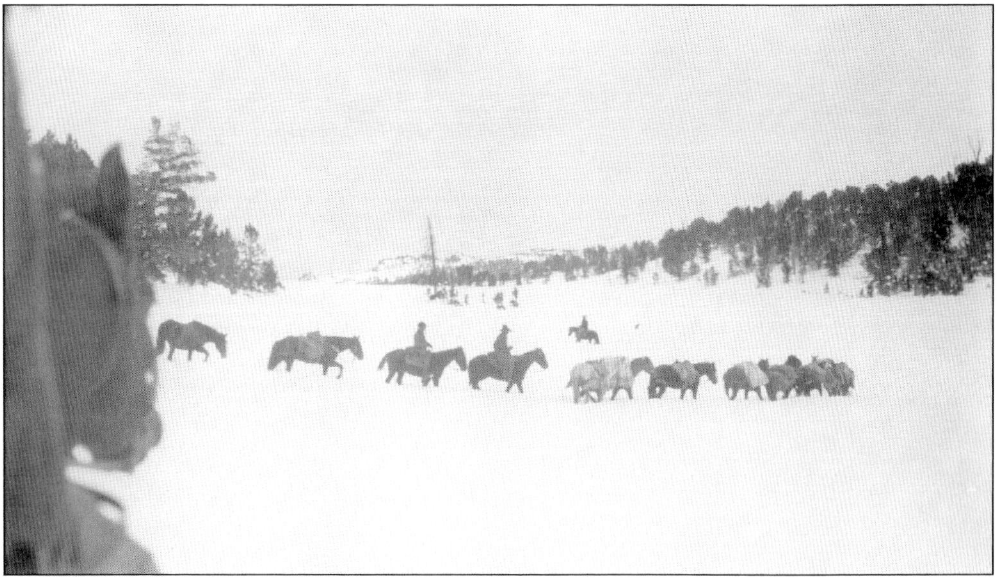

A Triangle C pack string is pictured in the 1930s as it breaks a trail in the snow.

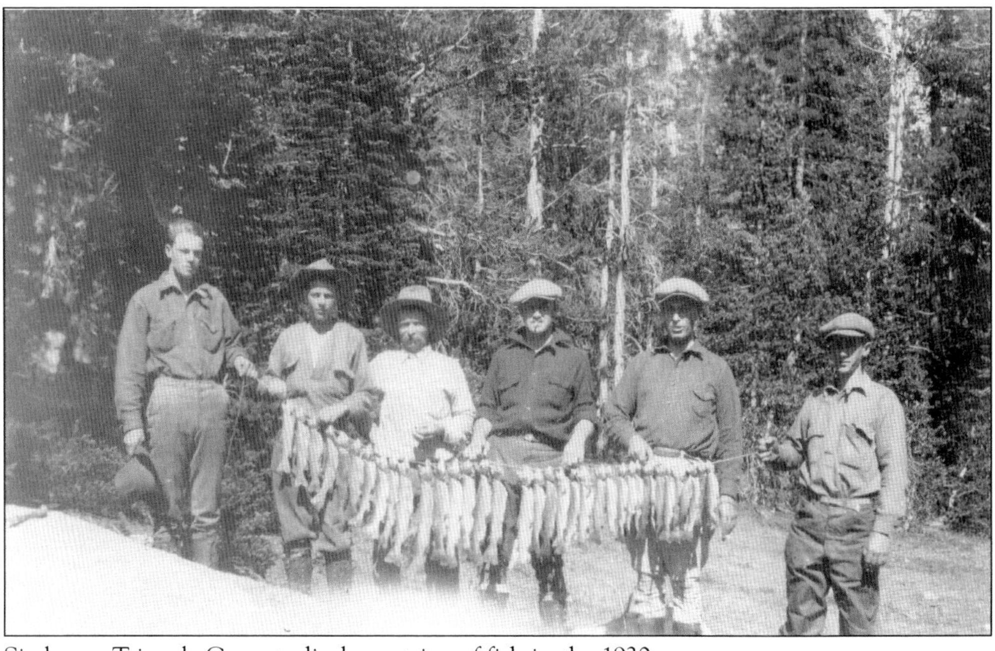

Six happy Triangle C guests display a string of fish in the 1930s.

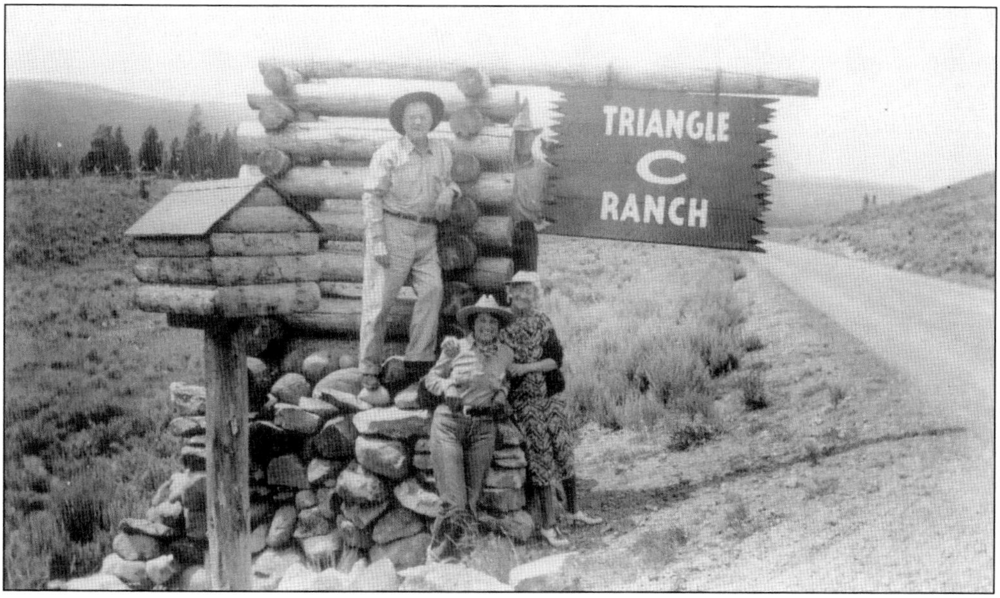

Guests pose under a Triangle C Ranch sign in the late 1930s.

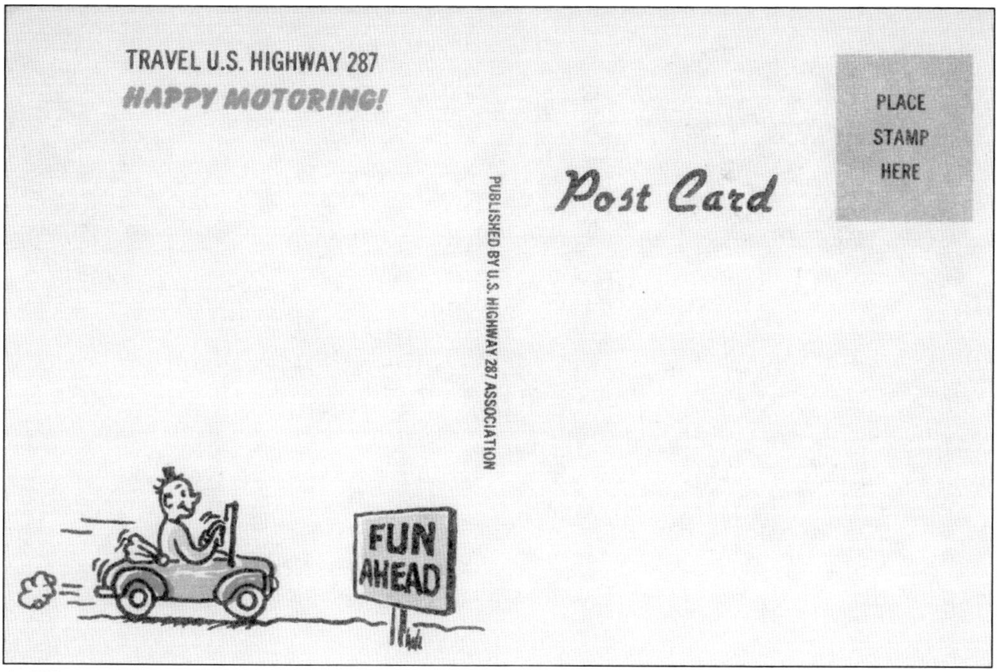

A Wyoming Tourism Commission postcard hints at the recreational opportunities available along US Highway 287.

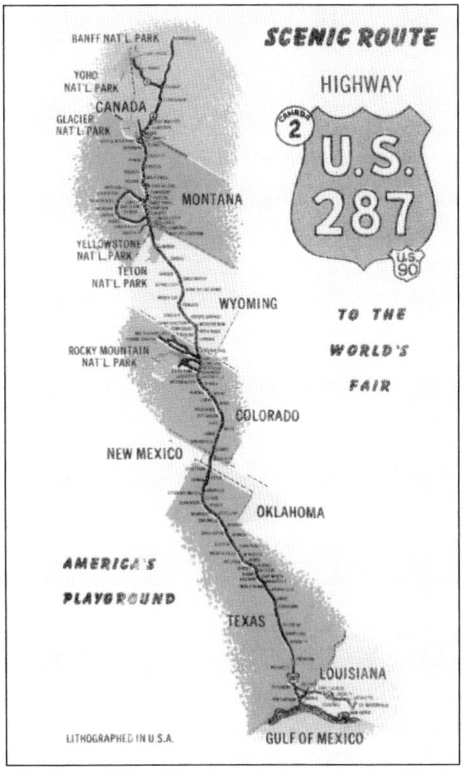

An early poster from the Wyoming Tourism Commission urges visitors to have fun along US Highway 287. It was likely developed for the 1962 World's Fair in Seattle.

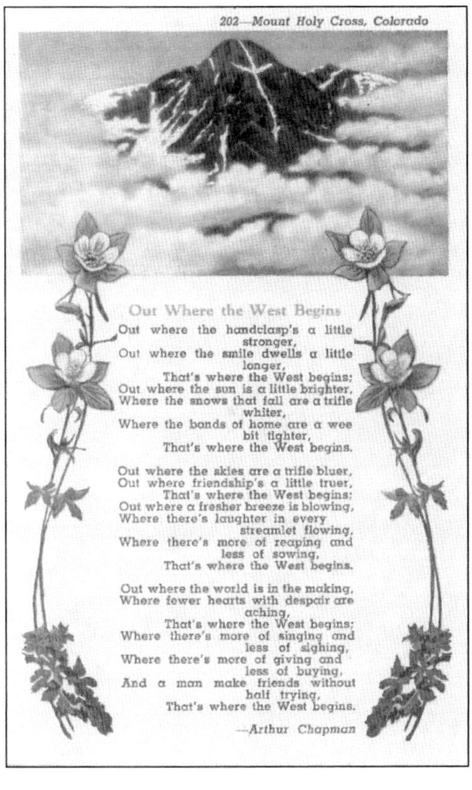

This early postcard featured a Colorado Mountain, but it was popular with Dubois guest ranches because of the poem.

Five

EARNING A LIVING FROM THE FOREST

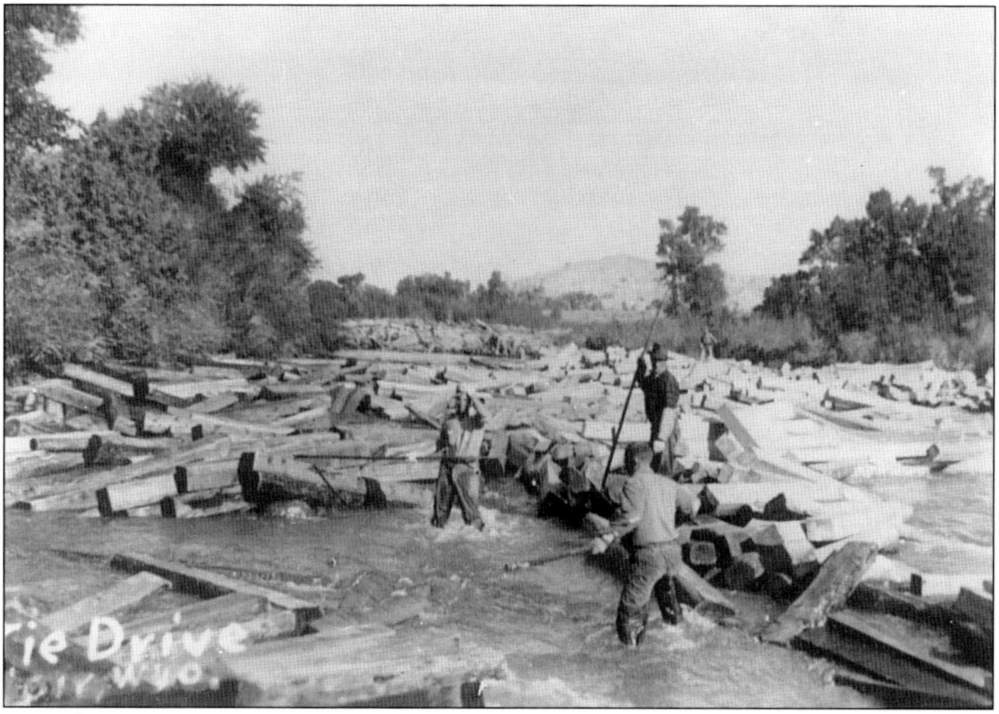

Six tie hacks (loggers who cut railroad ties) are pictured moving ties in a jam on the Wind River in 1934. The annual spring tie drive, a float of completed railroad ties down the river to the Chicago & North Western rail yard in Riverton, was a colorful part of the history of the upper Wind River Valley for over 30 years. The Scandinavian tie hacks that cut ties for Wyoming Tie and Timber Company left a lasting legacy of their culture in Dubois.

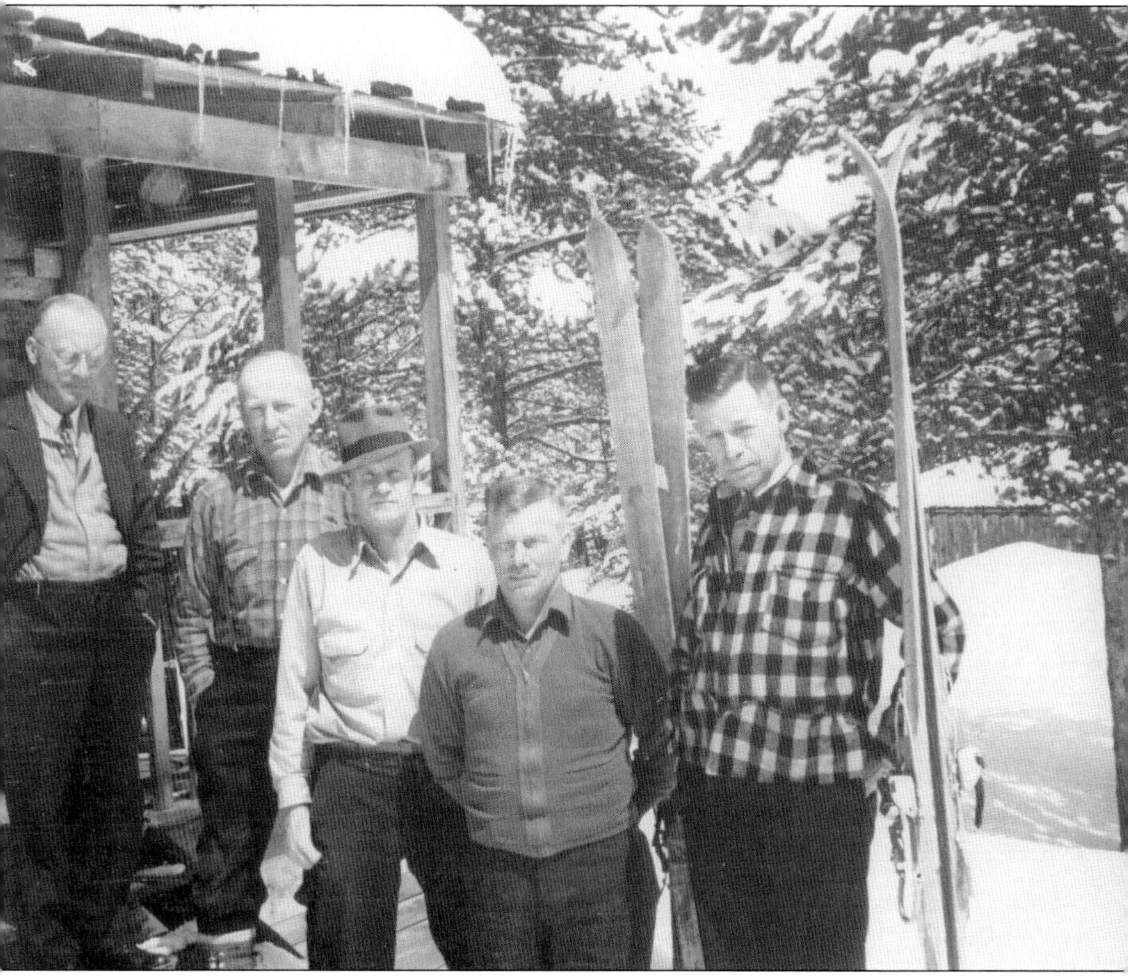

Wyoming Tie and Timber Company's top managers are shown at a meeting in the Warm Springs headwaters camp in the late 1930s. Pictured from left to right are Martin Olson, woods boss; John Selig, camp boss and tie inspector; Jerry Cobb, sawyer; Alfred Olson (Martin Olson's brother), tie inspector and drive boss; and Ricker Van Metre, company president.

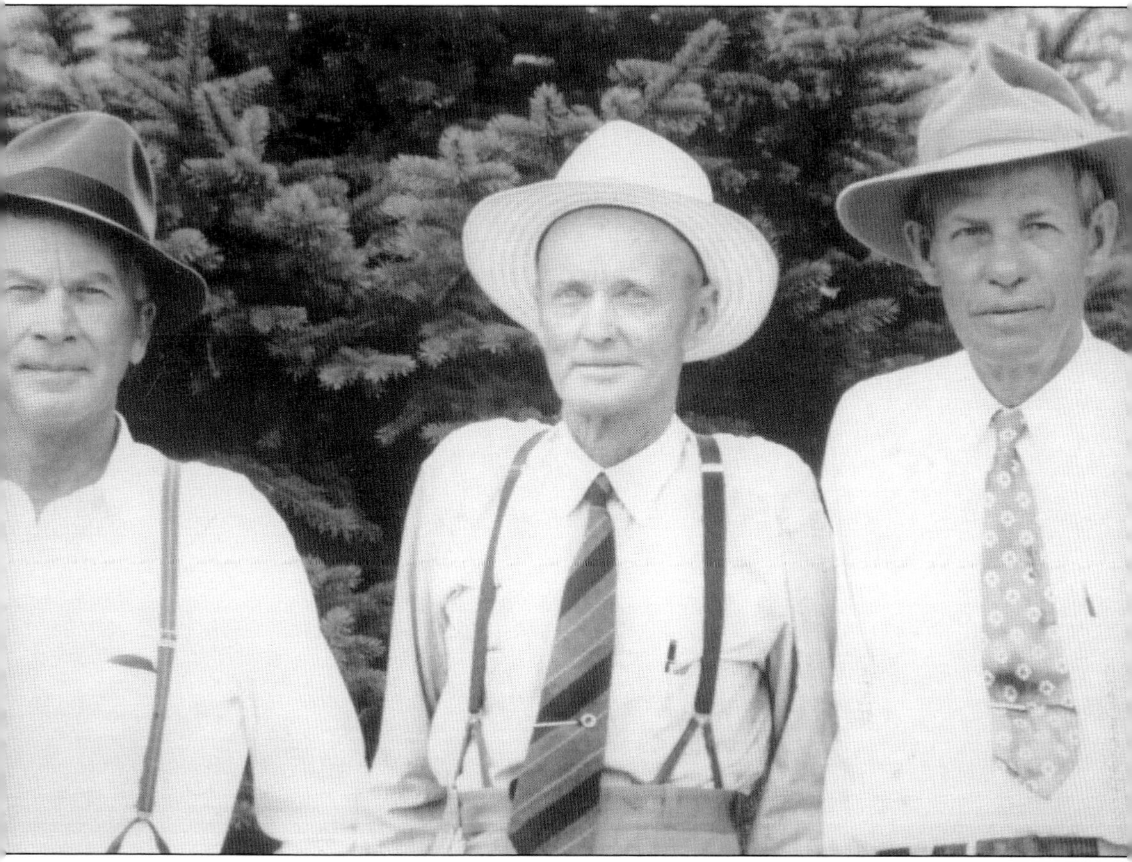

A 1930s photograph shows the three men who successfully guided the Wyoming Tie and Timber Company's tie-cutting operation from 1916 to 1947. Pictured from left to right are Martin Olson, woods boss; William H. "Billie Mac" McLaughlin, Riverton tie yard superintendent; and Ricker Van Metre, company president. Olson, who emigrated from Namsos, Norway, in 1897 when he was only 17, was even then a seasoned lumberman who had taken part in river drives in his home country.

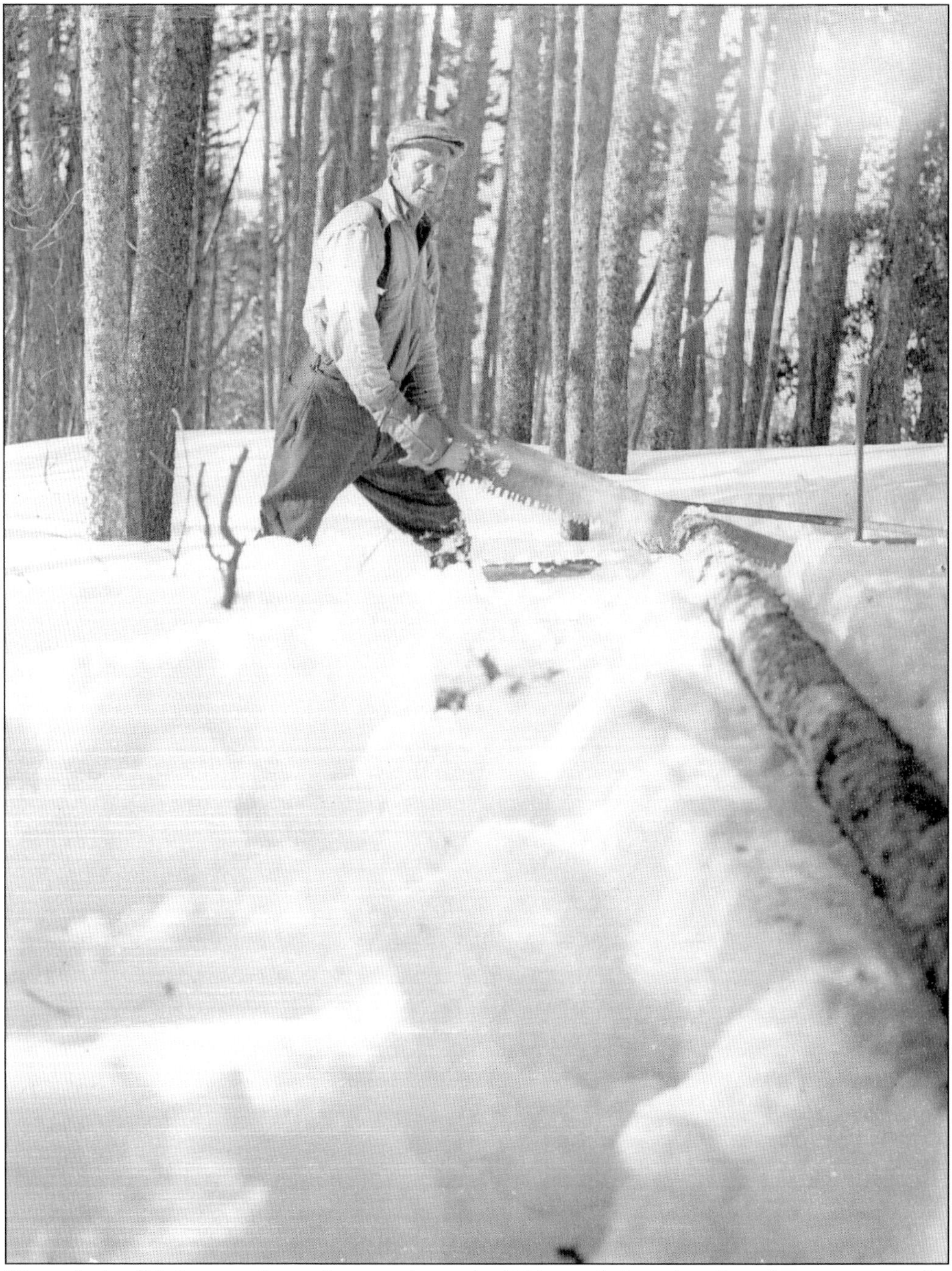

"Squeak Axel" Johnson, shown here in the early 1930s, and the other Scandinavian tie hacks felled their own trees and carved them into precise eight-foot lengths. The skillful, hardworking tie hacks deserved a lot of the credit for Wyoming Tie and Timber Company's successful operation in the upper Wind River Valley.

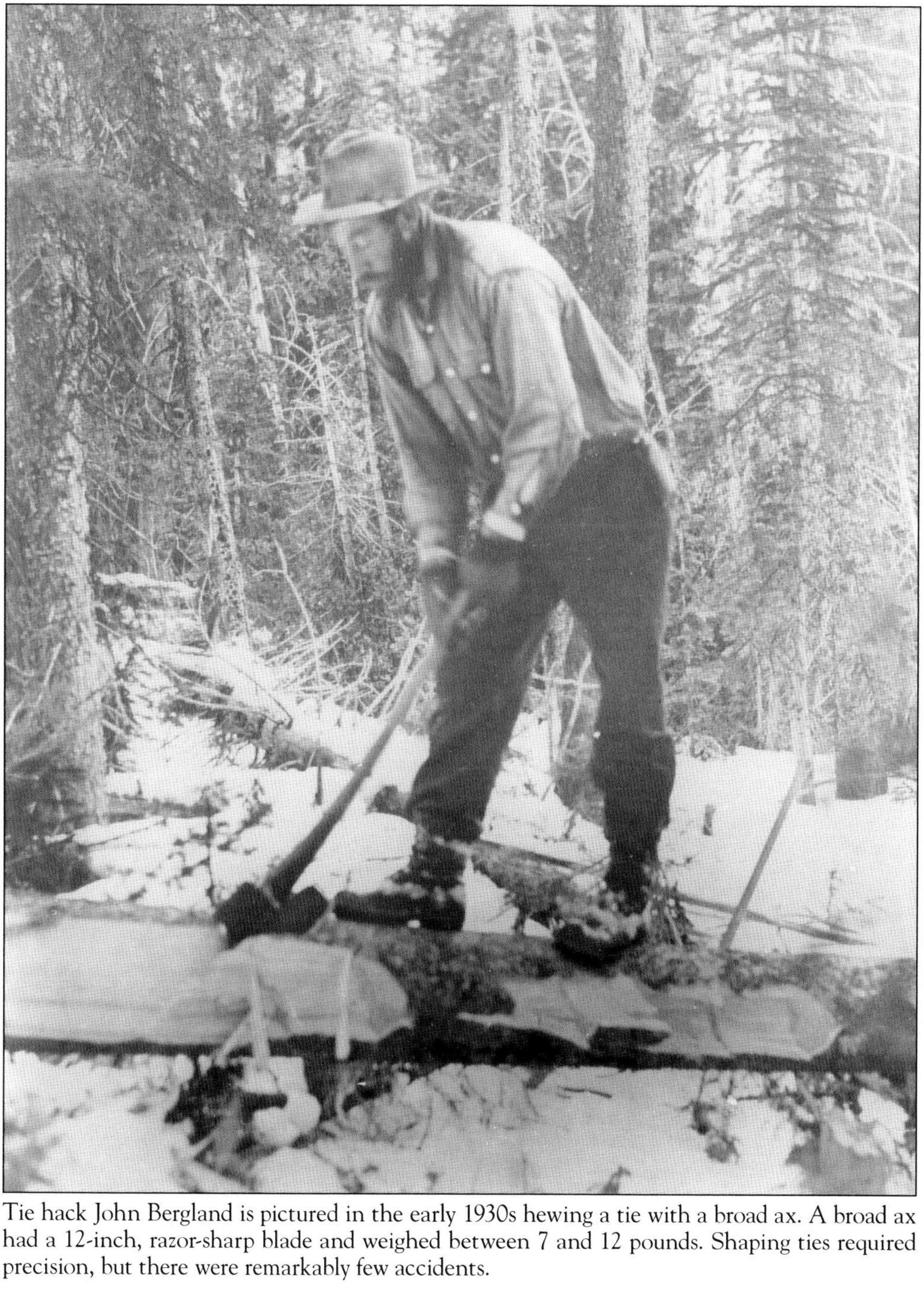

Tie hack John Bergland is pictured in the early 1930s hewing a tie with a broad ax. A broad ax had a 12-inch, razor-sharp blade and weighed between 7 and 12 pounds. Shaping ties required precision, but there were remarkably few accidents.

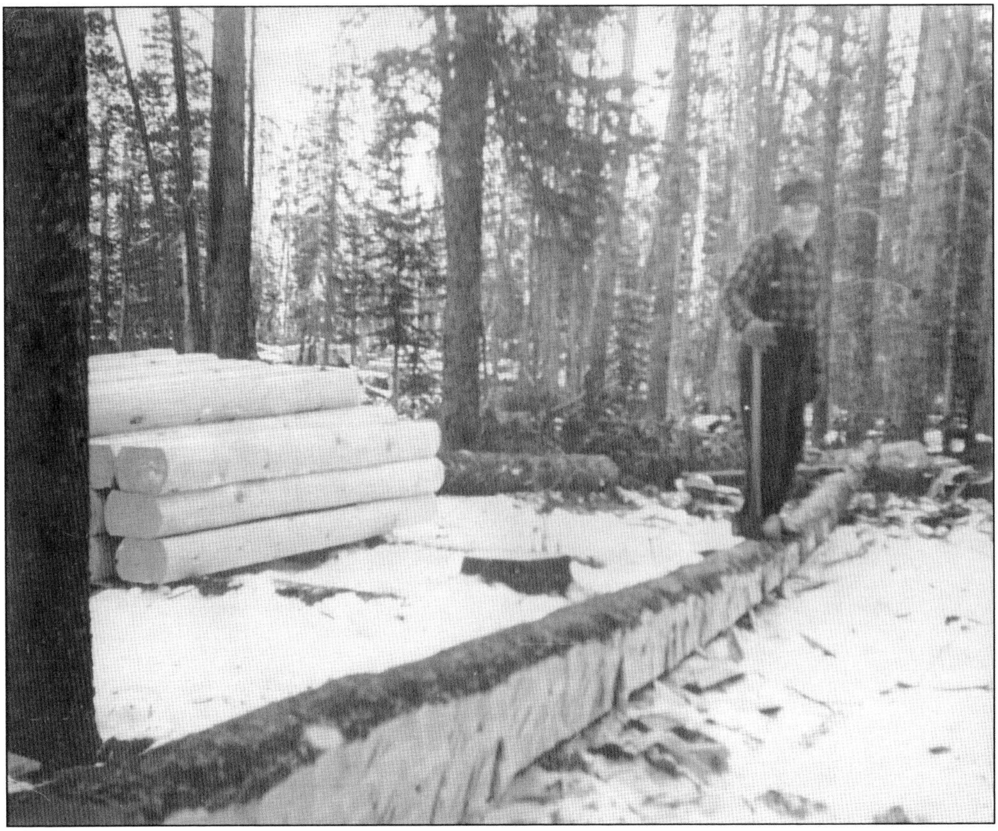

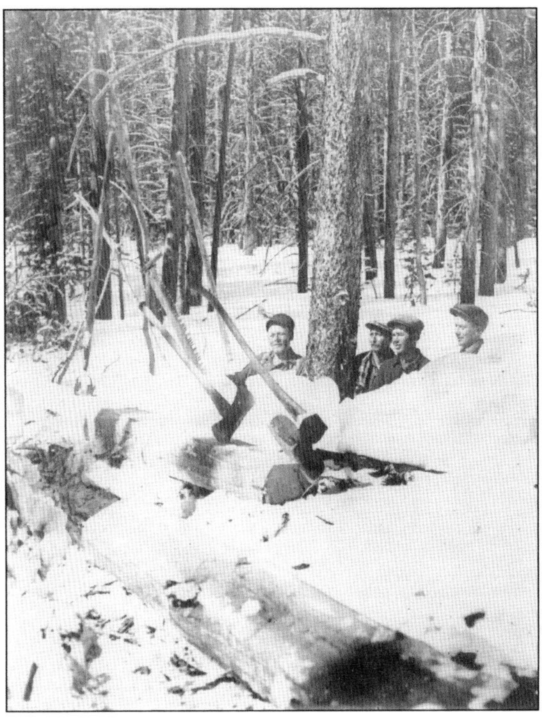

Ted Berg demonstrates the process of shaping ties that began with removing limbs and scoring the felled tree. Behind him is the stack of ties cut that day. The tie hacks were justifiably proud of their skill and precision.

In this image, tie hacks enjoy a lunch break in deep snow. Tie hacks cut timber during the winter months and worked in the extreme conditions of winter at high-elevation sites.

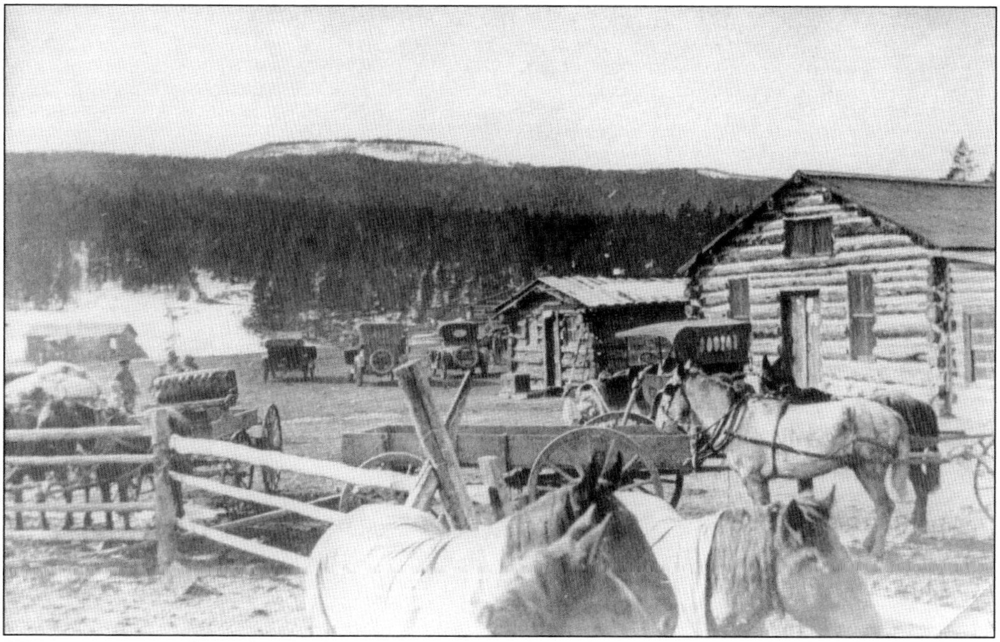

Wyoming Tie and Timber Company's first headquarters camp at the base of the Wind River Mountains, near Sheridan Creek's confluence with the Wind River, is pictured around 1918.

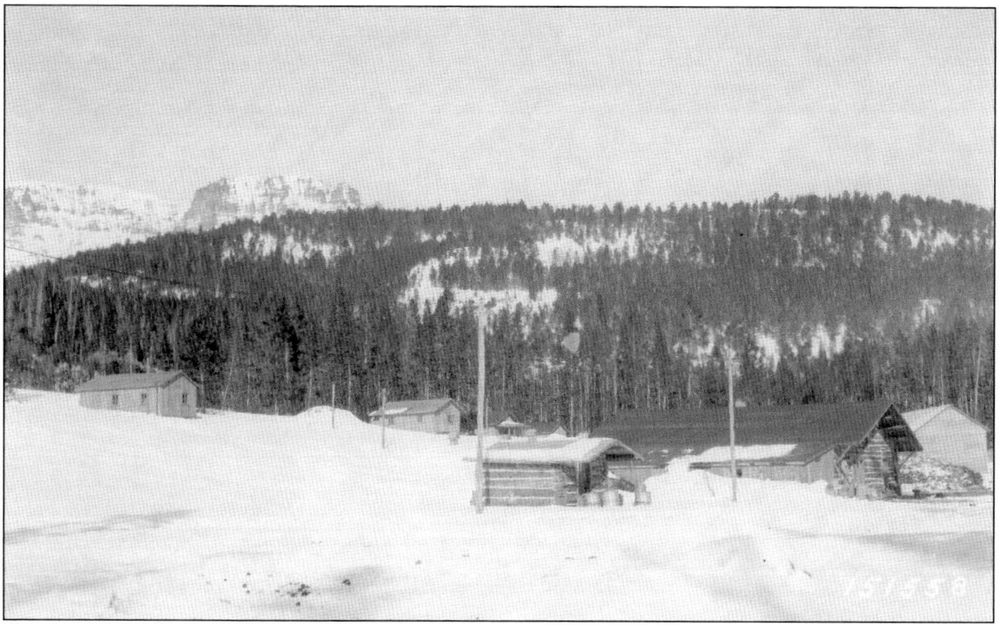

A second Wyoming Tie and Timber Company headquarters camp on the West Fork of the Dunoir River is shown in 1924 with Dunoir Butte, a distinctive landmark in the Absaroka Mountains, as part of the skyline to the left of the camp. The Dunoir River is a tributary of the Wind River.

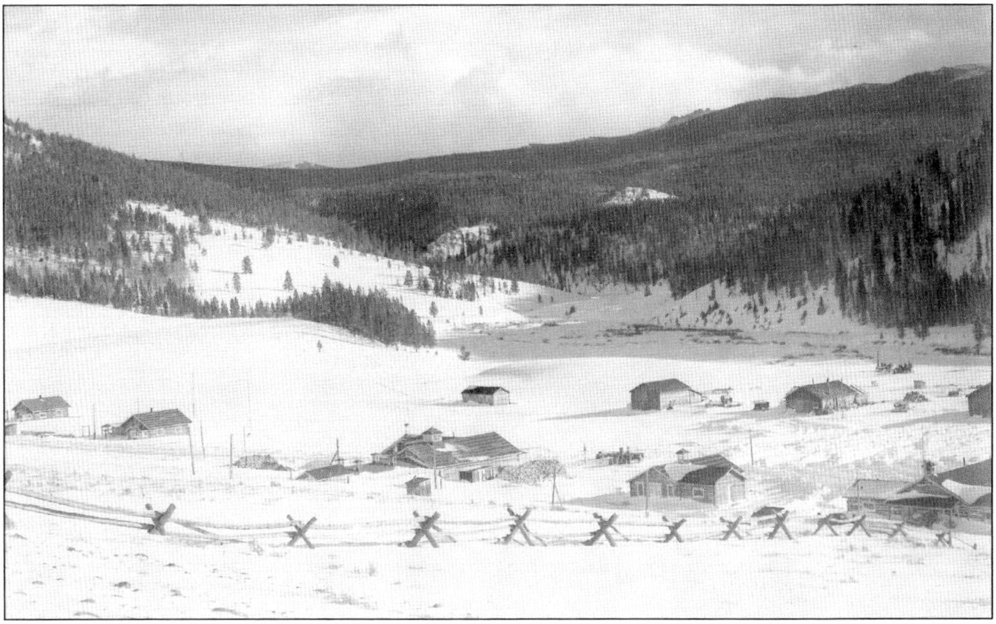

This 1930s photograph shows the east end of the headquarters camp on Warm Springs Creek during the winter. The camp, constructed in 1928, was also known formally as Dunoir Headquarters Camp because that name had been given to the camp post office when it was at the West Fork of Dunoir site. Headquarters camps were self-contained villages consisting of an office, store, post office, school, blacksmith shop, and several hay barns and storehouses.

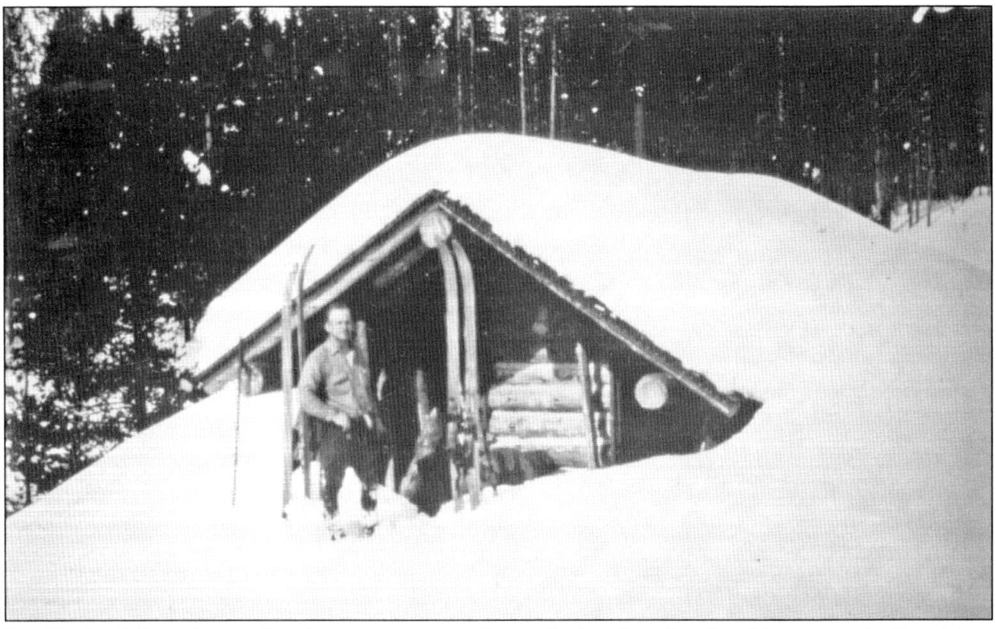

Tie Hacks did not live at headquarters camps. Instead, they lived in bunkhouses or built cabins, similar to the one shown in this 1930s photograph, near the stands of timber they were cutting at the time. Tie hacks traveled across deep snow on wooden cross-country skis, similar to those pictured in front of the cabin. Tie hacks led a lonely, isolated life, and their brawling and drinking bouts were legendary.

A.B. "Treg" Trego, photographed at work in his office in the Warm Springs camp, was secretary and bookkeeper for Wyoming Tie and Timber Company. During his years with the company, Trego became an excellent photographer who recorded headquarters camp life.

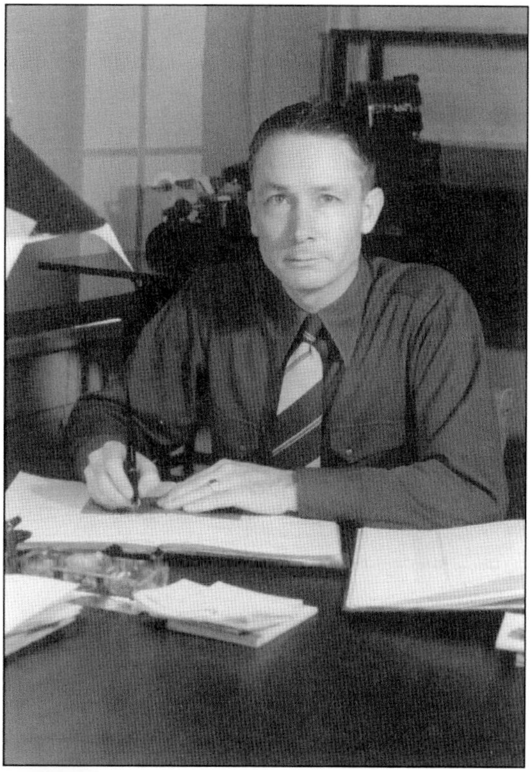

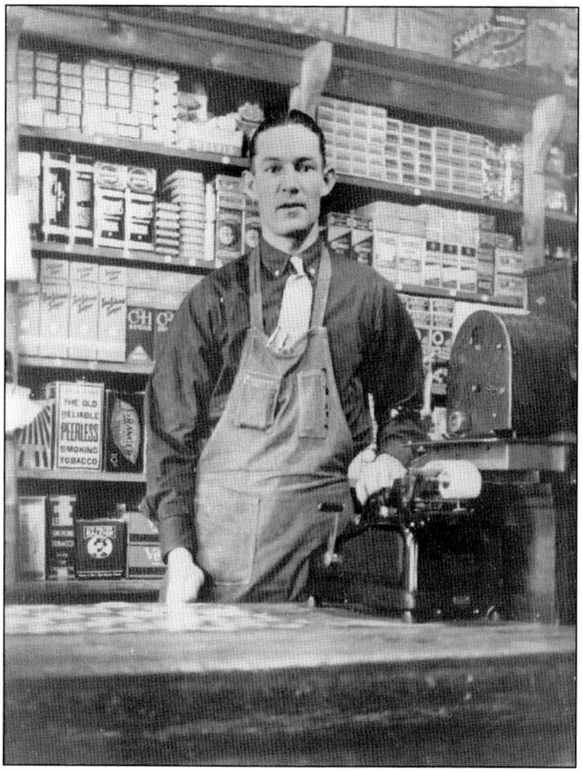

Tony Dolenc was the storekeeper at the headquarters camp on Warm Springs Creek. Smoking tobacco was one of the most popular items at the store for tie hacks, and he kept that handy at his cash register.

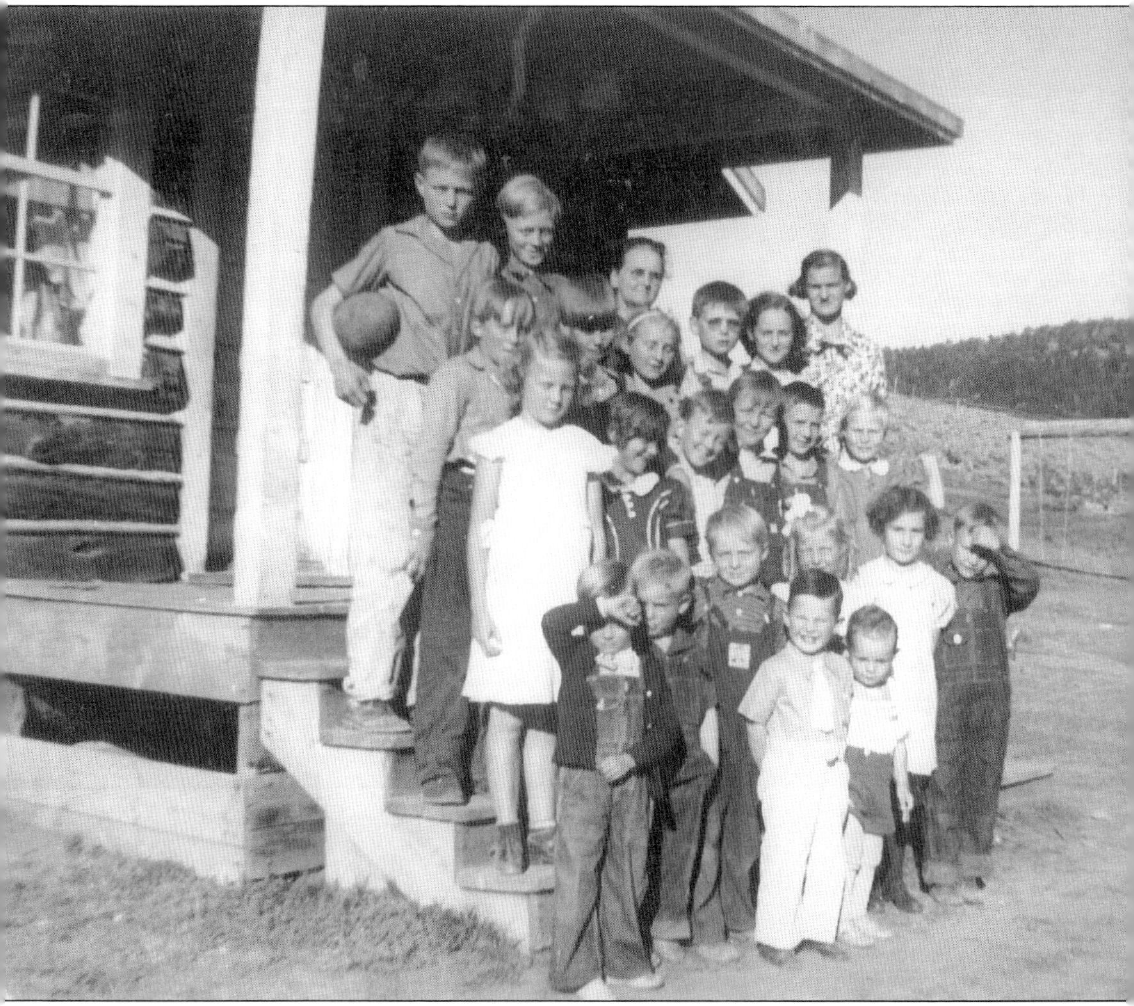

Schoolchildren ranging in age from 5 to 17 pose for a photograph on the first day of school at a headquarters camp in 1938. Although 10 was the average number of students at the school, one year 17 students attended. Teachers were replaced several times that year.

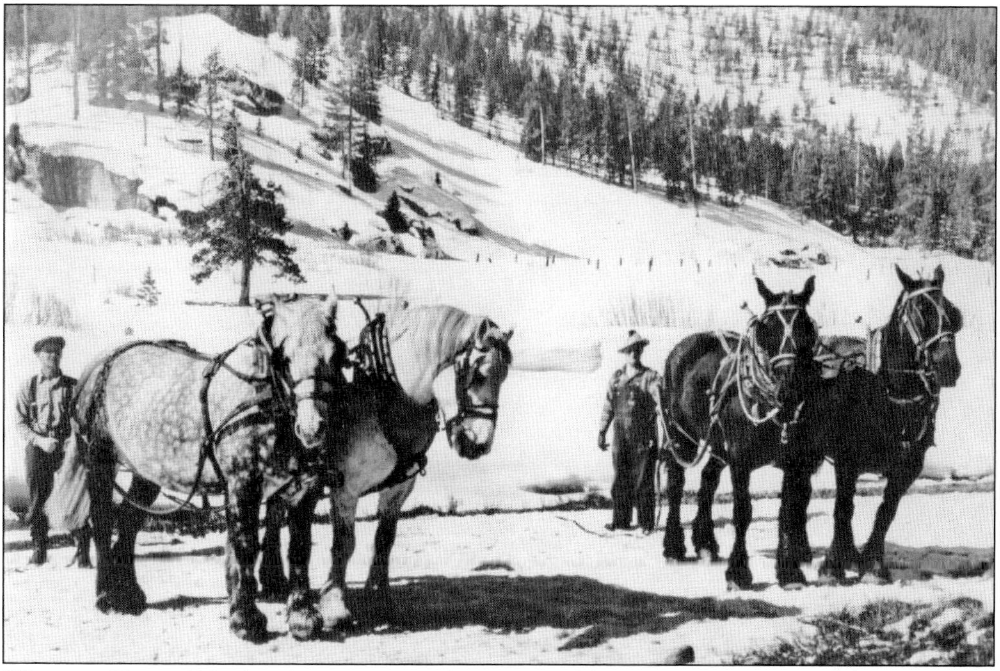

Wyoming Tie and Timber Company's sturdy Texas workhorse teams are pictured at work in the early 1930s. These horse teams pulled logs, sleds, and wagons and were considered indispensible in the early years of the tie-cutting operation.

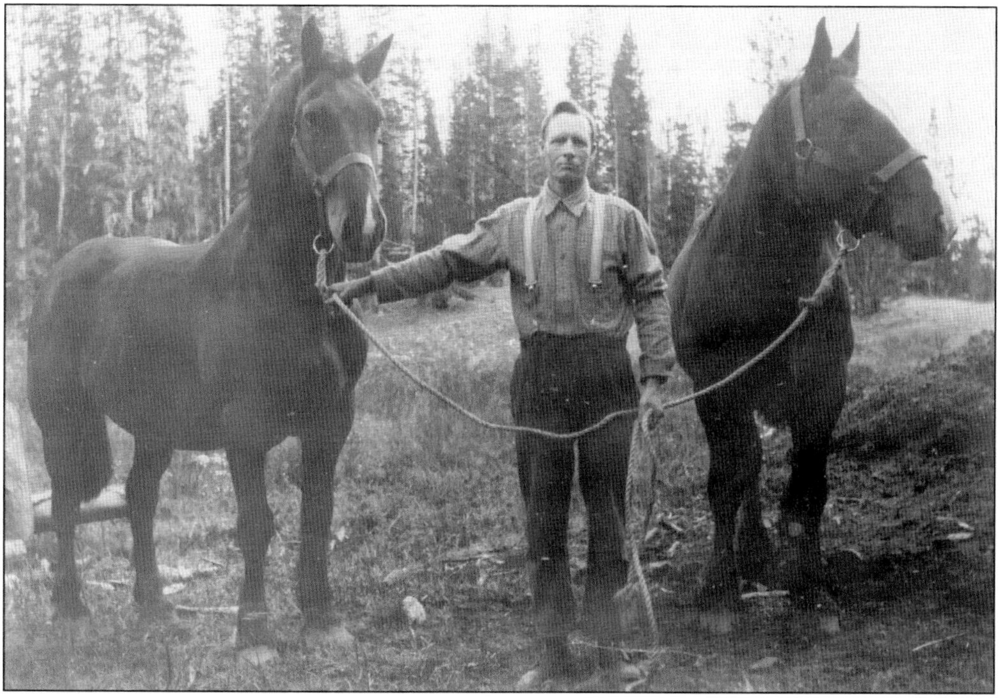

Driver Burt Engstrom stands between two of Wyoming Tie and Timber Company's workhorses in a photograph taken in the early 1930s. Engstrom considered his horses as "smart as we were." Bulldozers replaced the once vital horse teams in the last years of the tie-cutting operation.

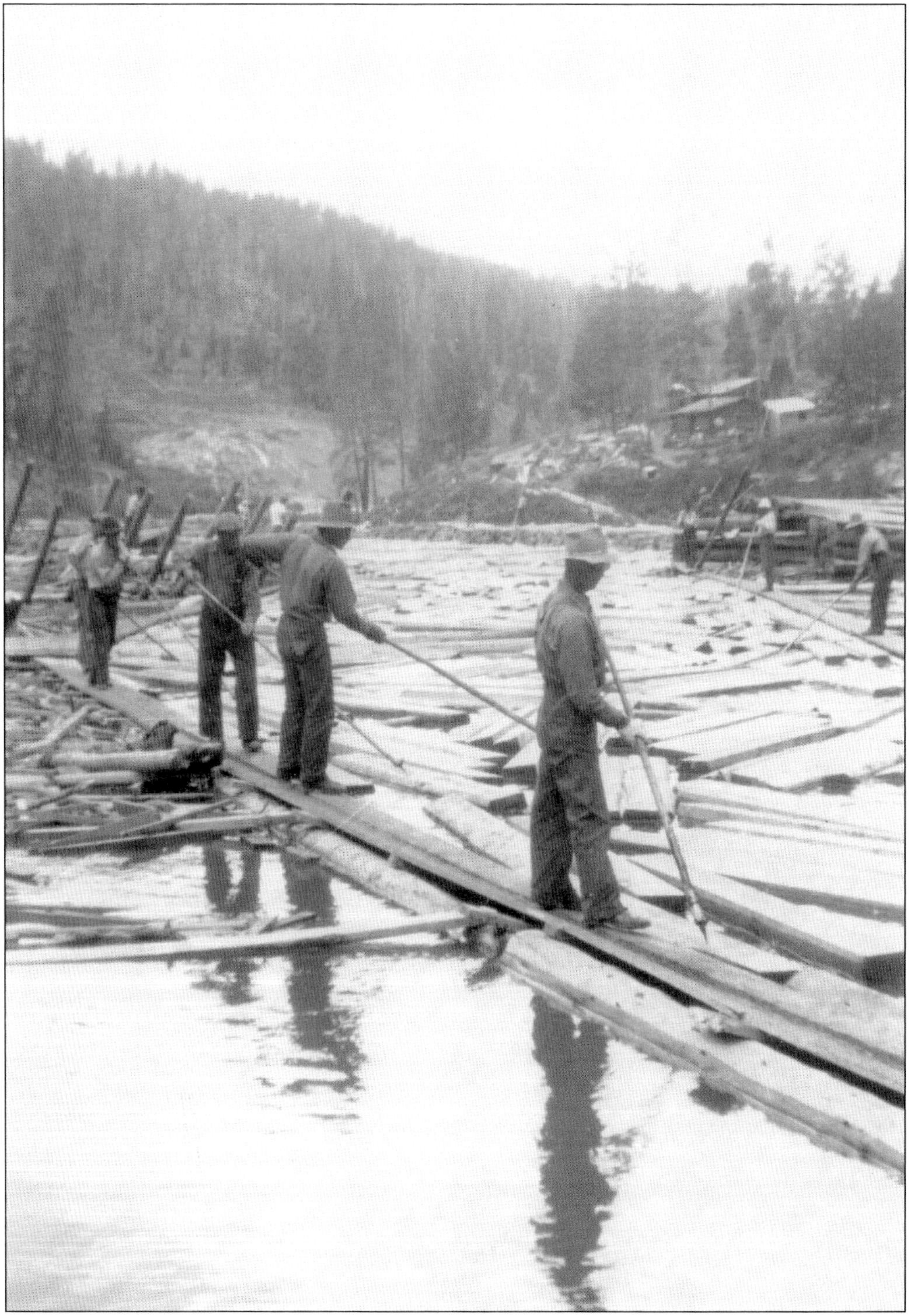

Tie hacks work ties in a holding pen on Warm Springs Creek before they are herded down the flume. When spring came, tie cutting ended, and it was time to move ties down the Wind River to the Riverton rail yard.

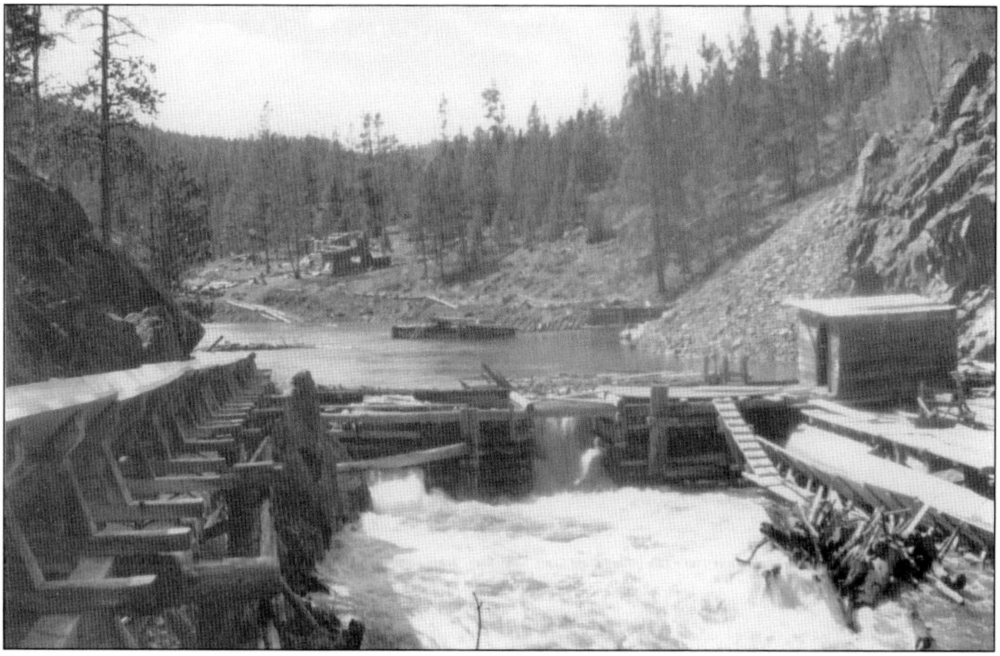

A 1930s photograph shows the dam across Warm Springs Creek, looking upstream. A boom that blocks an opening in the dam has been removed to allow ties to flow into the Warm Springs Flume. The Wild Cat Flume that brought ties to the creek from cutting areas above Warm Springs Creek is shown to the right in the photograph, and the Warm Springs Flume is to the left.

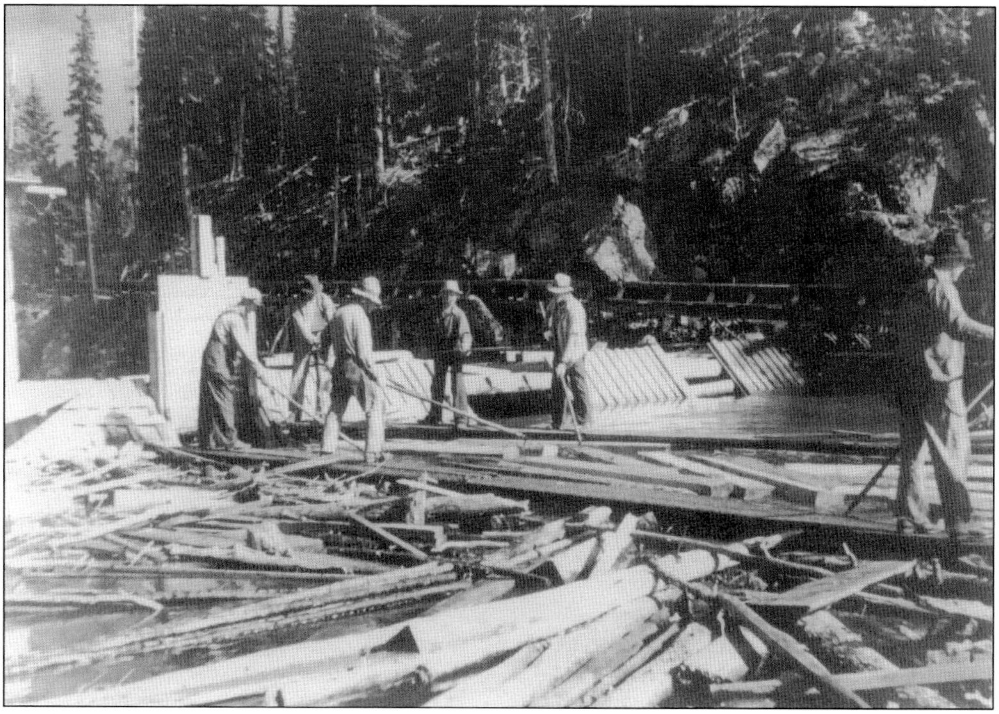

Tie hacks funnel ties through an opening in the dam into the mouth of the flume in the 1930s.

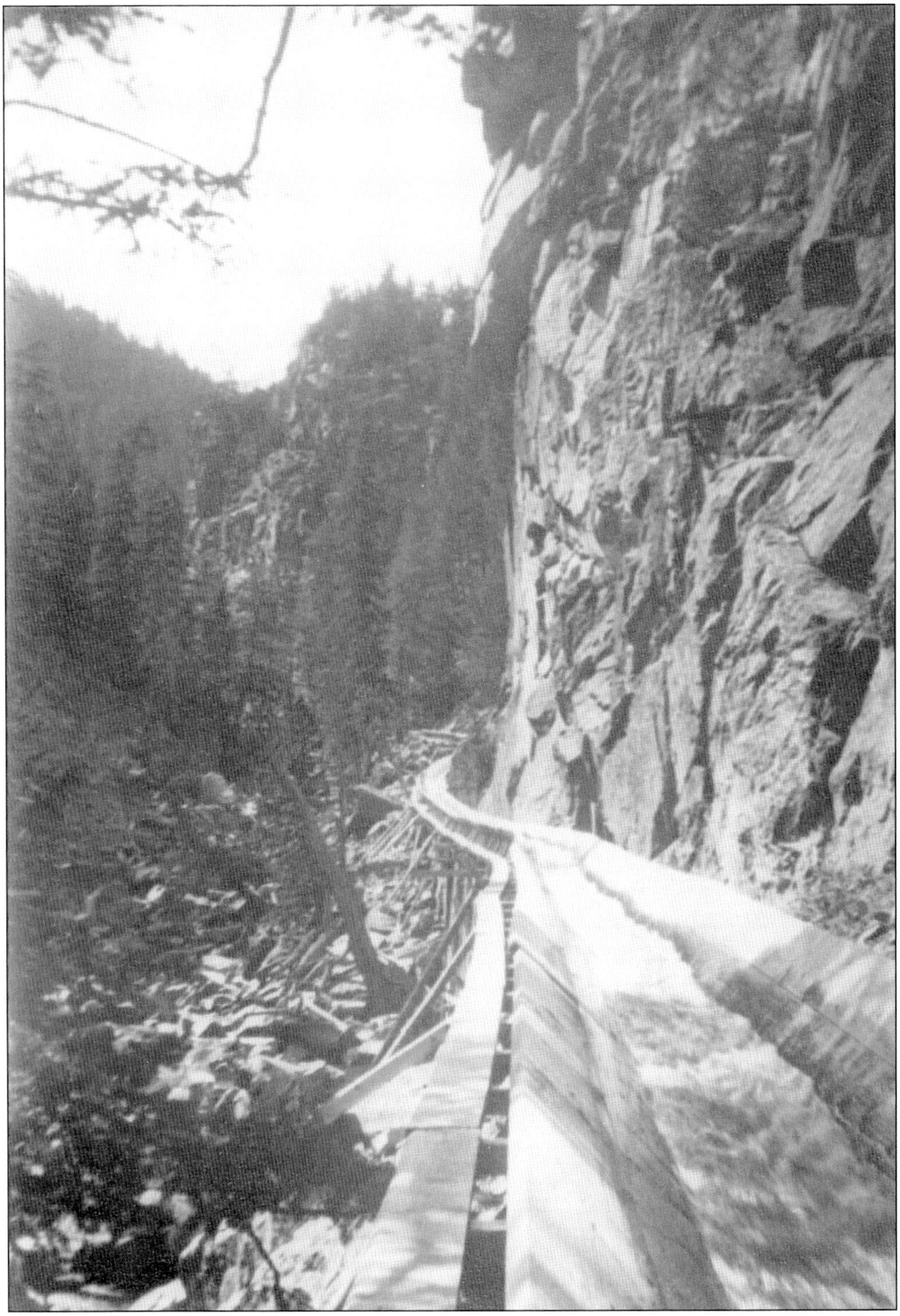

The Warm Springs Flume carries ties down the precipitous slope of Warm Springs Canyon to the Wind River between 1928 and 1942. Many people said a flume could not be built on the sheer canyon walls, but Wyoming Tie and Timber Woods Boss Martin Olson knew it could be done.

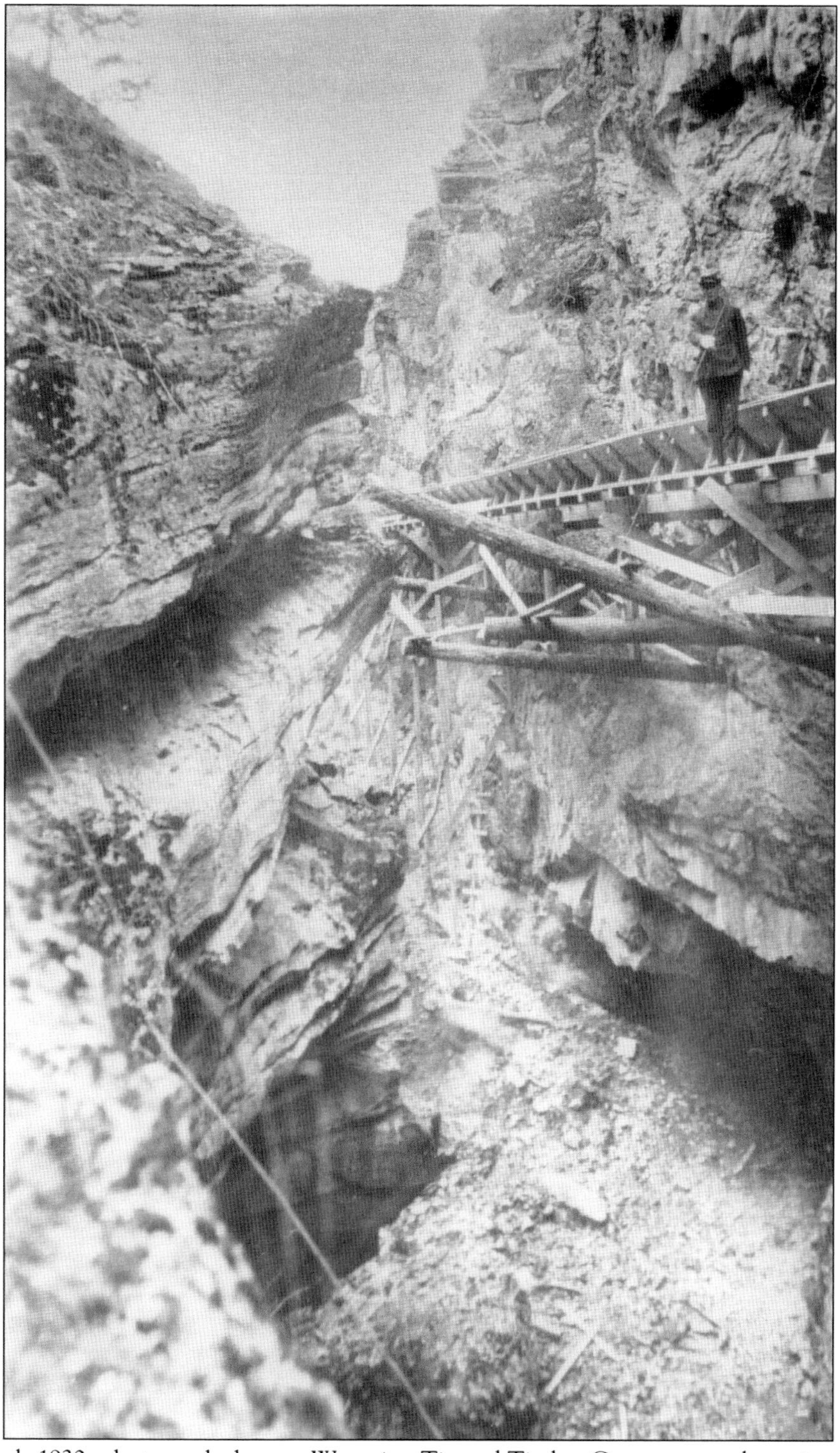

This early-1930s photograph shows a Wyoming Tie and Timber Company employee inspecting the Warm Springs Flume at a point where it is suspended by cables from almost vertical canyon walls.

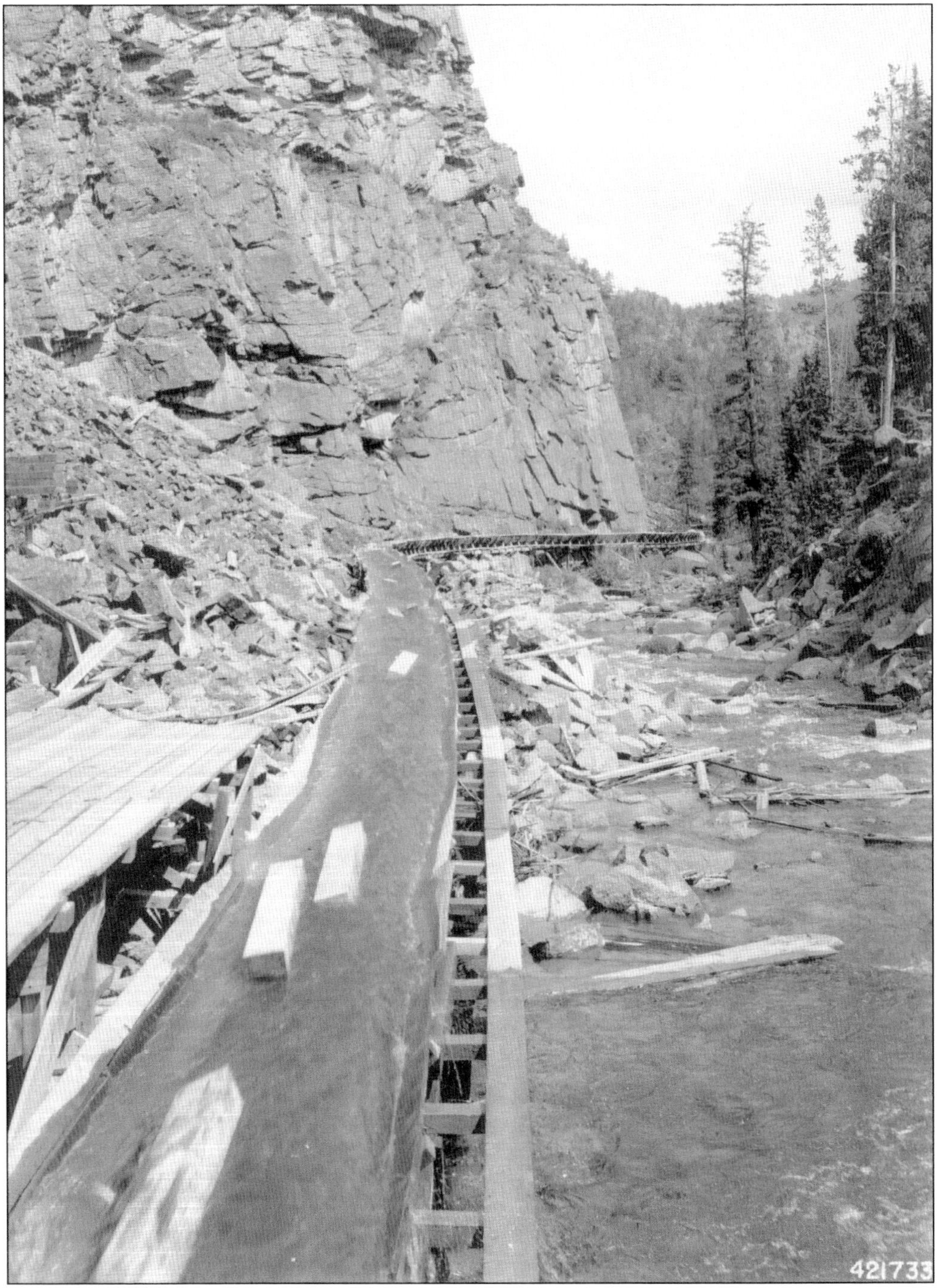

Completed railroad ties travel down the Warm Springs Flume on a stream of water diverted from the creek. Ties floated down the flume and landed with a splash in the Wind River at the end of the flume.

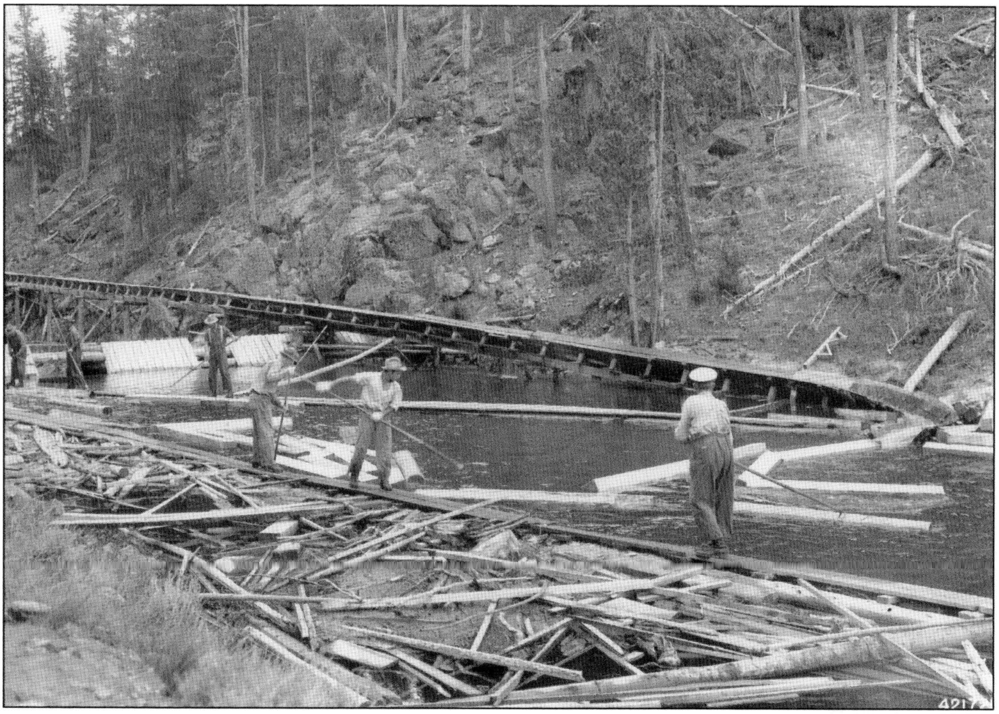

In this 1930s photograph, tie hacks move ties in the Wind River at the base of the Warm Springs Flume.

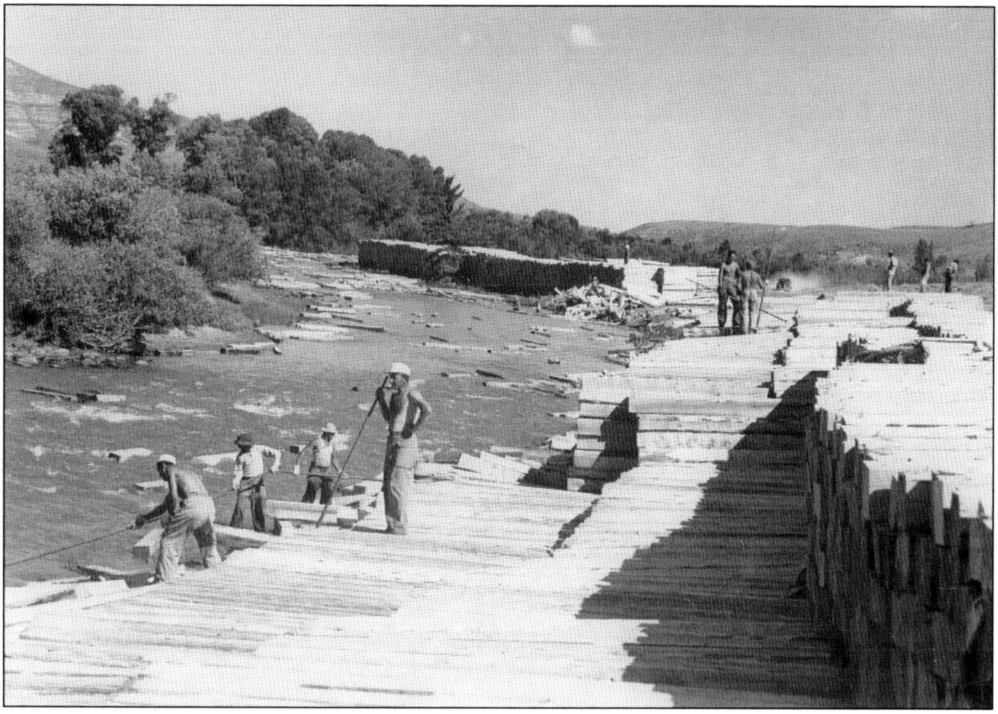

Ties are stacked along the Wind River, ready to begin the 100-mile tie drive, or float, to Riverton.

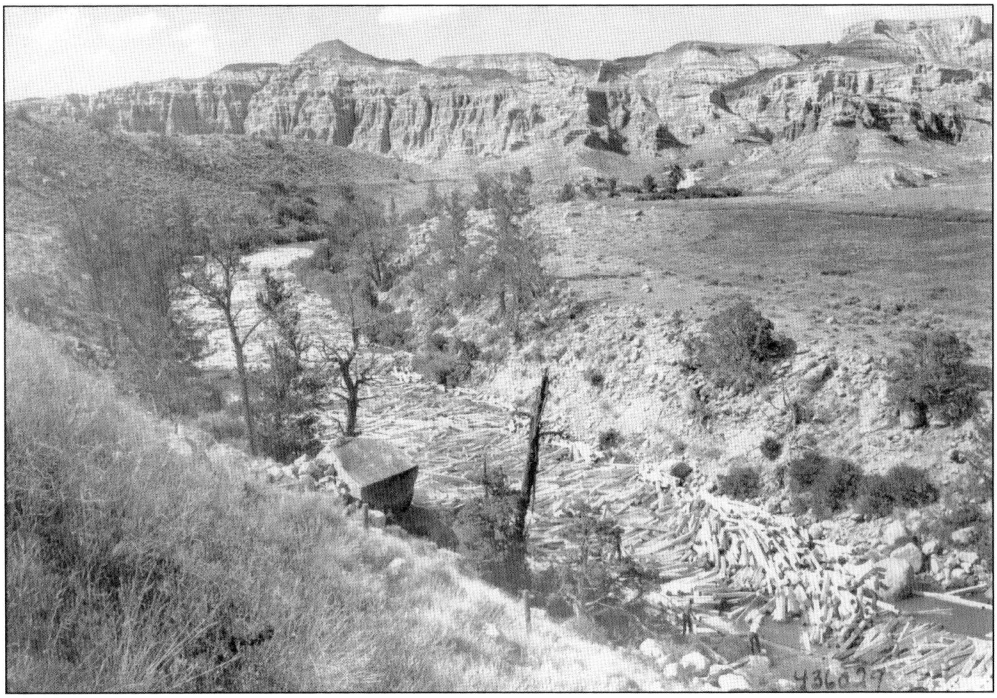

A tie jam has formed on the Wind River a few miles downstream from the base of the Warm Springs Flume. Tie hacks work to break it up in this 1930s photograph.

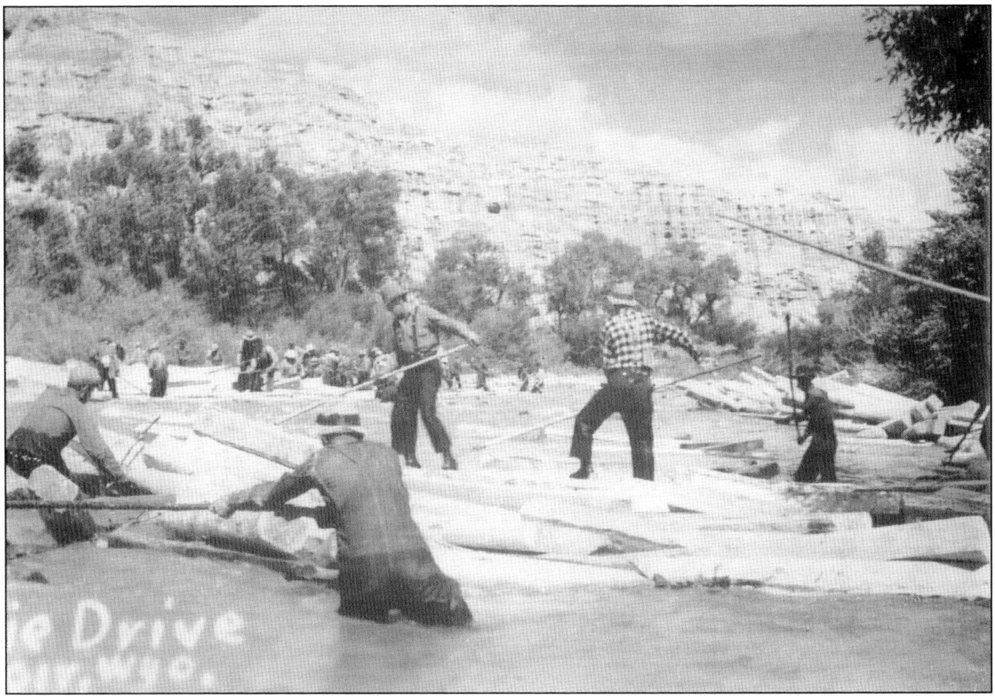

Tie hacks are pictured in 1934 breaking up a tie jam using a device called a pike pole to return ties to the river. Driving ties was hard, dangerous work, but no deaths were reported in all the years ties were floated down the river.

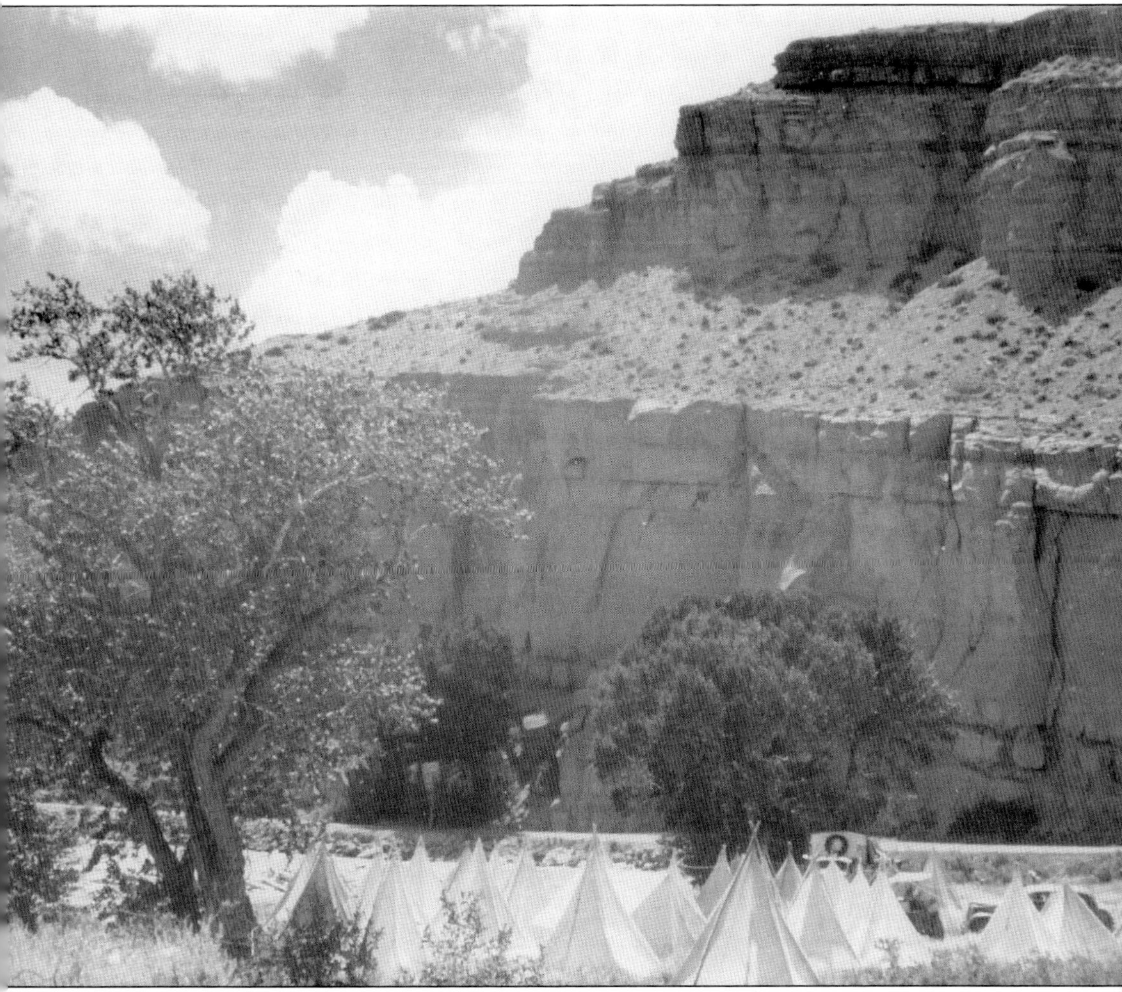

A white teepee city, pictured around 1930, nestles along the river bank at the edge of red cliffs southeast of Dubois. During the weeks-long river drive, teepee tents were set up each night at landings along the Wind River as temporary bunks for the tie hacks.

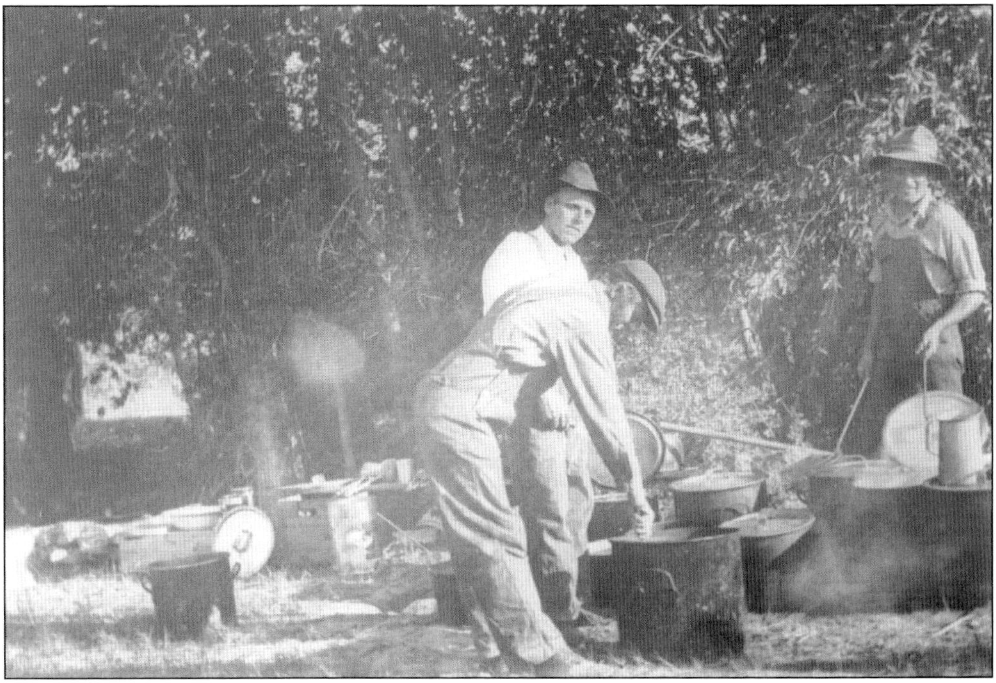

During the weeks-long river drive, camp cooks prepared the same food they served at the headquarters camp, but everything was cooked in Dutch ovens over hot coals in open trenches. Cook John Tangden is pictured stirring a pot of stew while Adolph Solum (left) and Alfred Bolin watch.

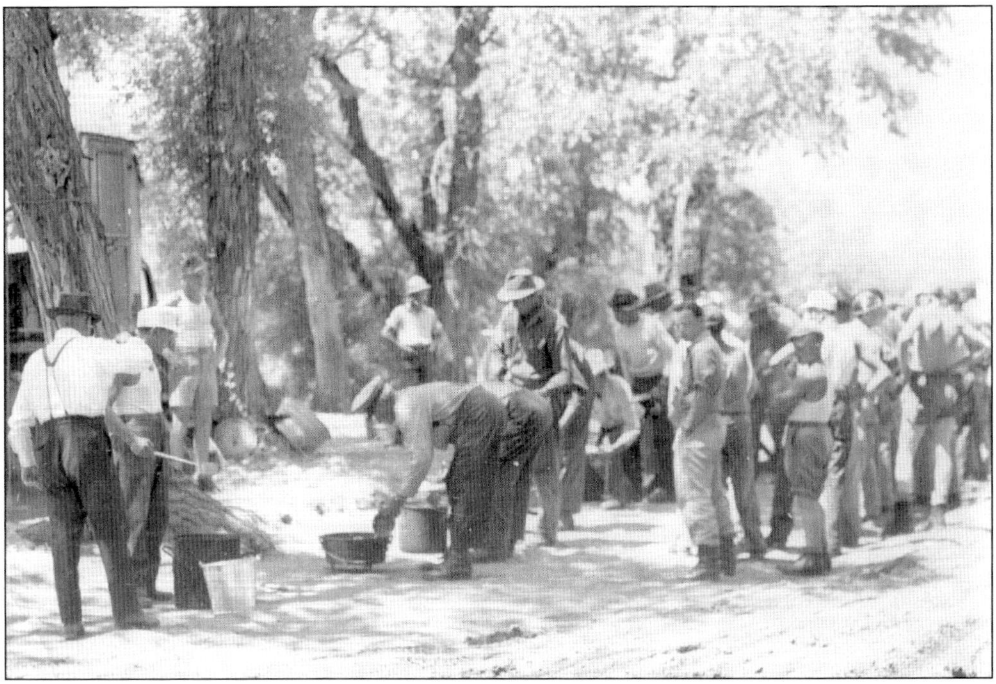

German prisoners of war (POWs) go through the food line where food is served directly from Dutch ovens during a 1945 river drive. They were served the same Dutch oven–cooked food as the tie hacks.

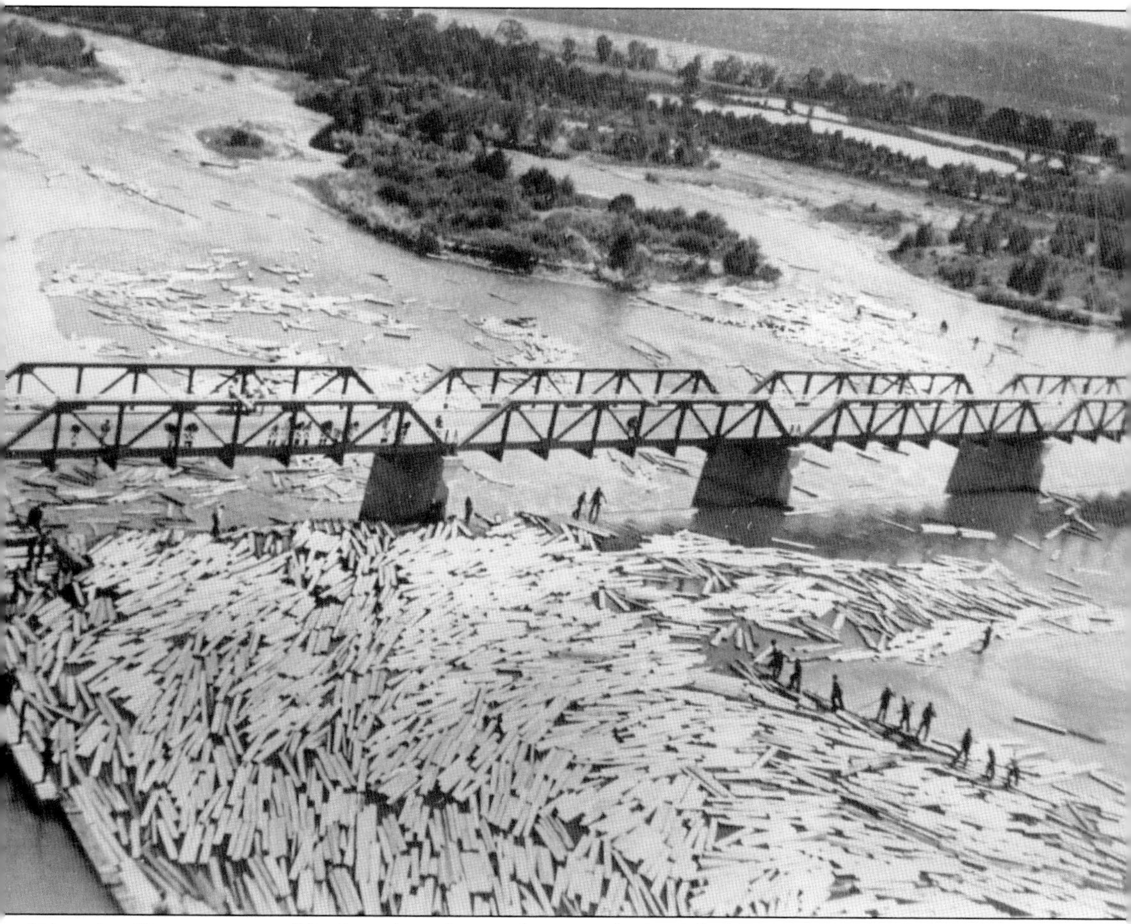

Diversion Dam was one of the last obstacles on the river drive to the Riverton rail yard. Tie hacks are pictured channeling ties over the dam's spillways in 1934.

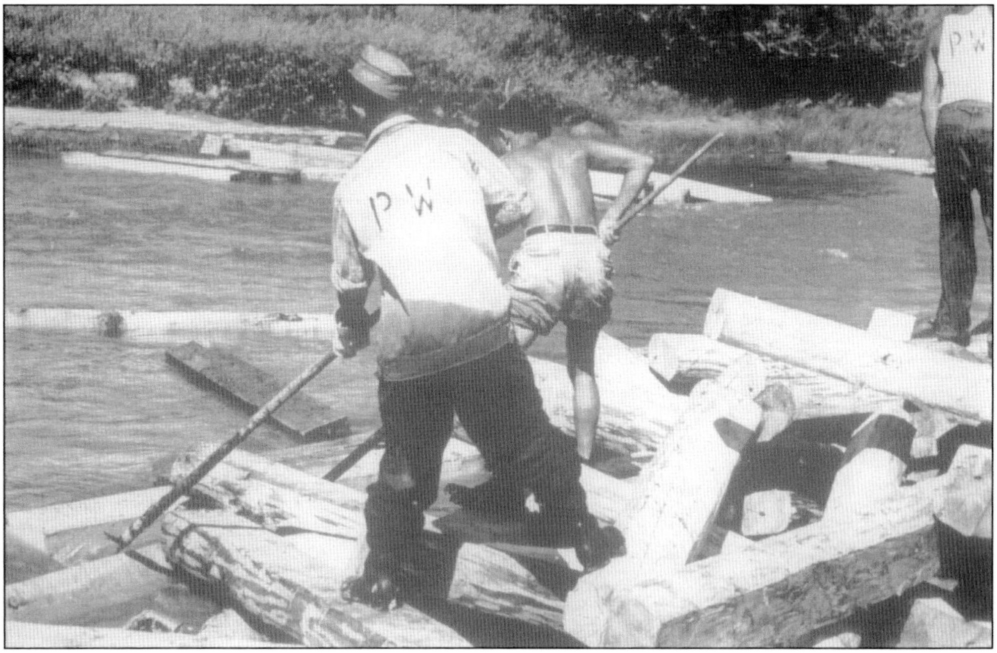

During World War II, German POWs took over the job of producing cross-ties at portable sawmills and floating them down the Wind River. POWs are pictured during the next-to-the-last river drive in 1945. Only 5,000 hand-hewn ties went into the Wind River that year, cut by aging tie hacks, and the other ties were mill-sawn ties.

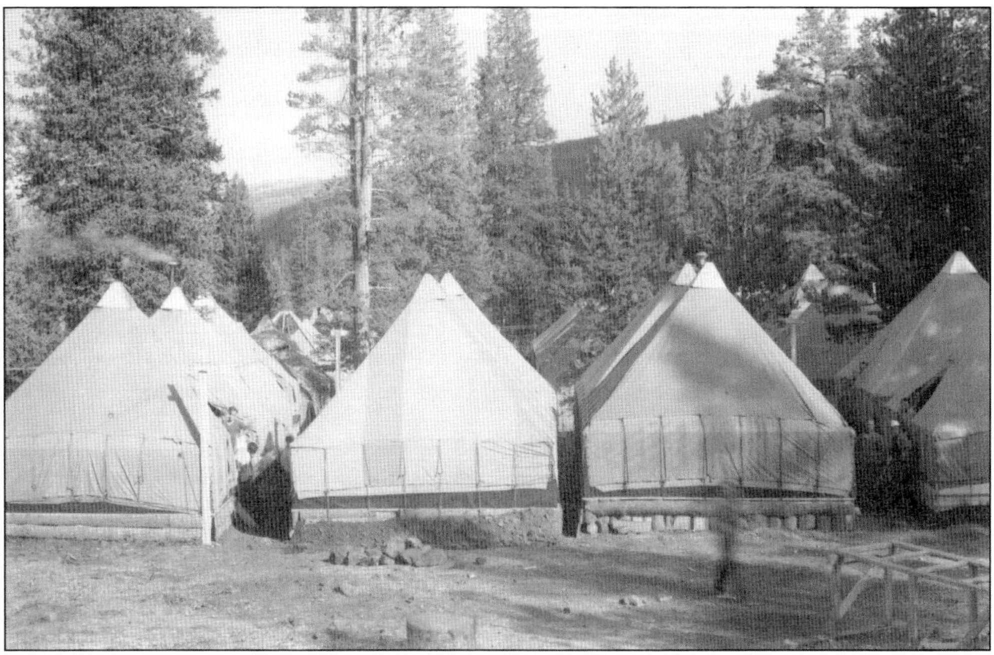

German POWs cutting ties for Wyoming Tie and Timber Company were housed in heated tents near the Warm Springs sawmill. Scandinavian tie hacks had lived in unheated cabins or bunks. The POWs were said to have enjoyed their work, and a few even returned for visits after the war ended.

Mechanization changed the process of making railroad ties during the final years of operations. A portable sawmill was moved from site to site to cut ties to the required size.

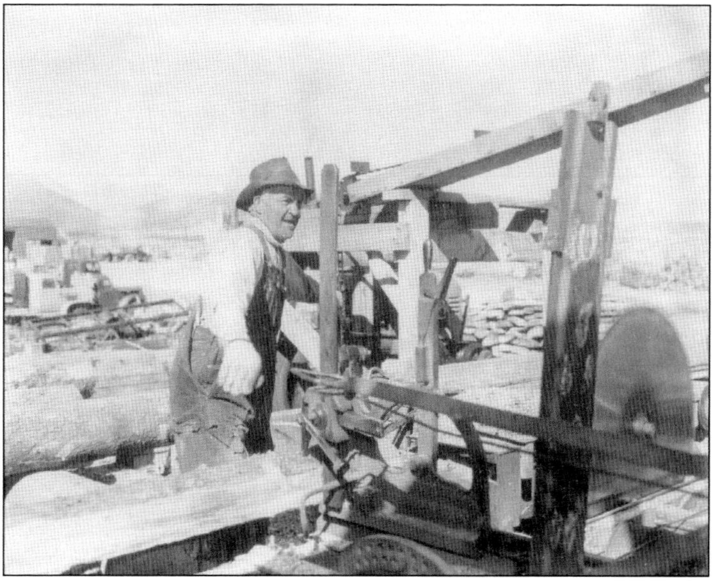

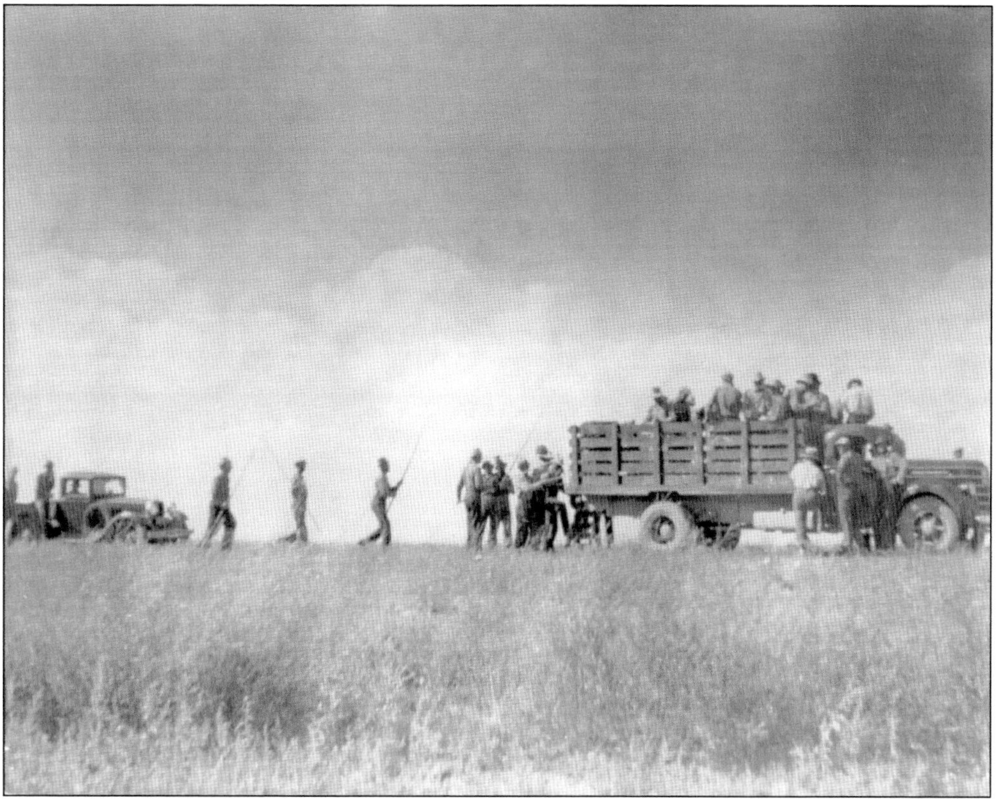

In this 1930s image, tie hacks ride to the river in trucks, carrying their long pike poles with them to prod ties away from the banks of the Wind River and into the main channel of the river. The tie drives ended in 1946, and 150,000 ties were sent down river that year.

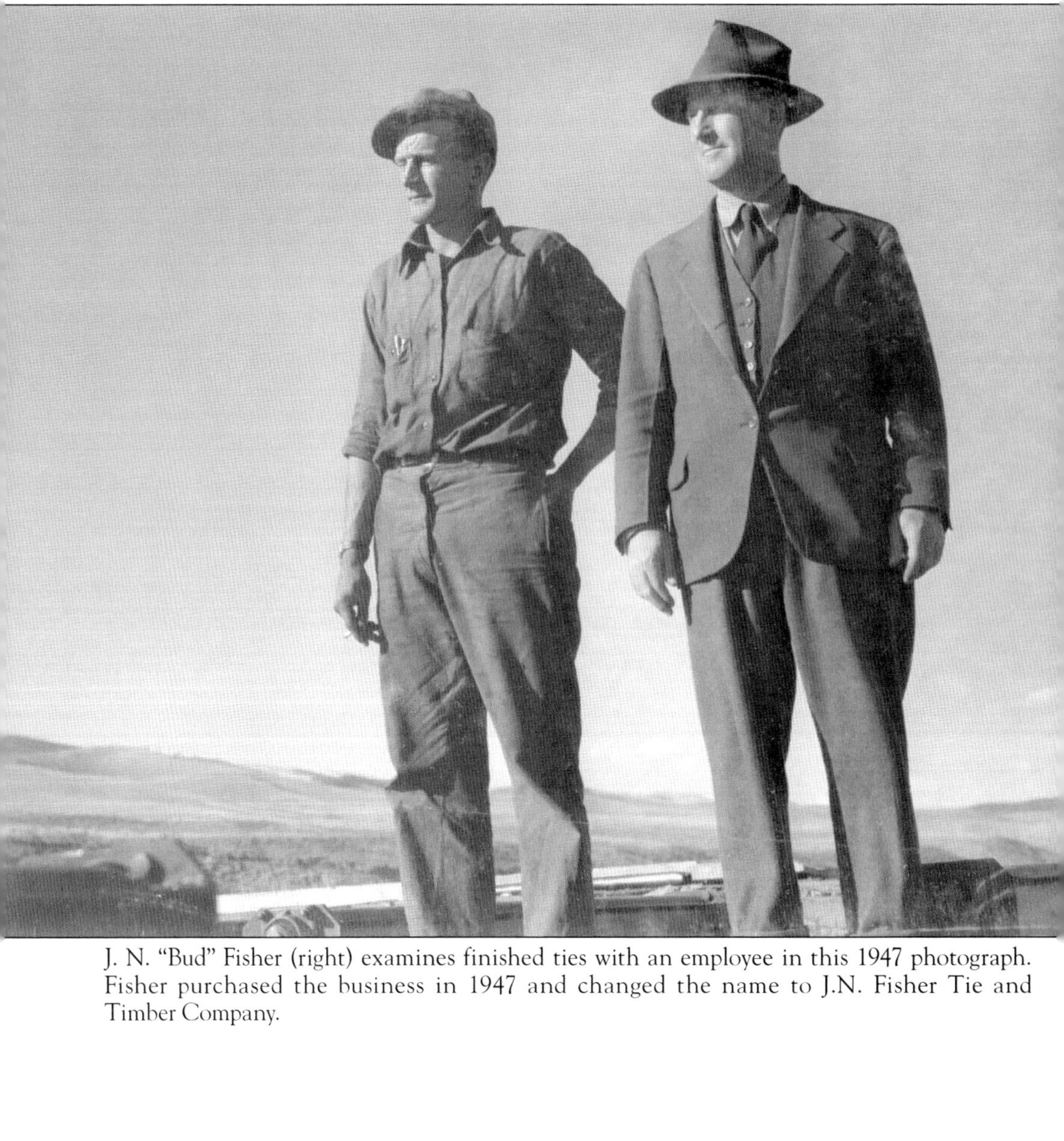

J. N. "Bud" Fisher (right) examines finished ties with an employee in this 1947 photograph. Fisher purchased the business in 1947 and changed the name to J.N. Fisher Tie and Timber Company.

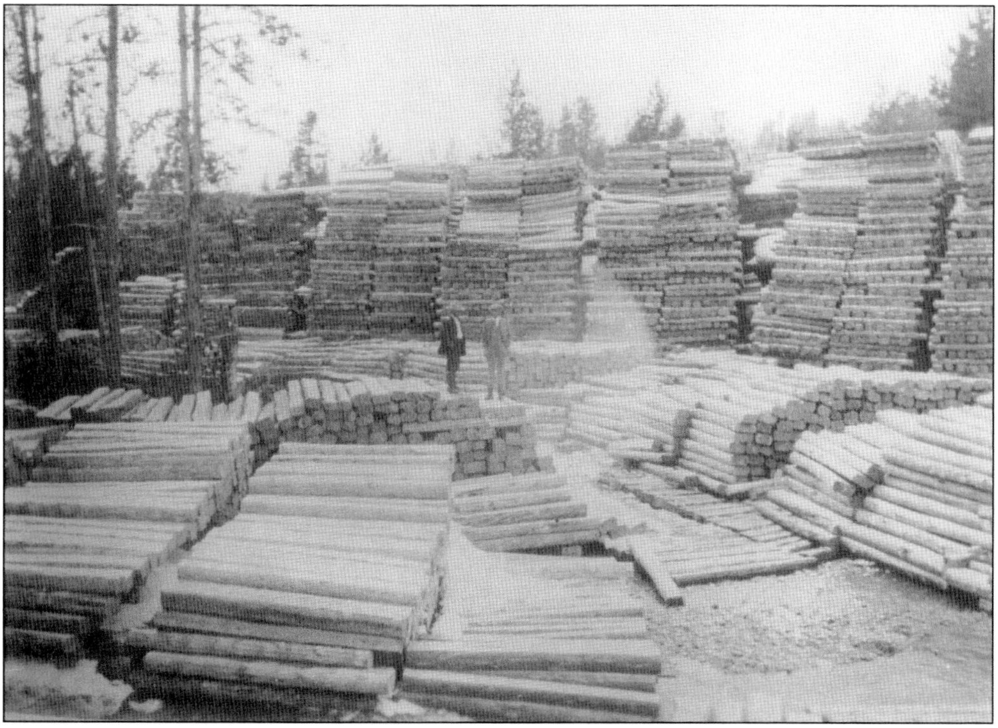

Bud Fisher (right) discusses the tie operation with woods boss Martin Olson, who retired when Fisher purchased Wyoming Tie and Timber in 1947.

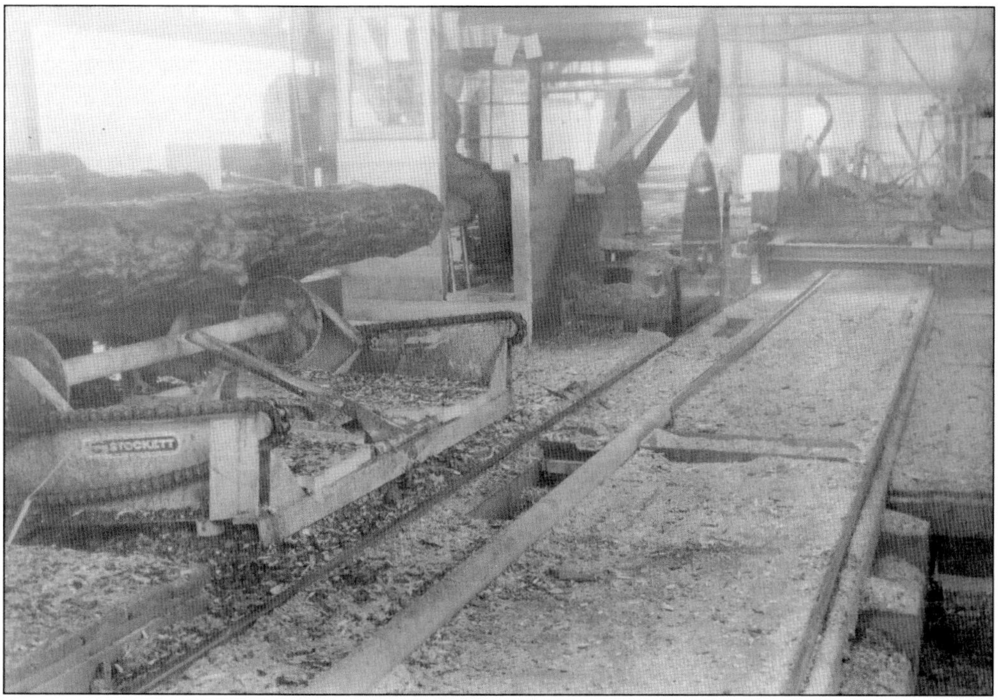

A 1947 photograph shows the interior of the J.N. Fisher Tie and Timber Company sawmill.

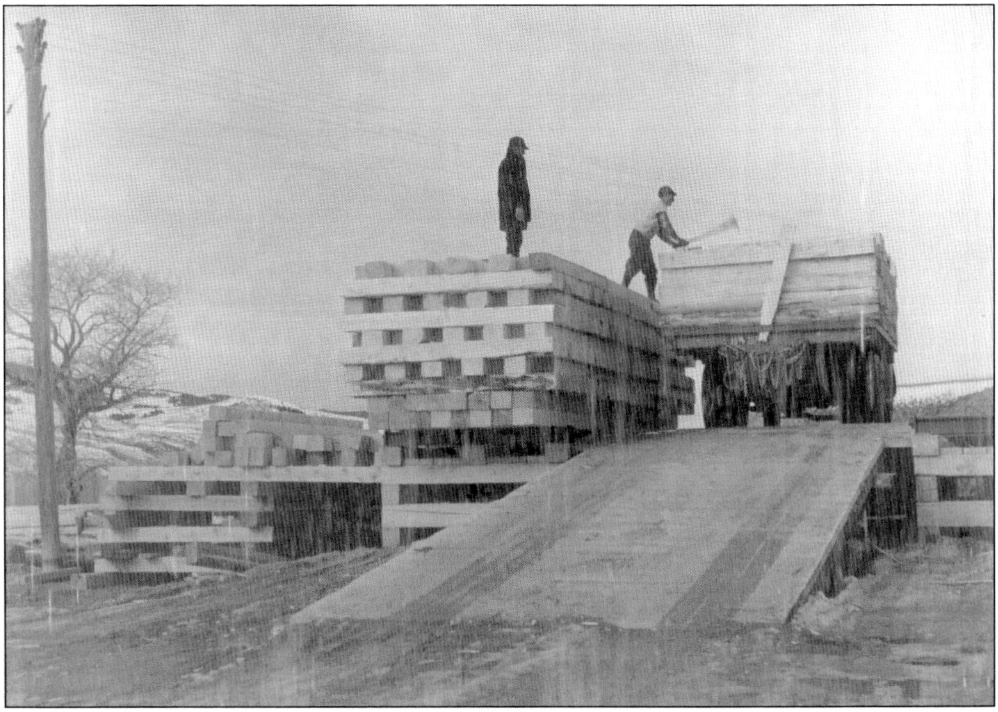

J. N. Fisher Tie and Timber Company Trucks replaced the Wind River tie drives after new owner Bud Fisher purchased roller trucks that could carry between 360 and 420 ties to the Riverton rail yard at one time.

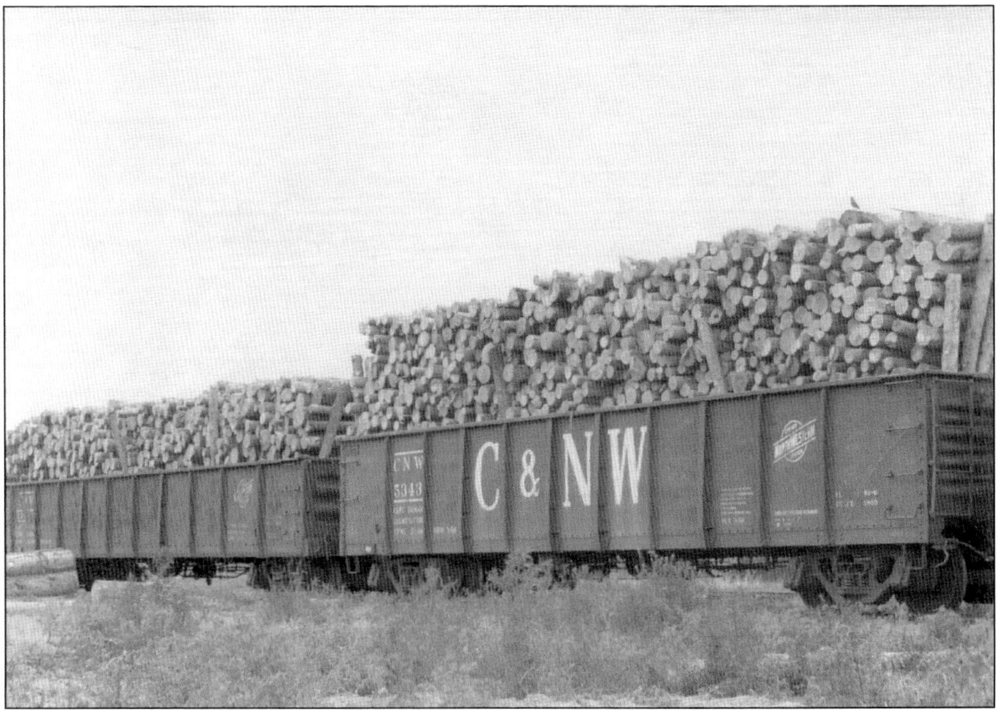

A trainload of J.N. Fisher Tie and Timber Company posts leaves the Riverton rail yard in 1947.

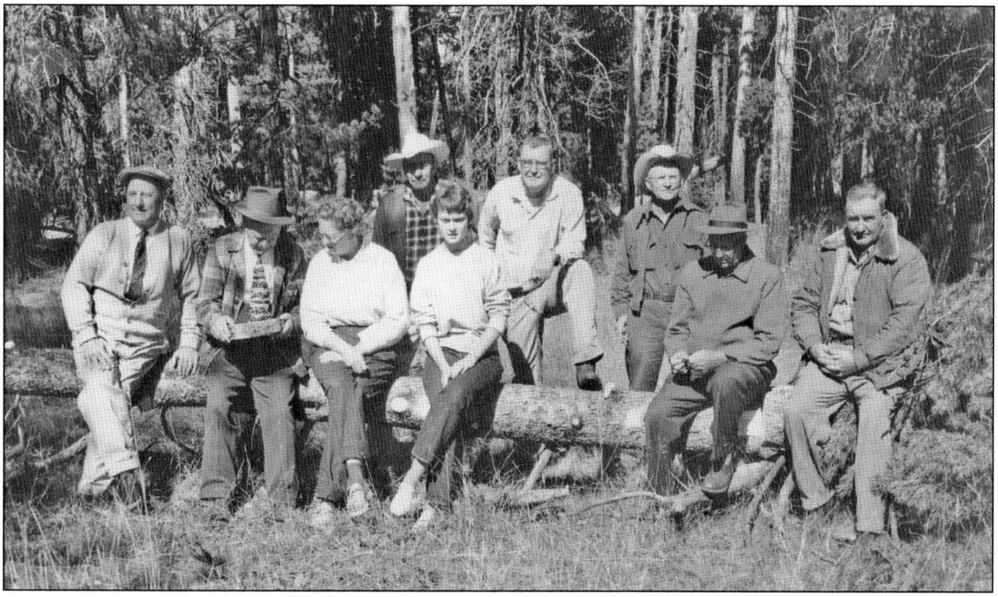

Martin Olson retired in 1947 after 50 years in the woods and built a home in Dubois that he named Dunloggin. Olson, second from left, reminisces with old friends during his 80th birthday celebration in August 1960. His wife, Lydia, and granddaughter are seated next to him.

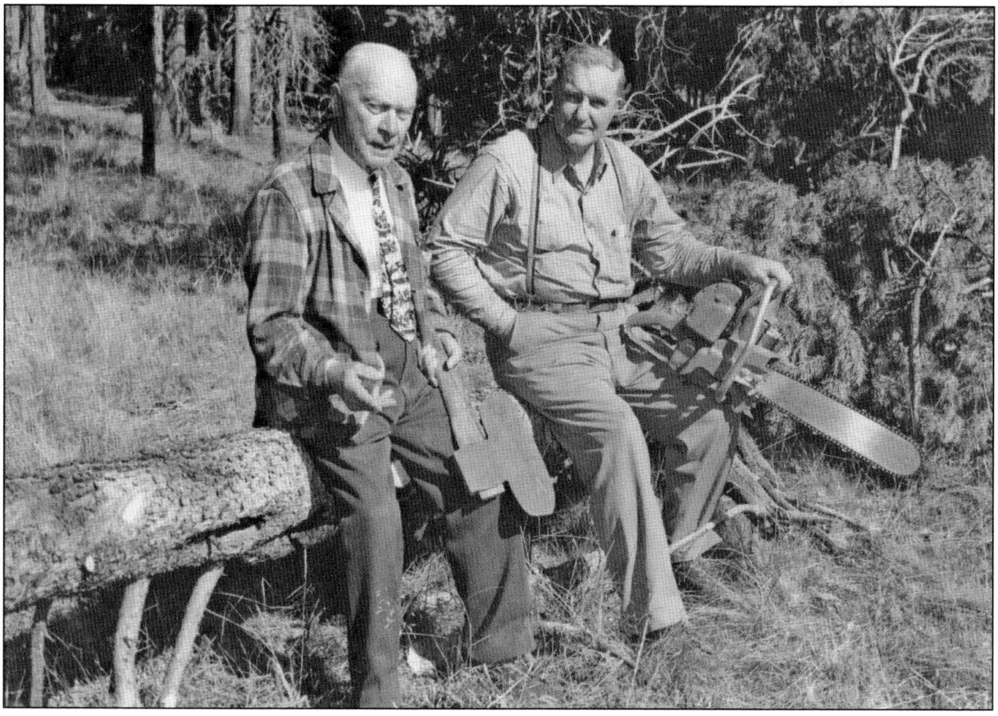

Martin Olson and Ralph Crow, old friends from their years with the Wyoming Tie and Timber Company, compare broad axes and chainsaws during a nostalgic moment at Olson's 80th birthday party. Many former tie hacks had died by 1960. Thirty were buried in a tie-hack section of the Riverton Cemetery with single hand-hewn cross-ties marking their plots. However, a few tie hacks were still alive and living in Dubois or Riverton at the time of Olson's birthday celebration.

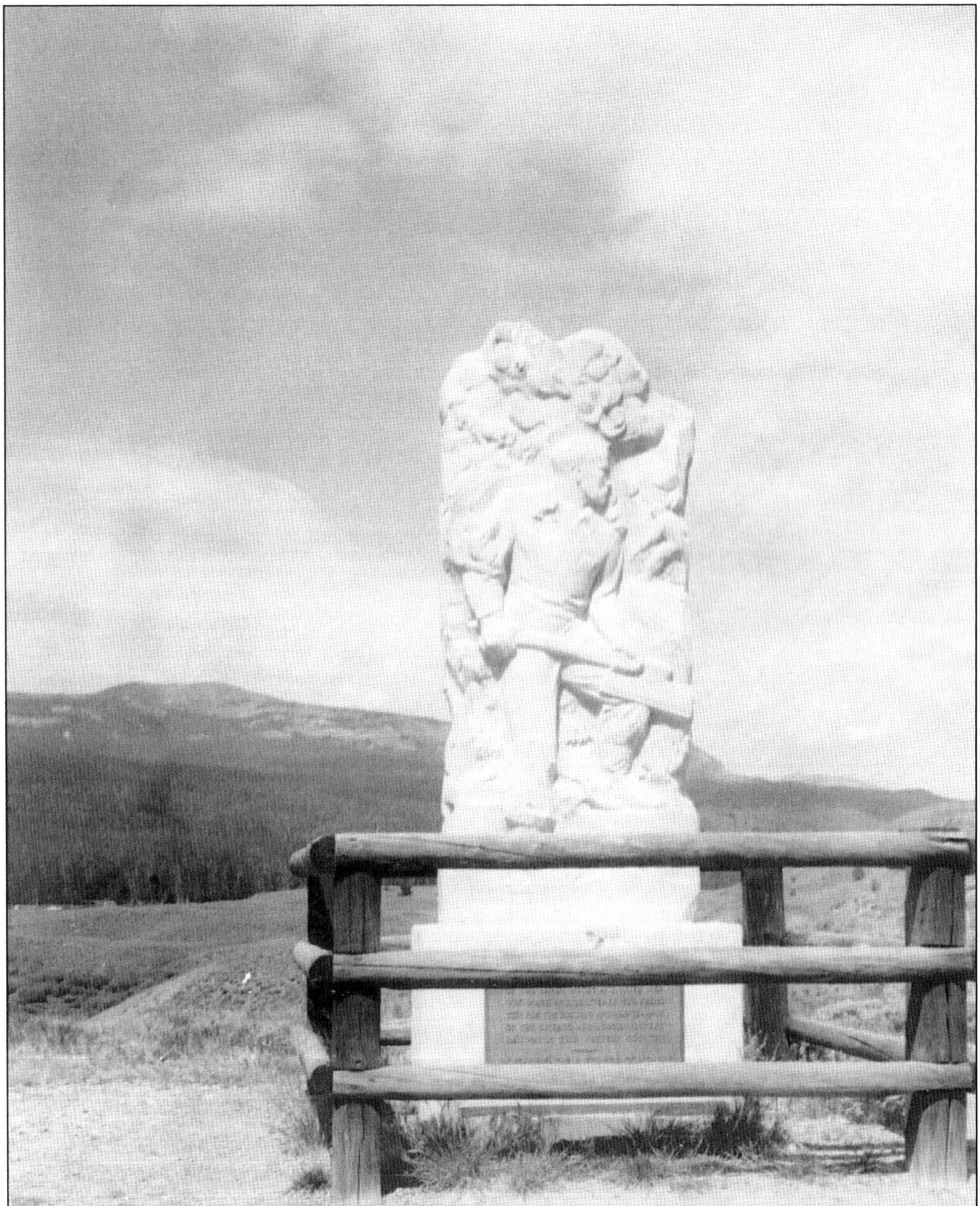

In 1947, the Wyoming Tie and Timber Company erected a 14-foot-high monument in the Shoshone National Forest Dubois along US Highway 26/287, about 18 miles northwest of Dubois, as a tribute to the tie hacks. The memorial was officially named a historic site in a 1974 rededication ceremony, through cooperation of the US Forest Service, Wyoming Recreation Commission, Wyoming Highway Department, Federal Highway Administration, and the Bureau of Outdoor Recreation.

Bibliography

Allison, Mary. *Dubois Area History*. Dubois, WY: self-published, 1990.

Gould, Lewis L. *Wyoming from Territory to Statehood*. Worland, WY: High Plains Publishing Company, Inc., 1989.

Larson, T.A. *Wyoming, A History*. New York, NY: W.W. Norton & Co., 1977.

Pinkerton, Joan Trego. *Knights of the Broadax*. Caldwell, ID: The Caxton Printers, 1981.

Schlissel, Lillian. *Women's Diaries of the Westward Journey*. New York, NY: Schocken Books, 1982.